Research Methods in Interpreting

Other titles in the *Research Methods in Linguistics* series:

Research Methods in Interpreting

A Practical Resource

SANDRA HALE AND JEMINA NAPIER

B L O O M S B U R Y

LONDON • NEW DELHI • NEW YORK • SYDNEY

Bloomsbury Academic

An imprint of Bloomsbury Publishing Plc

50 Bedford Square	1385 Broadway
London	New York
WC1B 3DP	NY 10018
UK	USA

www.bloomsbury.com

Bloomsbury is a registered trade mark of Bloomsbury Publishing Plc

First published 2013
Reprinted 2014

© Sandra Hale and Jemina Napier, 2013

British Library Cataloguing-in-Publication Data
A catalogue record for this book is available from the British Library.

ISBN: HB: 978-1-4411-4770-7
PB: 978-1-4411-6851-1
ePDF: 978-1-4725-2473-7
ePUB: 978-1-4725-2281-8

Library of Congress Cataloging-in-Publication Data
Library of Congress Cataloging-in-Publication Data
Research methods in interpreting: a practical resource/Sandra Hale and Jemina Napier.
pages cm. – (Research Methods in Linguistics) Includes bibliographical references and index.
ISBN 978-1-4411-4770-7 (hardback) – ISBN 978-1-4411-6851-1 (paperback)
– ISBN 978-1-4725-2473-7 (ebook (pdf)) 1. Translating and interpreting–Study and teaching.
2. Translating and interpreting–Research–Methodology. 3. Translating services.
4. Linguistic models. I. Napier, Jemina. II. Title.
P306.5.H35 2013
418'.020721–dc23
2013020288

Typeset by Deanta Global Publishing Services, Chennai, India
Printed and bound in Great Britain

To our husbands and children

CONTENTS

LIST OF FIGURES

LIST OF TABLES

ACKNOWLEDGEMENTS

We would like to acknowledge all the Masters and PhD candidates we have worked with over the years, who have contributed to our thinking about the most effective approaches to conducting interpreting research and also led us to identify the need for this book. We would also like to recognize Emeritus Prof Christopher Candlin for inspiring us both as researchers, as PhD supervisor for Sandra and a research mentor for Jemina. He has always been a supportive role model to us and countless other PhD students in applied linguistics. We would also like to acknowledge the diligent work of our research assistants Julie Lim and Joshua Phillips, who assisted with the copyediting of the book.

CHAPTER ONE

What is research and why do we do it?

This chapter will:

- Explore the meaning of research and the reasons for doing it
- Provide a general overview of research concepts
- Discuss the different research approaches and paradigms
- Suggest practical ways to conduct research

1.1 Introduction

Exercise 1.1

Before you read this chapter, ask yourself the following questions and write down your answers.

- What is research?
- Why do research?

After you have read the chapter, ask yourself the same questions again, write your answers down and compare your answers before and after you have read the chapter. Once you have done that, you will have completed a mini research project, using the 'pre- and post- intervention method'.

You may have different motivations for wanting to conduct research into Interpreting. You may be a practising interpreter who is looking for answers to improve your practice and is considering enrolling in a research degree. You may be a research student already or an Interpreting educator who is about to embark on a research project. You may be an educator who teaches research methods or supervises research students. If you fall in any of the above categories, we can identify with you. We are both interpreters, we have both conducted our doctoral research into Interpreting in search of answers to our practical questions and we are also Interpreting educators, researchers and supervisors of research students. As such, we understand that 'research' may seem daunting and that without proper guidance, new researchers can find themselves lost in a maze of different terminologies, methodologies, ideologies and approaches that will discourage them and may lead them to quit.

We hope to demystify the research process by providing you with an accessible step-by-step guide to conducting research in Interpreting.

1.2 What is research?

If you have completed the first exercise at the beginning of this chapter, you would have reflected on this question and written down an answer. See if your answer matches what you are about to read in this section. Research is searching for new knowledge in a systematic, organized way. Dörnyei describes it as 'disciplined inquiry' (2007, p. 15; Sarangi 2005). It is finding answers to questions by collecting evidence from different sources that will support a logical conclusion. So, first of all, you need to know *what* it is that you want to find out, what the aims of your project are and what the problem your project will address is. This is where you will problematize a topic of interest to you. Problematizing means identifying an issue that can be addressed by research. In order to do this, you will need to clearly state the aims of your project and then formulate those aims into answerable research questions. You also need to know *why* you are conducting this research. There needs to be a valid justification for your research beyond simply stating that it is a topic that interests you. You need to justify your research by showing its merit and significance. In order to do this, you must read what has been written on the topic that you want to research and demonstrate that there is a gap in the knowledge that you intend to fill in some measure. The results of your research need to be of use to other researchers and/or to the community, depending on whether it is basic or applied research. The next step is to decide *how* you will answer your research question in order to address your aims by choosing an appropriate methodology. Your methodology can strictly follow a specific paradigm, such as quantitative or qualitative, or it can be less rigid and use mixed methods. The methodology will include the type of data that will be collected and the methods for collecting and analysing such data. Once the data have been analysed, you will draw conclusions that will lead to answers to your initial question/s. In sum, with any research plan or proposal, you need to answer three pivotal questions: What? Why? and How? However, this is not where your search for knowledge should end, as the answer to one question will lead to more questions for further research, and so the process will begin again. This process is often referred to as the 'research cycle' (Hall 2002).

1.3 Why do research?

The second question posed to you in Exercise 1.1 was 'why do research?' We conduct research to acquire knowledge that will help us find reliable answers to our questions. We may believe something to be the case based on factors other than scientific research. Our personal experiences, what we hear from others, especially people in positions of authority, traditions or common sense may all contribute to what is known as anecdotal evidence. Anecdotal evidence is useful to help us formulate research questions that can be answered by systematic research. For example, you may think that conference interpreters cannot interpret accurately if they do not have visual access to the speaker, based on what a number of Interpreting educators, who are also experienced practitioners, have said. In other words, you can base your belief on an authority. Similarly, you may believe that community interpreters prefer to interpret in the third person rather than in the first person based on your own experience or observation of some interpreters. Neuman (2000) speaks of the pitfalls of basing our assertions on things other than research: authority, tradition, myths, common sense and personal experience. When discussing personal experience, he warns against 'overgeneralization', 'selective observation', 'premature closure' (when we stop once we got the evidence we want) and the 'halo effect' (when we believe what 'important' or prestigious people say). If we go back to the assertion above made by some conference interpreters, research could be conducted to ascertain whether interpreters' levels of accuracy deteriorate when the speaker is not seen, or whether it is simply a matter of preference for some interpreters. Similarly, with the assertion about community interpreters, research can be conducted to quantify the number of community interpreters who prefer to interpret using the indirect approach. Our own experience is very limited and cannot be used to make generalizations. Research can therefore confirm or disconfirm other sources of knowledge. However, the same warnings that apply to anecdotal evidence also apply to empirical evidence. We must beware not to overgeneralize our results beyond what our sample can represent. For example, if our sample of community interpreters includes only untrained interpreters, then we cannot claim that all community interpreters, trained and untrained, prefer to use the indirect approach.

We also conduct research to test, correct or enhance previous knowledge. This means that research is never static and is never infallible. Empirical research leads to evidence that can help us arrive at conclusions and to refine concepts or theories. However, such knowledge or theories are always open to scrutiny, challenge, debate and ultimately change. Further research can either confirm or refute existing theories. As Rudestam and Newton state:

> The only universal in scientific knowledge is a general commitment to using logical argument and evidence to arrive at conclusions that are recognized as tentative and subject to further amendment. Good scientists in action often deviate from an "official" philosophy of science and a prescribed methodology (2001, p. 23).

If scientists had not questioned the 'official' philosophies, we would still be believing in discredited theories such as 'the earth is flat'. Research carried out by humans is prone to error. The methodology may be flawed or the conclusions may be incorrect or there may be limitations due to the size of the sample or other constraints. Time and changed circumstances can also lead to different results. For example, we may conduct a study now and find that conference interpreters who are not accustomed to interpreting remotely will not perform very well, but if we repeat the study with conference interpreters 20 years from now, the results may be very different. With the advances in technology, it may very well be that in 20 years, all conference interpreting will be conducted remotely and that interpreters will be very comfortable with working in that manner. The results then may show no difference between the quality of remote or on-site interpreting. Alternatively, we may find that the results of the second study corroborate those of the first, in which case the original hypothesis will be proven. There are also some topics that are beyond the scope of science. In other words, although scientific methods of enquiry are much more rigorous and reliable than informal methods, we cannot suppose that science can answer all questions.

You may be asking yourself at this point, why bother with research if it cannot tell us absolute truths? Gile comments that interpreters who embark on research may find it difficult to '. . . come to terms with the reality of research, and with the idea that their project will probably not bring forth the ultimate solution or answer' (2001, pp. 19–20). Often, new researchers want to find the answers to all questions in one research project, but the reality is that each research project can make only a small contribution to the whole body of knowledge. Gile (2001) proposes three main types of contributions: empirical, conceptual and methodological.

Research will bring about new data that can be analysed, interpreted and compared with previous data. It will also contribute to the refinement, creation or refutation of concepts or theories. New research will also often contribute to new research methodologies – to how to conduct research in more effective, efficient, innovative and valid ways. New research, therefore, needs to build on what has already been done by continuing on the same lines, testing and critically analysing what has been found and by confirming or refuting previous findings. The more research is conducted, the closer we will get to the truth or to useful answers.

1.4 What is a theory?

In the foregoing section we have used the word 'theory' without giving any explanation of its meaning. This section will attempt to clarify what theory means in the context of research.

> Theory frames how we look at and think about a topic. It gives us concepts, provides basic assumptions, directs us to the important questions, and suggests ways for us to make sense of data. Theory enables us to connect a single study to the immense base of knowledge to which other researchers contribute . . . (Neuman 2000, p. 60).

One often hears practitioners disparaging 'the theory' because it is of no relevance to 'the practice'. Students also often speak of 'the theory' as if it were a single, all compassing homogenous concept. They usually refer to 'theory' as what is learned in the classroom, and to 'practice' as what actually happens in the real world. However, there is no such thing as one theory or one practice. Theories and practices can be varied and even contradictory. For example, there are different theories about the role of the interpreter, some based on ideology, some on personal experience, some on descriptive research and some on experimental research. Similarly, there are different practices that support or contradict the different theories. Interpreting research has drawn from many different theoretical frameworks and disciplines such as linguistics, discourse analysis and psychology. Some researchers base their research on one single theoretical framework, whereas others draw from a combination to generate their own theories. You may become interested in conducting research into Interpreting because you have studied a particular theory and may want to apply it to an interpreting problem to test its validity. Alternatively, you may be motivated by a practical problem and are interested in solving it by researching it. If you fall in the first category, you will probably conduct basic, explanatory, quantitative research within a hypothetico-deductive paradigm. If you fall in the second category, you will probably conduct applied, exploratory or descriptive, qualitative research within an inductive paradigm. Theory is much more prominent in basic research that 'deduces' or generates hypotheses from it. In applied research, theories are usually 'induced' from the data. This, however, does not mean that qualitative studies are conducted in a theoretical vacuum. Neuman explains that in qualitative research, '. . . researchers use theory . . . to refine concepts, evaluate assumptions of a theory, and indirectly test hypotheses' (2000, p. 60). The theory is identified through a thorough review of the relevant literature in the field. This will help place your study within a particular debate and guide you in the interpretation of your data. Scientific research needs to go beyond the simple collection of data. As Rudestam and Newton argue, a question such as '. . . "I wonder if there are more women than men in graduate school today?" is totally banal as a research question unless the answer to the question has conceptual or theoretical implications that are developed within the study and into conclusions that can have theoretical implications' (2001, p. 6). Your understanding of the current theories will help you decide what your research question will be and what methods you will use to answer it. In sum, all research is theory based. The predominance or application of theory will be determined by the research paradigm.

In qualitative research that does not follow a specific theory, it is useful to develop a 'conceptual framework' for the study (Maxwell 2013; Miles and Huberman 1994). A conceptual framework 'explains, either graphically or in narrative form, the main things to be studied – the key factors, constructs or variables – and the presumed relationships among them. Frameworks can be rudimentary or elaborate, theory-driven or commonsensical, descriptive or causal' (Miles and Huberman 1994, p. 18). Basically, a conceptual framework helps you to think through what is going on in the area that you want to study. By identifying key issues you can conceive:

> [a] model of what is out there that you plan to study, and of what is going on with these things and why – a tentative theory of the phenomena that you are investigating. The function of this theory is to inform the rest of your design – to help you to assess and refine your goals, develop realistic and relevant research questions, select appropriate methods, and identify potential validity threats to your conclusions (Maxwell 2013, pp. 39–40).

Figure 1.1 below illustrates an example of a conceptual framework, which is based on a real study developed by researchers and a healthcare interpreting service regarding healthcare needs of a particular linguistic community in Australia (Napier and Sabolcec 2012).

The conceptual framework will then guide development of the actual research questions. Below you can see a list of research questions that emerged from the conceptual framework in Figure 1.1.

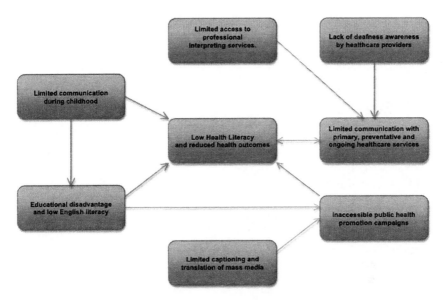

FIGURE 1.1 *Conceptual framework for study of Deaf Auslan users' access to healthcare information.*

- What is the state of access for CALD[1] communities in terms of health and ageing and access to information?

- How and where do CALD communities access preventative healthcare information?

- Are there sufficient healthcare information resources in the minority languages of CALD communities (i.e. translated policies, brochures, etc.)?

- How do CALD people access healthcare assessments (e.g. for dementia, depression, or for entry into a nursing home) if they have low English literacy?

- What are the preventative healthcare needs of CALD people according to gender and age?

1.5 What to research?

A number of different factors will help you determine what to research: your interest in a topic; the interests or expertise of your supervisors or of the department in which you are enrolled as a student; the interests of a government or other external entity who need concrete answers to inform policy; the desire to find specific answers to practical questions raised by your experience as interpreter; and even the availability of data and resources and time limitations. Most students start their research journey with very vague ideas. The literature review will help you narrow down those ideas and focus on a research problem that can be addressed by a single research project, within the time and resources available to you. Hale (2007) conducted a survey of practising interpreters where they were asked to indicate problems they would like addressed by research. Table 1.1 presents some of these interpreters' answers. Their answers are examples of very general issues of interest to them, but in order for research to address any of these issues, they must be refined into researchable questions.

Table 1.1 Practising interpreters' suggested topics for research

1. 'Variations in practice around the world in different settings'
2. 'How to optimise chuchotage during court hearings'
3. 'Compliance with the code of ethics and uniformity by all practitioners'
4. 'A comparison of the performance of trained and untrained interpreters'

(*Source*: Hale 2007, pp. 159–60.)

1.5.1 *The research question*

Whether your research paradigm is quantitative or qualitative, it is very useful to start your project with a research question (Phillips and Hardy 2002, p. 60). Bryman argues that 'no research questions or poorly formulated research questions will lead to poor research' (Bryman 2004, p. 20). The research question acts as a plan for your project. It will determine the type of data to be collected and the methods to be used. We will explain the differences between quantitative and qualitative methods in detail in a section below. However, generally speaking, quantitative studies require very specific questions to confirm or disconfirm a hypothesis. A hypothesis is a statement that presents a conclusion based on a theory or on results of previous research. The statement will then be tested by the new proposed research. The results will either confirm (the answer will be 'yes') or disconfirm (the answer will be 'no') the stated hypothesis/es. Quantitative studies generally operate within a hypothetico-deductive paradigm, where hypotheses are deduced from the theory. Qualitative studies will use more general questions that will elicit much more complex answers. The answers will not confirm or disconfirm hypotheses, but provide descriptions and interpretations of problems. In qualitative studies, the data generate the theory in what is known as an inductive paradigm. This is sometimes referred to as grounded theory, as the theory is constructed from the ground up. For any type of research, however,

Exercise 1.2: Formulating research questions

Choose one of the suggestions from Table 1.1 above and formulate one or more research questions.

the initial research question or questions must be able to be answerable by the research project. Composing 'researchable questions' is a difficult task.

Let us look at suggestion 3 in Table 1.1.

3. *'Compliance with the code of ethics and uniformity by all practitioners'*

This issue seems to be one that concerns the interpreter who suggested it. We can surmise that this interpreter believes that not all practitioners abide by the code of ethics. This assumption is most probably based on his/her own experience and observations of other interpreters; this is called anecdotal evidence. However, the statement alone is not clear about what s/he wants to know. We can speculate on the following questions:

- Does s/he want to prove that not all practitioners abide by the code of ethics?

- Does s/he want to know if all practitioners think they should abide by the code of ethics?

- Does s/he want to know why they do or do not abide by the code of ethics?

- Does s/he want to know if there are sanctions imposed on those who breach the code of ethics?

Many questions regarding this general theme can be asked that surround this general theme. We can assume that the problem is that there are various degrees of compliance of the code of ethics among interpreters. Now we need to refine the problem into a research question. Before we can arrive at the final research question, there are some further refinements that are needed. Below we list some suggestions on how to refine a topic to arrive at a research question.

1 Decide on the type of interpreting: conference interpreting or community interpreting (court, medical, other).

2 Decide on the geographical setting: country, state, institution.

3 Decide on a particular code of ethics: for example, if the sample is court interpreters in California, USA, the code of ethics may be the

NAJIT[2] code of ethics. If the sample is conference interpreters in Europe, the code of ethics may be the AIIC code of ethics . . . .'

4   Decide on what you want to find out: for example, interpreters' perceptions of the usefulness of the code of ethics; service providers' understanding of the code of ethics; actions taken when interpreters do not comply with the code of ethics.

5   Read what has already been written on the topic.

Let us opt for the following: court interpreting in Australia, AUSIT code of ethics, actions taken when code is breached.

Suggested research question: What actions are taken by the courts when interpreters breach the AUSIT code of ethics?
Suggested aim: To ascertain what actions, if any, are taken by Australian courts when interpreters are found breaching their code of ethics.

Now that the research question has been narrowed down, a suitable methodology must be chosen. We will come back to this research question and decide on the best methodology after we have discussed different methods in more detail later in the chapter.

Exercise 1.3: Refining your research questions

Go back to the research question you formulated in Exercise 1.2 and refine it further following the steps suggested above. This time add the aims.

1.6 Types of research

There are many different types of research, and different writers have listed many different classifications of them (Walliman 2005). You have undoubtedly already conducted some type of research as a university student or as a practitioner. You most probably have 'researched' a topic to find out more about it by reading what others have written on the subject in different sources or even by observing or by asking questions. These are all common methods of conducting informal research. Formal, scientific research also uses many of those methods. Reading about what others have written is called secondary research, and it is an important first step to conducting any research project. Another term for this type of research is conceptual research. Primary research refers to our own collection and analysis of data. Another word for primary, data-based research is empirical research. Williams and Chesterman (2002) define the purposes of these two types of research in the following way:

Conceptual research aims to define and clarify concepts, to interpret or reinterpret ideas, to relate concepts into larger systems, to introduce new concepts or metaphors or frameworks that allow a better understanding of the object of research. Empirical research, on the other hand, seeks new data, new information derived from the observation of data and from experimental work; it seeks evidence which supports or disconfirms hypotheses or generates new ones (p. 58).

They further argue that both approaches to research are crucial: '. . . You cannot observe anything without some kind of preliminary theory (concept) of what you are observing. . . . On the other hand, concepts that have no link to empirical data are not much use to science . . .' (p. 58).

Another major distinction is usually made between basic research and applied research. Basic research aims to advance knowledge regardless of its application, whereas applied research aims to investigate real-world problems with the aim to solve them. Again, as with the difference between conceptual and empirical research, it can be argued that basic research and applied research are also interrelated. Results of basic research can be used to inform applied research and vice versa. Nevertheless, the majority of Interpreting research has been applied research, as Interpreting is primarily a professional practice. Interpreting researchers have, for the most part, aimed to achieve what is outlined by Neuman:

Applied researchers try to solve specific policy problems or help practitioners accomplish tasks. Theory is less central to them than seeking a solution to a specific problem for a limited setting. . . . Applied research is frequently descriptive research and its strength is its immediate practical use (Neuman 2000, p. 24).

Williams and Chesterman agree that the primary aim of applied Interpreting research has been to improve the practice, but they also argue that applied Interpreting research has aimed to test theories against the practice (2002, p. 68). Under the banner of applied research, we can find what is referred to as action research. This is research conducted by practitioners, designed to solve real-life problems that affect the researcher/practitioner. This type of research is common in Interpreting research, as most researchers in the field are or have been practising interpreters or interpreter educators. Consequently, they will usually research aspects of the practice (either interpreting or teaching) that will affect their performance. This includes the analysis of their own work.

Three other important distinctions are: Exploratory research, Descriptive research and Explanatory research. Williams and Chesterman (2002, p. 65) attach three useful questions to each type: What can we find out about X? (exploratory); what is the nature of X (descriptive) and why and how X?

(explanatory). Neuman suggests different goals for each type of research, as outlined in Table 1.2 below:

Table 1.2 Goals of research

Exploratory	Descriptive	Explanatory
Become familiar with the basic facts, setting and concerns	Provide a detailed, highly accurate picture	Test a theory's predictions or principle
Create a general mental picture of conditions	Locate new data that contradict past data	Elaborate and enrich a theory's explanation
Formulate and focus questions for future research	Create a set of categories or classify types	Extend a theory to new issues or topics
Generate new ideas, conjectures or hypotheses	Clarify a sequence of steps or stages	Support or refute an explanation or prediction
Determine the feasibility of conducting research	Document a causal process or mechanism	Link issues or topics with a general principle
Develop techniques for measuring and locating future data	Report on the background or context of a situation	Determine which of several explanations is best
Answer 'what' and 'how' questions	Answer 'what' and 'how' questions	Answer 'why' and 'yes/no' questions

(*Source*: Neuman 2000.)

You would normally conduct exploratory research in fields that have not been researched before in order to identify the current issues. Exploratory research would normally be followed by either descriptive or explanatory research. Sometimes researchers triangulate methods to increase the reliability and validity of the results. Triangulation refers to the use of different methods applied to the same data (often referred to as 'mixed methods' research). Generally speaking, a method is considered reliable if it can be replicated by other researchers, or by the same researcher at a later time, and obtain similar results. A method is considered valid if it investigates what it is meant to investigate. In the main, quantitative methods are high in reliability and low in validity and qualitative methods are high in validity but low in reliability, this is why many researchers argue for the use of both methods.

Suggested research question: What actions are taken by the courts when interpreters breach the AUSIT code of ethics?

Suggested aim: To ascertain what actions, if any, are taken by Australian courts when interpreters are found breaching their code of ethics.

Decide on the type of research this question fits into: Exploratory, Descriptive or Explanatory?

1.6.1 Research philosophies

Research is not 'neutral', but reflects a range of the researcher's personal interests, values, abilities, assumptions, aims and ambitions. In the case of your own proposed research, your own mixtures of these elements will determine the subject of the research and will influence your approach to designing the research study. It is important to consider in advance what approach you will decide to take with your research – and why.

There are essentially two main research philosophies, although there can be overlap between the two – and both positions may be identifiable in any research project, as seen in Figure 1.2 below:

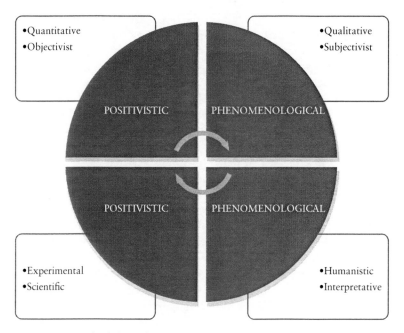

FIGURE 1.2 *Research philosophies*

The research philosophy can have an impact on the methodology adopted for the research project. The term methodology refers to the overall approaches and perspectives to the research process as a whole and is concerned with the following main issues:

- **Why** you collect certain data
- **What** data you collect
- **Where** you collect it
- **How** you collect it
- **How** you analyse it

A research method refers only to the various specific tools or ways data can be collected and analysed (e.g. a questionnaire; interview checklist; data analysis software etc.).

1.6.1.1 Characteristics of positivistic and phenomenological philosophies

Positivistic approaches to research are based on research methodologies commonly used in science. They are characterized by a detached approach to research that seeks out the facts or causes of any social phenomenon in a systematic way. Positivistic approaches are founded on a belief that the study of human behaviour should seek to identify, measure and evaluate any phenomenon and to provide rational explanation for it. This explanation will attempt to establish causal links and relationships between the different elements (or variables) of the subject and relate them to a particular theory or practice. There is a belief that people respond to stimulus or forces, rules (norms) external to themselves and that these can be discovered, identified and described using rational, systematic and deductive processes. For the most part, positivistic methodologies are quantitative.

Phenomenological approaches view research from the perspective that human behaviour is not so easily measured. Human motivation is shaped by factors that are not always observable, so it can become hard to generalize. Furthermore, people place their own meanings on events; meanings that do not always coincide with the way others have interpreted them. This perspective assumes that people will often influence events and act in unpredictable ways that upset any constructed rules or identifiable norms. Phenomenological approaches are particularly concerned with understanding behaviour from the participants' own subjective frames of reference. Research methods are chosen, therefore, to try and describe, interpret and explain events from the perspectives of the people who are the subject of the research. Typically, phenomenological approaches are qualitative.

1.6.2 *Quantitative versus qualitative research*

. . . quantitative and qualitative research represent different research strategies. . . . However, the distinction is not a hard-and-fast one: studies that have the broad characteristics of one research strategy may have a characteristic of the other. Not only this, but many writers argue that the two can be combined within an overall research project . . . (Bryman 2004, p. 20).

As the words imply, under quantitative methods, concepts are converted into numbers and are quantified. Quantitative research questions ask 'how many' or 'how much'. They also ask about the strength or significance of relationships or correlations between things (variables) and about the predictability of events (causes). Under qualitative methods, the quality or characteristics of concepts are explored, described and interpreted. Qualitative research questions ask about 'how things are'. However, most research has qualitative and quantitative aspects to some degree. We can say that quantitative methods look at the big picture, at results that can be generalized to a population from representative samples, whereas qualitative methods look at the detail, at the specific trends and themes within a particular sample. Table 1.3 below summarizes the differences between the two as suggested by four different authors:

Table 1.3 Camparison of quantitative and qualitative approaches

Quantitative approach	Qualitative approach
Underlying assumptions	
Facts and data have an objective reality	Reality is socially constructed
A research study must test a theory. This is known as the hypothetico-deductive approach: a theory leads to a hypothesis that is tested empirically. The hypothesis is deduced from the theory. A tight, clearly articulated hypothesis is necessary.	A research study can generate theory. This is known as an inductive approach, where the data can generate (induce) a theory. The word 'hypothesis' can be used loosely to refer to a speculation or informed guess about the possible results. Many qualitative studies do not have a hypothesis at all.

(Continued)

Table 1.3 *(Continued)*

Quantitative approach	Qualitative approach
Purpose	
To predict, to test and verify hypotheses, to generalize and find causal relationships Results can be inferred to wider populations	To identify trends and themes, describe and interpret them, to discovery and explore and speculate on relationships Results apply to specific samples
Data	
Constructed	Naturally occurring
Tightly designed data elicitation techniques (controlled experiments, validated instruments)	Unstructured elicitation techniques (interviews, observations, focus groups, authentic interpreted renditions or written texts)
Analysis	
Uses statistics to describe phenomena and to infer conclusions	Uses personal descriptions of phenomena and speculates on conclusions
Variables can be identified and measured	Variables are complex and interwoven and difficult to measure. The term 'variable' is rarely used
Data analysed objectively mostly using statistical packages	Data evaluated subjectively by the researcher's own analytical ability
Orientation	
Natural science model – positivist epistemological orientation	Interpretivist epistemological orientation
Objectivist ontological orientation	Constructionist ontological orientation
Strength	
High in reliability	High in validity

(*Source*: Bryman 2004, p. 20; Burns 1994, p. 242; Krathwohl 1998, p. 5; Rudestam and Newton 2001.)

We will now look at some illustrative examples of potential research projects using quantitative or qualitative approaches.

Example 1.1: Quantitative, hypothetico-deductive approach

Research Problem: Teaching interpreting skills is a difficult task. Different educators use different techniques depending on how they were taught, what their theoretical background is or on their practical experience as interpreters. The prevalent model for many years has been the 'master-apprentice' model (see Pöchhacker 2010b) where experienced interpreters teach students how to do it based on their vast experience. A hypothetical interpreter educator has a theoretical background in Systemic Functional Grammar. S/he wants to know whether teaching interpreting by applying a functional systemic linguistic theory will achieve better results than when more traditional master-apprentice teaching methods are used. The research problem needs to be narrowed down to a more specific research question. One suggestion is presented below.

Research Question: Do Chinese-English introductory interpreting students acquire consecutive interpreting skills more effectively when taught using a Systemic Functional linguistic approach than when taught using a traditional master-apprentice model?

Hypothesis: Teaching interpreting by applying a Systemic Functional linguistic theory will achieve better results.

Method: Two classes will be studied – the one that uses the traditional teaching methods will become the control group. The one that uses the new method will become the experimental group. After a period of instruction using the different methods, the students will take a consecutive interpreting test. The test results will be quantified and compared using statistical analyses to ascertain whether there are significant differences. If the experimental group achieves significantly better results, the hypothesis will be confirmed. Further analyses can be conducted to ascertain whether there are any correlations between different variables, for example, the dependent variable: rate of success (high marks) and different independent variables: for example, gender, age or anything else that may be particular to the sample.

This is a basic example of a quantitative, hypothetico-deductive approach (see Chapter 6 for more detail on conducting experimental research). After completing this phase of the study, the researcher may want to know more about the reasons why one method was more effective than the other.

S/he may do this by using some qualitative methods such as observing the way the different teachers taught the lessons, interviewing the teachers and interviewing the students or even doing a detailed discourse comparative analysis of the original texts used and the interpreted versions to identify specific features that improved with the new method of teaching.

Now let us go back to the research problem on compliance with the code of ethics. A question about how many interpreters abide by the code of ethics would call for a quantitative approach, whereas a question on what interpreters believe about their obligations to comply with the code of ethics would call for a qualitative approach. For the first question, a questionnaire asking interpreters to self-report on whether they abide by the code of ethics can be one way of eliciting numerical data. However, self-reporting may not be the most reliable method to obtain truthful information. Interpreters may say yes because they know that is what is expected of them or because they may honestly think they do comply but they have never been tested on it and may not be able to reliably answer the question. A qualitative approach using naturally occurring data would be a much more valid way of finding answers to such a question. However, since the researcher has no way of controlling the situation, ethical dilemmas may not arise spontaneously. This is the reason why, with naturally occurring data, the approach is usually exploratory and descriptive. Let us elaborate on this in Example 1.2 below.

Example 1.2: Qualitative, inductive approach

Research Problem: Although there is a generally accepted Code of Ethics for Community interpreters, anecdotal evidence seems to indicate that not all practising interpreters comply with its requirements.

Research Aim: To explore and describe the way interpreters apply the code of ethics when confronted with potentially ethical dilemmas

Research Question: What do interpreters do when confronted with potentially ethical dilemmas when interpreting in domestic violence cases?

Method: A number of interpreted interviews with police, lawyers and counsellors will be video recorded. The contents of the interviews will be transcribed and analysed using discourse analysis methods. Instances of potential ethical dilemmas will be identified and the different approaches taken by the different interpreters described and interpreted. Interpreters will also be observed in context. Conclusions will be drawn from the data on the extent to which interpreters comply with the code of ethics.

Example 1.2 is an example of a qualitative research study using discourse analysis (see Chapter 5 for more detail on conducting discourse analytical research). In order for the researcher to show trends and tendencies, some quantification is necessary. This can be done by first identifying the categories under which interpreter choices fall and counting the different choices. The frequencies can then be converted into percentages of the sum of choices. By doing this, although the research is essentially qualitative, it also resorts to some quantitative methods to draw more reliable conclusions.

To further strengthen the reliability of the above results, the researcher may want to select a number of ethically problematic instances from the authentic data and conduct a quasi-experiment, as illustrated in Example 1.3.

Example 1.3: Triangulation of methods

Method: Four of the main ethical dilemmas found in the authentic data will be selected. The situations will be re-enacted by actors and video recorded. The re-enacted vignettes will be shown to a group of practising interpreters with various levels of training and experience and with different language combinations. They will be asked to fill in a short questionnaire to indicate how they would have acted in a similar situation. The questions on the questionnaire will be closed, with multiple-choice answers drawn from the results of the previous study. The results of this study will be analysed quantitatively and compared to the results of the first study.

Exercise 1.5

Go back to your refined question in Exercise 1.3 and decide whether it will be best answered by using qualitative or quantitative methods. Write the aims and methods for the above question.

1.7 Why Interpreting research?

As mentioned above, many practitioners tend to be sceptical about the usefulness or relevance of theory and research to their practice (see Chesterman and Wagner 2004, for a discussion on the relevance of research to translators which can be equally applicable to interpreters). This is understandable perhaps in the case of difficult theories that seem too detached from reality. However, research into Interpreting can be applied in order to address practical problems faced by interpreters, interpreter educators, interpreting students and interpreting service users. The research questions can be generated by real-life problems affecting anyone who has any link to Interpreting. In a previous publication, Hale (2007) has argued for the need for a cross-fertilization between research, training and practice, where the practice generates questions, the research takes them up and finds answers, the training applies the answers and generates more questions and the cycle continues. Of course, many answers will come from the practice, in the form of the results of descriptive research. So you may ask yourself, what is the point of descriptive research if it is going to tell interpreters what they do and already know? The point is that descriptive research will systematically document what more than just one or two interpreters do and find general tendencies and trends. Descriptive research can also lead to further investigations of causes and predictions using different methodologies.

Exercise 1.6

Reflect on the statement below and try to answer the questions: 'Community Interpreters should be advocates for the minority language speaker'

Do you agree with this statement?
If you do, how do you justify it?
If you do not, how do you refute it?
How can research help us decide on an answer to this claim?

You may have been told in the course of your Interpreting training about what interpreters should or should not do, should or should not be, should or should not say. Some of these prescriptions are based on the results of research, but most are based on educators'/practitioners' own ideas or experience. You will not always be able to find a research project that will justify a certain position. Indeed, the body of research in Interpreting, especially community interpreting, is so small that most questions are yet to be formulated and researched. This in itself is a good reason to conduct Interpreting research: to fill a noticeable gap in the knowledge. So, how can you use research to help you decide on whether community interpreters should or should not be advocates for the minority language speaker? The first step is to review the literature on the topic to become familiar with the debate: what have people written about this topic? What are their arguments? What do they mean by the word 'advocate'? What settings are they referring to? What are they basing their arguments on? You should also read about the opposite view. What does the other side of the debate propose? Why do they argue for impartiality? What do they mean by the word 'impartial'? This first step will clarify some concepts and will generate further questions. The next step could be to formulate answerable research questions from the above statement. One obvious initial question is to ask: *What do minority language speakers and service providers expect of community interpreters?* This preliminary question will lead to an exploratory study where you will find out what the users of interpreting services want. You may find many conflicting and competing expectations, with some expecting the interpreter to be completely impartial, others completely partial and others taking somewhat of a middle view. You may then want to quantify the positions and see which is the view of the majority. This may help you take a position. However, finding that a majority of people take one position may not be enough for you to share their view. You may then want to pursue the research further and analyse the performance of interpreters who claim to be advocates and those who claim to be impartial. The research question for this second enquiry could be: How do interpreters' perceptions of their role as either advocate or impartial professional affect their performance as interpreter? The results of this second project will then lead to another, and the search for knowledge will continue. You may at some stage be able to take a position based on the results of research. The rest of this book will cover the steps you need to take to conduct a research project and provide you with an overview of the main research methods used to investigate questions about Interpreting.

1.7.1 *A note about collecting data through interpreters*

When generating data in multilingual, cross-language or cross-cultural research contexts, researchers need to decide if they will use an interpreter; however, they need to recognize that interpreters may not be able to convey linguistic and cultural issues from a completely neutral position if they are not suitably trained or qualified, which may impact on the integrity of the data. Thus, consideration needs to be given as to whether to use bilingual-bicultural researchers who can conduct interviews directly; or whether to involve interpreters actively as part of the research team (Edwards 1998; Liamputtong 2010; Temple 1997; Temple 2002; Temple and Edwards 2002). As an interpreting studies researcher, if you are considering doing a cross-linguistic study (e.g. comparing how interpreters of different languages interpret the same source text), then you may also need to give consideration to this issue.

1.8 Conclusion

In this chapter, we have given you an overview of what research is, how research can be conducted and why it should be conducted. The following chapters will concentrate on the second topic: how research can be conducted, by covering the main research methods and designs to conduct Interpreting research. You may need to refer back to this chapter as you read the subsequent chapters, for some of the main principles that will be further elaborated upon in the rest of the book.

Further reading

Garzone, G. and Viezzi, M. (eds) (2002). *Interpreting in the 21st century. Challenges and opportunities*. Amsterdam and Philadelphia: John Benjamins.

Nicodemus, B. and L. Swabey (eds) (2011). *Advances in interpreting research. Inquiry in action*. Amsterdam and Philadelphia: John Benjamins Publishing Company.

Liu, M. (2011). Methodology in interpreting studies. A methodological review of evidence-based research. In B. Nicodemus and L. Swabey (eds), *Advances in interpreting research. Inquiry in action*. Amsterdam & Philadelphia: John Benjamins Publishing Company, pp. 85–119.

Shlesinger, M. (2009). Crossing the divide: What researchers and practitioners can learn from one another. *Translation & Interpreting*, 1(1): 1–14.

Notes

1   CALD: Culturally and Linguistically Diverse.
2   National Association of Judiciary Interpreters and Translators.

CHAPTER TWO

Critical reading and writing

This chapter will cover the following topics:

- The literature review
- Writing the research proposal
- Obtaining ethics approval

2.1 Introduction

This chapter will take you through three crucial preliminary steps needed to embark on your own research project: the literature review, the research proposal and the ethics approval process. You will need to complete these three steps before you can start collecting and analysing your data. At this stage, you may be asking yourself questions such as 'Why are these three steps crucial?'; 'Can't I start collecting and analyzing the data and then cite the literature when I am ready to write?'; 'Why do I need a research proposal?'; 'Why do I need ethics clearance when the project will not involve any clinical trials?' Many students have asked their supervisors the same questions. This chapter will attempt to answer them for you.

2.2 The literature review

. . . the literature review plays several roles: structural for its positioning of the thesis, contextual for its scene setting, inspirational for helping develop an argument, and operational for defining scope, limitations and originality (Crowley 2007, p. 208).

The aim of a literature review can be one or more of the following: an attempt to integrate what others have done and said; to criticize previous studies; to build bridges between related topic areas; to identify the central issues in a field. (Hall 2008)

The above quotations give us an indication of the multiple functions of the literature review. We can view the literature review as both a process and a product. The process involves searching, reading, selecting and critically reviewing what you read; and the product involves the presentation of your review as part of the written proposal, thesis or research article. We will discuss the different purposes of the literature review under these two broad headings.

2.2.1 *The process*

Table 2.1 summarizes the first three phases involved in the process of reviewing the literature.

Table 2.1 The process of reviewing the literature

Phase 1: Exploring the topic	Learning about the topic: What are the issues? What are the debates? What are the underlying theories and concepts?
	Learning about previous research: What research has been done? What questions have been answered by previous research? What methodologies have been used? What are the strengths and weaknesses of previous research?
Phase 2: Finding a gap in the knowledge	Refining your research questions: Have my original questions been answered by previous research? What questions have not been answered by previous research?
	Justifying your research: How can my research fill a gap in the knowledge about interpreting?
	Establishing the significance of your research: What will my research contribute to the research community, to interpreting educators and to interpreting practitioners that previous research has not contributed before?
Phase 3: Positioning your research	Where does my research fit in relation to other research?
	Is my research replicating, developing or creating a research methodology?
	Is my research positioned within an established theoretical framework or is it breaking new ground and proposing new theories?

2.2.1.1 Phase 1: The exploratory phase

The first phase is exploratory: to read as widely as possible to discover what others have said, done and found on the topic. You need to be thoroughly familiar with the field in which you will become an expert. Before you start to explore the topic, you need to find the relevent literature to read. Table 2.2 provides a list of the different types of resources that are available to you to explore, with an explanation about the nature of each type of publication.

Table 2.2 Literature types

Type of literature	Purpose
Edited books An edited book is a compilation of chapters written by different authors on a related topic. The editor/editors select the theme of the book, call for papers or invite specific experts to contribute to the volume. The editor/editors then send the papers to referees to be reviewed (normally two referees are used). A referee is a peer reviewer, that is, an expert in the same field who can comment on the merit of the research presented, the adequacy of the methodology, the appropriateness of the writing style and the general quality of the paper. A referee will write a detailed report on the paper s/he has reviewed and recommend one of the following options for the editor: reject submission; re-submit subject to major revisions; minor revisions required or accept without revisions. Very rarely will a paper be accepted without any revisions required. The editor/editors will base their final decision on the referees' reviews and on the revised	Edited volumes are a useful resource to start exploring the topic, as they present similar topics from different authors with usually different perspectives and approaches to the subject and to research. Each of the chapters will contain a list of references used by the authors. These lists of references are extremely useful for helping you find further literature on the topic in question. Try to always find and read the primary sources cited by others, rather than simply quote what others have quoted without reading the original publication. You will find that you may have a different interpretation of the original source when you read it yourself, and sometimes, you may even find that the original was in fact misquoted. Below are some very useful edited volumes on Interpreting issues: Pöchhacker, F. and Shlesinger, M. (eds) (2002). *Interpreting studies reader.* London: Routledge. Garzone, G. and Viezzi, M. (eds) (2002). *Interpreting in the 21st century. Challenges and opportunities.* Amsterdam and Philadelphia: John Benjamins. Napier, J. and Roy, C. (eds) (in press). *The sign language interpreting studies reader.* Amsterdam: John Benjamins.

(Continued)

Table 2.2 (Continued)

Type of literature	Purpose
version of the paper upon re-submission. The best papers will then be chosen for inclusion in the edited volume as chapters. Edited volumes normally have an introduction written by the editor/editors introducing the theme, summarizing the chapters and providing a conclusion which ties the chapters together under the same theme.	The *Critical Link* series – 1–6 (Brunette et al. 2003; Carr et al. 1997; Hale et al. 2009; Roberts et al. 2000; C Wadensjö et al. 2007). *The Research on Interpretation* series published by Gallaudet University Press (Metzger et al. 2003; Metzger and Fleetwood 2007). Valero, C. and Martin, A. (2008). *Crossing borders in community interpreting.* Amsterdam: John Benjamins. Russell, D. and Hale, S. (eds) (2009). *Interpreting in legal settings.* Washington DC: Gallaudet University Press. Leeson, L., Wurm, S., Vermeerbergen, M. (eds) (2011). *Signed language interpreting: Preparation, practice and performance.* Manchester: St. Jerome, pp. 2–11. Malmkjaer, K. and Windle, K. (eds) (2011). *The oxford handbook of translation studies.* Oxford: Oxford University Press.
Books There are many different types of books: textbooks, introductory books, research books, theoretical books. Books can be written by one or more authors. It takes approximately 3 to 4 years to write and publish a book, so books can never be completely up to date with the latest research results.	Books are a good source of information on theories, research methods and general concepts. It would be impossible to list here all the many good books that have been written on Interpreting. However, below are some key books in the field: Wadensjo, C. (1998). *Interpreting as interaction.* London and New York: Longman. Berk-Seligson, S. (1990). *The bilingual courtroom. Court interpreters in the judicial process.* Chicago: The University of Chicago Press. Gile, D. (2001). *Getting started in interpreting research: Methodological reflections, personal accounts and advice for beginners.* Amsterdam: John Benjamins. Pöchhacker, F. (2004). *Introducing interpreting studies.* London & New York: Routledge. Hale, S. (2004). *The discourse of court interpreting.* Amsterdam: John Benjamins.

Table 2.2 (Continued)

Type of literature	Purpose
	Hale, S. (2007). *Community interpreting.* Basingstoke: Palgrave Macmillan. Napier, J. (2002). *Sign language interpreting: Linguistic coping strategies.* Douglas McLean. Napier, J., McKee, R. and Goswell, D. (2010). *Sign language interpreting: Theory & practice in Australia and New Zealand* (2nd edn). Sydney: Federation Press. Metzger, M. (1999). *Sign language interpreting: Deconstructing the myth of neutrality.* Washington, DC: Gallaudet University Press. Roy, C. (2000). *Interpreting as a discourse process.* Oxford: Oxford University Press. Angelelli, C. (2004). *Medical interpreting and cross-cultural communication.* Cambridge: Cambridge University Press.
Refereed Journals A *journal* is a periodical publication that specializes in a field of enquiry. Most journals publish two issues per year. Journals normally have one or two editors who play the same role as the editors described for edited books. The only difference is that journal editors normally do the job for many years. Journals also have editorial boards comprising international experts in the field who sometimes help with the editing of special issues and often with refereeing of submitted papers. Editorial work is done for free.	A journal article is published regularly (normally twice yearly). For this reason, journals are up to date with the latest research. Journal articles are also more detailed, more specialized and often more complex than book chapters or books. It is crucial for any literature review to adequately review the relevant journal articles in addition to other sources. Some of the leading journals that publish interpreting research articles are: *Interpreting: International Journal of Research and Practice* *Target: International Journal of Translation Studies* *Translation and Interpreting: The International Journal of Translation and Interpreting Research* *Meta: The translators' Journal* *Babel: International Journal of Translation* *The Translator* *The Interpreter & Translator Trainer* *International Journal of Interpreter Education* *Sign Language Studies* Although some of these journals have 'translation' and not 'interpreting' in the title, they publish articles that focus on interpreting as well as translation studies.

(Continued)

Table 2.2 (Continued)

Type of literature	Purpose
Reports A report presents the results of a study that has usually been funded by an external body such as a government department or private company.	Some examples of reports that are relevant to Interpreting are: Law Institute of Victoria 'Interpreting Fund Scoping Project' www.liv.asn.au Ozolins, U. (2004). *Survey of interpreting practitioners. Report.* Melbourne: VITS. www.vits.com.au/downloads/VITS%20 Survey%20Report-Final.pdf Hale, S. (2011). *Interpreter policies, practices and protocols in Australian Courts and Tribunals. A national survey.* Melbourne: Australian Institute of Judicial Administration. http://www.aija.org.au/online/Pub no89.pdf Napier, J., Spencer, D. and Sabolcec, J. (2007). *Guilty or not guilty? An investigation of deaf jurors' access to court proceedings via sign language interpreting. Research Report No. 14.* Sydney: Macquarie University & NSW Law Reform Commission.
Theses Master and doctoral theses are also useful resources. Some publish their theses as monographs, but many theses remain unpublished.	Many university libraries will digitize their students' theses for easy access. Others will have printed copies on their shelves.

Now that you know what types of literature to look for, you need to know how to find it. Table 2.3 provides a summary of the different ways you can locate the relevant literature.

Table 2.3 How to find the right literature

Walk into a university library	This approach may be seen as antiquated. However, there is merit in walking into a library, finding the shelves where the books on Interpreting are placed and physically inspecting them. As you look at the collection and read the titles and tables of contents, you may be led to explore areas you had not thought of before, you may become interested in different topics or be inspired by what you read.

Table 2.3 (Continued)

Seek help from the librarian	University libraries will have librarians dedicated to each discipline who can help you find the literature you need. You should also attend any workshops organized by the library on literature searchers.
Catalogues	All libraries now have on-line catalogues that will not only cover the collection for that particular library but also from other university libraries. If you are an enrolled student and your university library does not hold an item you need, you can request an inter-library loan. This means that you in fact have access to most libraries around the world, not just your own local library.

Databases	Databases are very important tools that will help you find relevant literature according to particular themes. They provide abstracts of articles that have been published in the field. All university libraries subscribe to different databases and have guidelines on how to search them. Some relevant databases for Interpreting research articles are:
	
	    Linguistics and Language Behavior Abstracts
	    Linguistics Abstracts Online
	    Communication and Mass Media Complete

Google Scholar	Unlike the databases listed above, Google Scholar covers books and book chapters as well as journal articles, and it is freely available on the internet. Tip: Search for articles in Google Scholar via your university library database list, as any article you find will automatically be linked to any electronic journal subscriptions in your library that you can quickly download.

(*Continued*)

Table 2.3 (Continued)

Reference lists	It is also a very good idea to use the reference lists provided at the back of relevant books and journal articles to find further references. These lists have been compiled by researchers who have conducted their own literature reviews. They are, therefore, a very useful resource for anyone interested in similar topics. As mentioned above, find the references that interest you, and review them yourself, rather than rely on what others have said about them.
Conferences and seminars	Attending conferences and seminars on your topic of interest is another way of reviewing the literature indirectly. You will hear about what other people are researching, you will have the chance to ask them specific questions and to hear about new publications that you may not have found. Many speakers will distribute a list of references used in their presentation to the audience. We will discuss the role of conferences and seminars in our final chapter of the book, when we discuss their role in disseminating your research and getting feedback. However, it is important to highlight that attending conferences and seminars plays a very important role in the initial phase of your research project as well.

As you start to refine your search, you will also need to read outside of the strictly Interpreting and Translation studies field, into areas relevant to your research question that have not been addressed by the Interpreting field. For example, if your research is about the professionalization of interpreting, you may want to read the literature in the field of Sociology that relates to definitions of professionalism, for example; if you are interested in researching interpreting testing, you may want to read the literature on language testing and assessment and evaluation in general.

By reading widely, you will familiarize yourself with the issues, debates, theories, concepts and research methods in the field. If you are uncertain about what you want to research, this first step will help you clarify your thoughts and ideas. Much of what you read in this first phase of your literature review will never make it into the final product. You will go through a process of elimination and only keep what is relevant to your research questions and to your argument. One common comment from teachers on the margins of students' literature reviews is 'how does this relate to your research question?' Students are often reluctant to exclude anything that they have read, falsely assuming that if they do not include it in the final product, their reading has been in vain. You need to accept that sifting through the literature is a crucial part of the review process. We can compare this process to a funnel. You start reading widely and gradually narrow your focus down to your very specific research questions, discarding what is not strictly relevant and keeping only the references that you can link to your research questions and aims. During this first phase, you are also looking for answers to your research questions or to similar research questions as well as for the ways similar questions have been addressed through the different methodologies. Keep in mind that you will come back and revise your literature review later once you have refined your study, and again once you have collected your data, so that you can tailor the review to your findings. So you do not need to get it perfect at this stage in terms of writing style either, as the more you write, the more polished the review will become.

Exercise 2.1

Go to your university library and find an edited volume, a book and a journal on Interpreting. Follow the different suggestions outlined above.
    Book a session with the librarian to learn how to search databases. Then start searching literature on a particular topic that interests you.

2.2.1.2 Keeping track of your searches

It is very important that you do not lose track of the literature that you have searched and found and the literature that you have discarded. In order to avoid wasting time duplicating your efforts, you need to devise a good tracking system, where you document all your searching efforts, including the databases you have searched, the keywords you have used, the date of the searchers, the results you have obtained and so forth.

    Equally important is for you to devise a system for citations. One method is to record verbatim quotes that you think you may use in different files under themes. You can then go back to those thematic files and read all of the quotations from different authors and review their different positions together. The files can be simple Word documents, or they can be part of a software package. When copying quotes, make sure that you make no mistakes and that you clearly document the sources of the quotes, including author, publication details, year and page number. If you do not have the full reference details, you will not be able to use the quote and it may take too long to look for its source again.

Another important tool in this phase is a reference management software system such as EndNote. Different libraries will subscribe to different systems. These software packages help you to organize your references for later easy access.

Exercise 2.2

Book a training session on how to use Endnote or another reference management package used by your university library.
Start your own electronic library on Interpreting.

2.2.1.3 Reading and taking notes

Ridley (2008, p. 46) discusses the SQ3R approach: Survey, Question, Read, Recall and Review. The first letter in this approach could also stand for 'Skim', as this is what you are doing when you first find an article or a book: you skim through it, read the abstract or the book summary and table of contents and decide whether it is of relevance to your research. Once you have decided that it is relevant, you start reading it in an active, directed way. You will need to approach research literature differently from the way you would approach a novel, which you read for entertainment and enjoyment. When you read research literature, you must ask yourself questions such as: What is the article about? What research questions is the project attempting to answer? What are the aims of the research? What research methods did the author use to answer those questions? Can I replicate those methods or build on them? Is the methodology adequate? Were the original aims of the study met? What are the findings of the research project? Are they convincing? What are the strengths and weaknesses of the research study? How does this research relate to my own?

Ridley suggests that after each section, you stop, recall what you read and review it. This entails taking notes and writing your own summaries, impressions and opinions about it for later use.

Exercise 2.3

1 Find three research articles on similar aspects of Interpreting. Read each of them following the SQ3R approach.

2 Now answer the following questions for each article:

What are the aims of the research?
What are the research questions?
What is the methodology used?
Who were the participants and how were they recruited?
What are the results of the research?
What are the author's conclusions?
What are the strengths of the study?
What are the weaknesses of the study?

3 Write a 150-word summary for each article using your own words.

4 Then review the three articles in connection to each other by comparing and contrasting the results and approaches of each, and in connection to your own research study. Position your research in the debate.

2.2.2 *Phase 2: Finding the gap*

The search in phase 1 will lead you to the second phase, where you must identify a gap in the knowledge that you will fill, to some measure, with your research project. If your original answers have already been addressed and answered adequately by previous research, then the first phase will have revealed this, in which case you need to devise new questions or revise them to address a different aspect of the problem.

The second phase is where you use the literature to support and justify your research. You need to demonstrate that your research project is significant because you have identified a problem that nobody has yet addressed or addressed adequately. This will support your claim for significance: demonstrating that your research is worthwhile because it will produce useful outcomes, it will make a valid contribution to the research community and the Interpreting community that has not been made before.

So, to sum up, through the review of the literature, you will identify an issue or a problem that needs to be addressed or you will corroborate that the problem you envisaged through your own practice is indeed a problem and has not yet been solved. You will then show that your research project will be able to address that problem, and you will justify its significance based on three general points: one, that there is a gap in the knowledge that no-one else has yet filled; two, that your project's methodology will be appropriate and effective in answering the research questions you pose; and three, that the results will be significant, because they will contribute not only to the addition of knowledge, but also, if it is applied research, to the improvement of the practice.

Exercise 2.4

Go back to the articles you reviewed in Exercise 2.3. Read them again and identify a gap in the knowledge: questions that these articles do not answer. Then pose research questions that can be answered by your research (refer to Chapter 1 on how to formulate research questions). Then justify the significance of your proposed research..

In Exercise 2.4, you are asked to review only three articles for the sake of the exercise. For your actual Literature Review, you will need to review many more in order to substantiate your claim that there is a gap in the knowledge. Many students will ask: how many articles is enough? When do I know that I have reviewed everything that there is to review? There is not a straight answer to these questions. It will depend on the topic that you are researching and on the discipline in which you are working. In established disciplines, where much research has been conducted over many years, there will be a lot more literature than in new and emerging fields. However, this is no excuse to only review a few articles. What changes is the specificity of the literature that you will read. In new and emerging disciplines, you will need to review literature that is not directly related to your research question, but that is indirectly related to it. For example, if you are interested in researching the discourse strategies used in class by Interpreting educators in the Chinese-English combination, you may not find many or any previous research in this area; so then you look for similar studies in other language combinations and if nothing can be found in that area either, then you look for studies on language teacher strategies, for example, and so on. Some of our own Interpreting students have told us that they cannot really do a Literature Review on their chosen topic because no research has been conducted in that area and hence nothing has been written on it. We have two responses to this proposition: 1. If what you say is true, that is what you want to find, because it means that your research can be justified. 2. How do you know that nothing has been written on it? If you have discovered this through reading the literature on Interpreting, then you have started your literature review already. Another way of knowing whether you have reviewed enough literature is by following the steps suggested in this chapter. If you have searched all the suggested sources, including the sources cited by others, you will reach a point where the citations will start to repeat. When you have read all the sources that others have cited, you can be sure that you have read most, if not everything that is to be read. Another way of knowing if you have read enough is when you stop asking yourself: 'I wonder if anything has been done on this or the other?' When you are confidently able to answer 'no' to these questions, then you have reached the end of your literature review. Of course, new articles will continue to be published as you do your research. You will constantly update your literature review during the duration of your project, but you will need to stop when you are ready to submit, without feeling that you have not covered all the literature.

2.2.3 Phase 3: Positioning your research

The third phase of this process is to position your research project in the context of other research. Your research will not appear in a vacuum. You need to establish your relationship with previous research. You may be replicating someone else's methodology, or you may be using a very different methodology to answer a similar question. You may be working within a specific theoretical framework, or you may be breaking new ground, using an inductive approach to allow your data to generate theory. You may be supporting previous research or you may be refuting it. Whatever it is you are doing, you need to make sure that you clearly state it and inform your reader of your position.

Exercise 2.5

Now write another section of the review where you position your research in relation to the research studies you have reviewed in Exercise 2.4.

Concurrently with the three phases outlined above, the process of conducting the review of the literature has the additional function of providing you with a model of the writing style in your discipline. As you read academic books and articles, you will learn the appropriate academic writing style, which you should emulate in your own writing. For example, it was once believed that it was inappropriate to use the first-person pronoun in academic writing. Hyland (2004) found that the personal pronoun is common in the Humanities and Social Sciences but not so in Science and Engineering fields. As you read Interpreting articles, you should be paying attention to the linguistic characteristics used by established authors.

Exercise 2.6

Conduct a linguistic analysis of the three articles you have read. Below are some points to guide you:

- Describe the structure of the article: List the subheadings.

- Analyse the use of voice: Does the article use the active or the passive voice? If it uses the active voice, does it use a personal approach? (first-person singular: e.g. 'I argue that. . .' or the first-person plural: 'We will demonstrate that . . .'), or an impersonal approach (e.g. '. . . the author suggests . . .' or 'This article will present . . .')?

- Analyse the use of verbs: List all the verbs in the articles and categorize them according to their propositional content (e.g. reporting verbs, opinion verbs, etc). Then identify the sections where the different categories of verbs appear (e.g. Introduction, Methodology, Results, Discussion sections).

- Analyse the use of cohesive devices: What cohesive devices do the articles use to link up different ideas and different paragraphs; to present supporting evidence and opinions; to question or challenge assumptions? etc.

2.3 The product

The product refers to your written review of the literature. There are two main approaches to the literature review in a thesis: the dedicated approach and the recursive approach (Ridley 2008). The dedicated approach is where you have the traditional chapter in the thesis called 'Literature Review' which reviews all the relevant references for your project. This approach is appropriate for a thesis, which concentrates on one large research project. Similarly, this is appropriate for a research chapter or article. If your thesis covers more than one research project, then you may want to opt for the recursive approach where each project is contained in one chapter, which commences with the review of the relevant literature.

Whichever approach you decide to take, the Literature Review needs to follow a structure. Different authors have suggested different structures, and there is no fixed single structure that must be followed. The structure will depend on your project and your aims. The first section of the Literature Review generally maps or contextualizes the field, identifies the gap and establishes the significance of your study. The second section shows how others have attempted to deal with the same or similar problem, and the third section critiques what has been done and again highlights what your research aims to do differently (Crowley 2007; Evans and Gruba 2002). Within each section, you will have subsections, introduced by titles and subtitles (a little like the chapter headings and subheadings in this book). In applied Interpreting research studies, the setting where the interpreting takes place will be crucial information, so a description of the setting normally appears first. This is where reports are a very useful source of information. Your review of reports will provide a chronological historical account of the setting of your research. This can be followed by a chronological review of the literature, (if your aim is to show the development of theories or of methodologies, for example), or by a thematic review, from those that are conceptually and philosophically very distant from your position to those closest to it. You must always remember that the literature review is not a list of summaries of loosely related articles, by author. The literature review critically presents aspects of different authors' writings that relate or contrast each other.

Think of your literature review as leading the reader on the start of a journey with you towards your research study. You are telling them a story about the broad topic of interest (e.g. dialogic interpreting): who has done research in this area, what they found, why it is interesting, what the strengths and weaknesses are and where the gaps are. You then narrow the focus to an element of the topic that is of most interest to you (e.g. turn-taking in multiparty interpreter-mediated communication): Why is this area of particular interest, what do we already know about this area, what don't we know about this topic and how do you propose to explore it further? Throughout the literature review you need to regularly link back to your own study: Why are you reviewing this particular chapter/book/article? What is relevant/unique/important about it? How has it informed your own research design? How does it relate to your research aims and questions?

Exercise 2.7

Look at your research question/s and aims and identify the headings and subheadings you would include in your literature review.

2.3.1 *Steps in the writing of the product*

Many steps are involved in the production of a final 'Literature Review'. The Literature Review is the most organic chapter of your thesis, because during the duration of your research (which may take from 6 months to 10 years!), you will keep adding to the Literature Review as new research becomes published. Nevertheless, you also need to realize that you will need to work on numerous drafts, not only of your Literature Review, but of all chapters. The following suggested steps, therefore, apply to all your chapters:

1 Step One: Write a plan. This will include the headings and subheadings you identified in Exercise 2.7 and a quick summary in point form of what you intend to review under each section.

2 Step Two: Expand on each section, including the appropriate use of quotes. Make sure that you have copied the quotes correctly and that you have referenced them fully.

3 Step Three: Read over your review and ensure that (a) your argument is coherent, (b) that everything that you mention has relevance to your research question, (c) that you make clear connections to your research aims, (d) that you maintain a sense of audience and make your position clear to the reader and (e) that you summarize your conclusions.

4 Step Four: Read the review again and ensure that your sentences are complete and grammatical, that you have no spelling mistakes, that you use apostrophes correctly and that your style is appropriate (modelling it after the literature that you have read)

5 Step Five: Leave it aside for a few days and then read the review again and ask yourself the following questions: (a) Does the review provide a clear summary of the context and the concepts relevant to my research? (b) Does the review demonstrate that I fully understand the literature I am reviewing? (c) Do I position my research clearly in the context of the academic debates and the research that has been conducted? (d) Do I clearly identify a gap in the knowledge that will be filled by my research? (e) Do I articulate the aims of my research in connection with what has already been conducted? (f) Do I convincingly argue that my research will be significant? (g) Is everything that is reviewed relevant to my research aims? (h) Am I reflexive enough? (i) Am I too critical? Do I substantiate any criticism of previous research?

Key pointers:

- What is already known about the topic?
- Why is it interesting?
- What are the gaps in the knowledge?
- Why am I interested in this issue?
- How can I improve our knowledge about this issue?

- How do I propose to investigate this issue?

- This is what I did

- This is what I found

- This is what I think it means

- This is how I think it can be applied in policy, practice and/or pedagogy

- These are my suggestions for future research

2.3.2 *Common flaws in novice researchers' literature reviews*

Below is a list of some of the most common flaws in students' or novice researchers' literature reviews, which you should try to avoid:

- Being too critical or not critical enough

- Using emotive language

- Making overgeneralizations, sweeping or unsubstantiated claims

- Using colloquial, spoken, non-academic language

- Straying from the main argument into irrelevant material

- Providing too much or too little information about previous research

- Presenting summaries of the literature without critically reviewing it and/or without making its relevance to their study clear

As you review the literature, you will need to maintain a balance between being too uncritical and too critical. If you are not critical enough, you run the risk of accepting everything that you read as the ultimate truth without questioning it. As you read, you need to reflect on what you read by asking yourself the questions suggested in Exercise 2.3. You will find that no single research project will be perfect or will answer all the questions. Some research projects may use flawed methodology or some may fail to answer the questions posed. When relevant, you may state these observations in your literature review. However, you must also beware of being too critical. Sometimes, the reason why a study may not be clear to you is because you do not fully understand the theories behind it, or the methodology or the style it is written in. Before you criticize a previous study, read it a number of times to make sure that you fully understand the claims made by the author. The author may also offer some caveats to the reader, acknowledging that the study has flaws and that further research is needed to make more reliable claims.

You must also beware of responding emotionally to research. You may have your own ideas and beliefs and may not agree with what you read. In your literature review, try to approach your review in a detached, objective way, avoiding emotive, judgemental or hyperbolic language. What you are reviewing is the robustness of the research study (the appropriateness of the methodology chosen to answer the research question, the validity of the sample, the extent to which the results can be generalized) and the logic of the argument and conclusions (Are the conclusions drawn from the results of the study? Is the argument logical? Does the author substantiate his/her claims?). This means that instead of criticizing the researcher, you are critiquing the research project, highlighting both its positive and negative points. As a researcher yourself, you will learn from the positive points by replicating them and from the negative points by discarding them. Other researchers will in turn learn from your future research positive and negative points.

Another common mistake is to make claims without any substantiation. This involves providing statements as fact without citing any sources. This tendency is also usually accompanied by exaggeration or overgeneralizations. This style of writing is acceptable in some genres, such as journalism, but not in the academic research genre. Example 2.1 is an excerpt from The Sydney Morning Herald, a daily newspaper, which exemplifies many of the traits that are unacceptable in academic writing. If we analyse the text in Example 1.2, we will see that it does not provide any sources to substantiate any of its claims. The only reference made by the author to support her claims is that 'some psychiatrists say' it, but she does not specify who the psychiatrists are and where they have written such information. Another characteristic of this excerpt that would be equally unacceptable in academic writing is the use of emotive and hyperbolic language that describe value judgements, such as 'it is obvious', 'ruthlessly exploited', 'useless products'. Another trait evident in this short text is the use of exaggeration and overgeneralization. Although she states that 'some psychiatrists say' this, it is impossible that everyone would be preoccupied with dieting and that such preoccupation has become a neurosis for the whole population of the world! Although she has most probably not meant to generalize in this way, that is the propositional content of her statement.

Example 2.1: Non-academic text

If we look back over the centuries, it is obvious that much of the dieting industry has ruthlessly exploited our shame. It has promoted fraudulent ideas and useless, sometimes dangerous, products. . . . In the 1920s, there were bile beans, laxatives with an extra bite that prevented your body absorbing fat. . . . By the 1950s, cigarettes were laced with appetite suppressants. Over the past century, our preoccupation with dieting has grown into a neurosis, some psychiatrists say. (Louise Foxcroft, 3/1/2012, The Sydney Morning Herald)

In contrast, Example 2.2 is an excerpt from the literature review of an academic chapter in an edited volume on Interpreting. The author describes the different angles from which simultaneous interpreting have been studied and described and provides references to research to substantiate each of her claims. Unlike Example 2.1, there are no pre-modifiers for each of the different phenomena presented. The author does not preface each phenomenon with her own opinion, but objectively states each of them.

Example 2.2: Academic text

Researchers have sought to understand and describe the process of simultaneous interpretation from a variety of different angles. One might choose to look at it as a sociolinguistic phenomenon, a 'mediated discourse event or communicative act' (e.g. Cokely 1992; Roy 2000). Alternatively, one might investigate neurologic phenomena (e.g. Gran 1989; Tomola et al. 2000/01), or use computational modelling (Londsdale 1996).

(*Source*: Harmer 2007, p. 76)

Exercise 2.8

Re-write the text provided in Example 2.1 as an academic text. As you do not know the sources to the claims, invent fictitious sources and change the writing style to an acceptable academic style.

A further oversight is to offer insufficient information to substantiate conclusions. In Examples 2.3 and 2.4, the sources are cited but there is not enough information for the reader to make judgements on whether the conclusions are justified or not.

Example 2.3

Empirical studies of interpreting in the United States and Australia (Berk-Seligson 1990; Davidson 2001; Hale 1997, 1999) suggest that professional practice is inconsistent with the theory.

In Example 2.3, we learn that empirical studies of interpreting have been conducted in Australia and the United States by at least three researchers. However, we are not told anything about these studies or about their results.

We are then presented with a conclusion that the practice is inconsistent with the theory. However, we are not told anything about the practice (Whose practice? In what context? etc) or anything about the theory (What theory? Whose theory? How is it inconsistent with a particular practice?). In Example 2.4, a number of studies are cited that supposedly suggest that interpreters are 'visible' participants in the interaction. Here we are presented with a metaphorical concept that is not explained: 'interpreter visibility'. The studies are not described either, so as the reader, we have no way of knowing what the cited studies have researched and what their findings are, unless we turn to the specific references to find out for ourselves. We are then confronted with a judgement: 'This clearly raises ethical issues for practitioners'. This bold statement does not present a good argument because first, we are not given enough information about the presumed evidence to decide for ourselves; and secondly, there is no discussion about the relationship between the unexplained concept of 'invisibility' and the unexplained concept of interpreter ethics.

Example 2.4

Studies of interpreters suggest that they are 'visible' participants in the interaction (Roy 1989; Wadensjo 1992; Metzger 1999; Angelelli 2004). This clearly raises ethical issues for practitioners.

Exercise 2.9

1 Try to locate the references cited in Examples 2.3 and 2.4. The examples provide only the name of the author and the year. Use your searching skills to find the full reference.
2 Read and review some of the references in relation to the concepts that are loosely discussed in the examples.
3 Write a review of the cited research studies and provide your own conclusions based on the results of the studies.

2.3.3 *Avoiding plagiarism*

Plagiarism means presenting others' work as one's own without acknowledging the author or authors. Even if you do not intend to plagiarize, you may inadvertently do so if you are not clear on how to reference your sources. As a general rule, the only times you do not need to cite your source are when you are making statements that are commonly known or accepted and when you are writing your own opinions, arguments and conclusions. Every other time, whether you have copied a verbatim citation or you have paraphrased what someone else has written, you need to appropriately reference the sources. There are different referencing systems, but the most common one in our field is the American Psychological Association (APA) system, which is what we are using in this book. If you are a student, you will need to ascertain which system your university would like you to use and be consistent throughout your thesis. If you are writing for publication, you will need to use the style prescribed by the journal or publisher. You can access most style manuals on-line. If you use a reference management system, such as Endnote, the software automatically adjusts the references to the chosen referencing system.

Throughout the Literature Review and the rest of your thesis, you will either cite verbatim quotations or paraphrase what others have said. All references used in your thesis must appear in the Reference list at the end.

Example 2.5: Verbatim quotation (from Swabey and Mickelson 2008, p. 57)

In Ethics and Decision Making for Interpreters in Health Care Settings (1990), Sandra Gish writes:

Professional ethics are standards or behaviors that have evolved over time to reflect the profession's desire to insure the well-being of its clients. They are expressed in a formalized code of behavior which describes the principles that are important to the profession. More importantly, they define the forms of behavior that are morally desirable by the profession in its service to consumers (Gish 1990, p. 21).

The examples below show the different ways to cite relevant sources.

In Example 2.5, Swabey and Mickelson provide a long verbatim citation from Sandra Gish. When text is cited verbatim, the page number needs to appear in the reference, as well as the name of the author and the year of publication. Verbatim quotations are used when they reflect exactly what we would like to say, when we are presenting a definition of a concept, when we want to contrast specific positions from different authors or when we want to create an effect that can only be achieved through someone else's exact words. Verbatim quotations need to be used sparingly, and they need to be adequately linked to your argument. Otherwise, you risk simply presenting a list of other people's ideas, without your own reflection. That is also considered to be plagiarism, even if you have appropriately cited the sources.

Example 2.6: Paraphrasing individual sources (Pöchhacker 2004, p. 121)

Early studies of cognitive operations in language processing by interpreters tested subjects for recall after interpreting and related tasks. Gerver (1974a), in an experiment with nine trainees and scripted texts, found that recall (as measured by content questions) was better after listening than after simultaneous interpreting or shadowing and identified simultaneous listening and speaking as the cause of impaired memorization. This was confirmed in subsequent work by Isham (1994), who concluded from the differential performance of signed-and spoken-language interpreters that post-task recall was not only a function of the interpreting process itself but reflected the impact of modality-related processing interference (see also Ingram 1992, p. 114)

In Example 2.6, Pöchhacker uses a topic sentence to introduce the theme of the paragraph. This is followed by descriptions of two studies that corroborate each other (Gerver 1974 and Isham 1994). He then makes further reference to one other study (Ingram), which is not summarized in his review. This excerpt is from a chapter that reviews research in Interpreting, which makes it impossible to review everything in detail. If you were writing a thesis on memory in Interpreting, then you would be expected to review all the relevant studies. Note the differences between Example 2.6 and Example 2.3.

Example 2.7: Paraphrasing a group of studies with results in common (Martinsen and Dubslaff 2010, p. 21)

Deviations from the norms, such as additions, omissions or register variations (e.g. Hale 1997, 2004; Jacobsen 2002), usually pass unnoticed by the primary participants involved because they cannot monitor the interpreters' renderings of their own or other participants' input.

In Example 2.7, Martinsen and Dubslaff cite Hale and Jacobsen as non-integral sources. The references to Hale and to Jacobsen support their claim that studies have shown that additions, omissions and register variations occur in interpreters' renditions. Having established this fact, they comment on the reasons why such deviations are usually undetected by the primary participants. Whereas in Example 2.6, the references were the subject of the text, in Example 2.7, they are secondary to the main argument presented in the text.

Exercise 2.10

Using the three articles that you have read for the exercises in this chapter, present a verbatim citation and two paraphrases following Examples 2.5–2.7. Provide the full references using the APA system.

2.4 The proposal

You should now be ready to start writing your research proposal. The application for any research degree programme will require a research proposal, which will be refined with your chosen supervisor. Although different universities will have slightly different proposal formats, all proposals have the same function, as explained by Kumar in the quotation below:

> Broadly, a research proposal's main function is to detail the operational plan for obtaining answers to your research questions. In doing so it ensures and reassures the reader of the validity of the methodology for obtaining answers to your research questions accurately and objectively (Kumar 2011, p. 218).

Your initial research proposal will be used to convince the admissions committee that your research is worth conducting and that you have a viable plan that can be completed within the time frame of the chosen degree. The proposal will be refined in consultation with your chosen supervisor, and it will become your blue print for the rest of your candidature.

The following are suggested sections that you should cover in your proposal. Refer to Chapter 1 to help you complete each of the sections:

Suggested research proposal template

Research Project Title:

Literature Review: Provide an overview of the current state of affairs, clearly demonstrate that there is a gap in the knowledge that you will attempt to fill with your proposed research. (Indicative length: 500 words)

Statement of Research Problem and Significance of Your Project: Based on the review of the literature, clearly state the research problem and highlight the significance of your project. (Indicative length: 250 words)

Research Aims/Questions: State the aims of your research project, and present them in the form of a number of clearly articulated research questions. (Indicative length: 200 words)

Methodology: Describe the methodology you will use to answer your research questions. This should include the type of study that you will be conducting (qualitative/quantitative, experimental/descriptive/survey, etc), the data that you will be collecting and the way you will be analysing the data. You may want to describe the theoretical approach that you will be taking in this section. (Indicative length: 500 words)

Timeline: Provide a draft timeline for the duration of your candidacy. A typical timeline includes: Year 1: Literature Review, Ethics clearance application, data collection; Year 2: Data analysis; Year 3: Writing of thesis. (Indicative length: 50 words)

Total length of proposal: Approximately 1500 words

Exercise 2.11

Write a research proposal for your project following the guidelines provided above.

2.5 Obtaining ethics approval

If you are a practicing interpreter, you will be familiar with the need to abide by a professional code of ethics. When conducting research, you will also need to abide by ethical requirements. There are two main aspects to ethical research: one has to do with consideration given to any human participant, and the other, with the way you collect, analyse and report the data.

2.5.1 *Research involving human participants*

Any research that will collect data from human participants, such as through questionnaires, interviews, focus groups or experiments, will need ethical clearance from the human ethics committee of the university in which you are enrolled and at times from external bodies where the research is being conducted. For example, if the research is about medical interpreters working in a hospital, the hospital will also require you to apply for ethical approval from their ethics committee. Research that uses publicly available information as data does not need ethics approval. Publicly available printed or on-line material, for example, can be used without the need to apply for ethical clearance because the information is already in the public domain.

Recruiting willing participants is always difficult for any research project. People need to volunteer to give of their time freely, and as researchers we must ensure that we do not abuse people's generosity to participate. In other words, we do not want to waste people's time in something that will not generate any benefits, either because the project has no merit or because we have not designed it well enough to achieve its aims. The research committee that will assess your application will be concerned with three major points: (1) the merit of your project, (2) the potential risk to any human participant and (3) the ethical conduct of your project.

You will need to convince the committee that your project has merit through your literature review and your argument about its significance, as explained in Chapter 1 and in previous sections of this chapter. You will also need to convince the committee that your chosen methodology will achieve the aims of your project. With regard to risk, for most Interpreting research, the risk to the participants will be negligible or minor. Negligible risk refers to the risk of participants being slightly inconvenienced by giving of their time to participate in the project. Minor risk may involve participants feeling uncomfortable with the content of material that they need to read or discuss. For example, if your research is on court interpreting and you choose a sexual assault case to simulate an interpreted situation where you want your participants to assess interpreters, the sensitive content of a sexual assault case may constitute minor risk in the form of emotional discomfort, especially if a participant has been the victim of sexual assault. Major risk refers to real potential physical or emotional harm that the research can cause to participants. Such risk is more likely in medical, clinical trials than in Interpreting research. Whatever the risk involved, you will need to justify it. Let us look at the sexual assault example. You may justify the choice of such material if you are researching how interpreters deal with sensitive material and how they interpret taboo language. If there is no link between your research questions and such sensitive content, then you should change it to something that is not potentially harmful to any participant. Another concern of ethics committees is to ensure that participants do not feel coerced to participate in a research project, and that there are no potential conflicts of interest. For example, if you are an interpreter educator that wants to conduct a study on teaching interpreting students, you will need to carefully consider how you recruit participants so that students do not feel that they have to participate in your study in order to get a good grade. These issues are not insurmountable, and a carefully designed project will receive ethics approval as long as it is clear that a risk assessment has been carried out.

The third point of interest to the research committee is that you conduct the research in an ethical way. This includes providing participants with enough information about the project and about what will be required of their involvement in order for them to give informed consent. Returning to the sexual assault example, potential participants who may be emotionally harmed by such material may choose not to participate.

2.5.1.1 Obtaining informed consent from human participants

Participants need to give you their permission to participate in any research. Before they can give you such permission, they need to have enough information to make an informed decision. They also need to know that they can withdraw their consent at any time if they change their mind. Different universities will have different guidelines on how to provide information to participants. Usually, each project will require you to produce an information sheet for the participant to read before they sign the consent form. Many universities produce standard pro-formas of information and consent forms, where all you need to do is fill in your details. Below are the main points that need to be covered in the information and consent forms.

The consent form will contain the details of the information sheet in first person. Below is a sample Consent Form.

Sample contents of an information sheet

1 Project title: The title needs to be short and clear.

2 Participant selection: Here you must outline the characteristics the participant must have in order to participate in the questionnaire. For example, the participants must be practicing interpreters in order to participate.

3 Description of the project in lay terms: Provide a short description of your project, stressing its significance, in language that anyone will be able to understand without any prior knowledge of the topic. Think about this section as an article in the newspaper that would attract the attention of the general public. This section is extremely important, as it will determine to a large extent whether someone will be willing to participate in a research project. They need to be assured that they will not be wasting their time in something that will be of no benefit to anyone.

4 Description of yourself as researcher: You need to show that you are qualified to conduct the research. If you are a doctoral student, you must name your supervisor as the expert in the field who will monitor your research.

5 Participant's involvement: Explain what the participant will be required to do and how long it will take.

6 Risks to participant: Mention any inconvenience, discomfort or potential harm to the participant.

7 Benefits: List the direct and indirect benefits of the research outcomes.

8 Dissemination of results: Explain how the results will be made public. This will include presentations at conferences and other public fora and publication.

9 Confidentiality: Ensure participants of the confidentiality of their personal information. For most Interpreting research, the identity of the participants will not be important, so they need to know that they will not be identified by name or by any personal details that may lead others to guess their identity. For example, if you conduct your research about interpreters who work for a small agency that employs only 5 interpreters of 5 different languages, the simple mention of the language will identify the particular interpreter.

10 Withdrawing consent: Participants need to know that there is no obligation at all for them to participate and that they can withdraw their consent at any time. In other words, they should not feel that they are entering a binding agreement to participate if they sign a consent form.

11 Further information: Tell them that they can ask anything about the project before they sign the consent form or afterwards. Participants will take a copy of the Information form with all your contact details and those of your supervisor's to contact you at any time after they have completed their participation.

12 Complaints: You need to include a section on who to refer any complaints to about the ethical conduct of your research. Usually, all complaints should be addressed to the university's ethics committee.

Sample consent form

Project Title:

I, (insert participant name), acknowledge that I have read the attached Information sheet and that I agree to participate in the above-mentioned project.

I understand that my participation is voluntary and that I can withdraw at any time. I also understand that all personal information will remain confidential.

Signed:

Name:

Date:

This study has been approved by (insert ethics committee name and approval number)

Exercise 2.12

Devise an Information Sheet and Consent Form for the research project you presented in your Research Proposal in Exercise 2.11

2.5.2 *Integrity in research conduct*

The second aspect of ethical research is integrity when collecting and analysing data and when reporting the results. This implies being as objective as possible so that our own opinions and views do not interfere with the results of our research. For example, it would be unethical to only include the data that will support our own opinions. Similarly, it would be unethical to only report the findings that agree with our position and ignore those that do not. Any attempt to deceive by selectively choosing, hiding or fabricating data is highly unethical conduct.

2.6 Conclusion

In this chapter, we have provided you with the steps and tools necessary to conduct the very crucial initial phases of any research project: the literature search, literature review, research proposal and ethics clearance application.

CHAPTER THREE

Questionnaires in interpreting research

This chapter will cover the following topics:

- What is the difference between a survey and a questionnaire?
- When to choose questionnaires?
- Question types
- Questionnaire design
- Sampling
- Questionnaire administration
- Questionnaire analysis
- Review of sample questionnaire-based research studies in conference and community interpreting research

3.1 Introduction

After reading Chapters 1 and 2 and completing all the exercises, you are now ready to decide on a method of data collection. The questionnaire is one of the most common methods of collecting large amounts of data relatively quickly. Dörnyei comments that its popularity '. . . is due to the fact that they are relatively easy to construct, extremely versatile and uniquely capable of gathering a large amount of information quickly in a form that is readily processible' (2007, p. 102). However, there is a lot more to conducting questionnaire research than simply writing a set of questions and giving them to a few people to answer. This chapter will discuss the complexities of devising, administering and analysing questionnaires and will take you through the different steps: from deciding on the method to analysing the results.

3.2 What is a survey?

A survey is a means of gathering information from particular sources to ascertain certain situations or conditions. Surveys can take different forms: observations, text analyses, interviews, focus groups and questionnaires. All of these methods can be used to survey a situation. However, surveys are more commonly associated with questions: both in the form of oral questions in an interview and written questions on a questionnaire. In this chapter, we will concentrate on the written questionnaire. Chapter 4 discusses interviews and other ethnographic methods.

One of the entries in The Macquarie Dictionary for the verb 'to survey' is '. . . to collect sample opinions, facts, figures or the like in order to estimate the total overall situation' (Delbridge et al. 2003, p. 1891). There are three key terms in the above definition: sample, estimate and total. A survey will not 'survey' everything or everyone; it will only survey a sample. A sample is a fraction of the whole population. From the information collected from the sample, an estimate will be made about the situation of the total population. A census is a questionnaire that aims to collect information from the whole population. A national census does this, normally every four years. In this chapter, we will discuss surveys, and not census. Later in the chapter, we will learn that the type of sample and the way the sample is chosen will determine how accurate or representative of the whole population the estimate provided by the survey is.

3.3 When to choose questionnaires as a research method

Before you embark on the design of a questionnaire, you need to decide if that is the best tool to answer your research questions. The first point to consider is that with any type of questionnaire, you are asking people's opinions about different issues, and that is all. You cannot ascertain whether what they say is true. So, for example, if you want to find out how well interpreters perform under different conditions, you will not obtain a very reliable result by asking them to tell you in a questionnaire. This is because their answers will be purely subjective and will not be measured against any valid instrument. Some very good interpreters may be very demanding on themselves and rate themselves low, whereas some not-so-good interpreters may overrate their performance. For such questions of performance, the best elicitation technique would be a valid and reliable testing instrument. What they may tell you may be interesting, but you can only report it later as what interpreters said they do, rather than what interpreters actually do. It may be an interesting research question to compare how self-rating differs from rating by other more reliable means. In that case, then the questionnaire can be used to elicit self-perceptions. Furthermore, questionnaires can be designed in such a way to cross-reference different question types to test the validity of respondents' answers. So although responses may be subjective, by asking the same information in different ways, you can assess the accuracy of their statements.

When you design your questions, you must endeavour to ask your sample about what they are able to accurately respond to. This has to do with your sample's age, background or situation. One way to ensure that only those who can answer the questions take part in the questionnaire is by clearly stating at the start of the questionnaire, the characteristics of the participants you are targeting. For example, if you want to survey interpreters about their court interpreting experience, you must specify clearly at the commencement of the questionnaire that only interpreters with court interpreting experience should respond. If you do not specify this, it is likely that you will attract others who do not qualify, and either they will find out half way through the questionnaire that they cannot answer it, or they will make up the answers. Similarly, the content of the questions needs to be appropriate for the sample that is being surveyed. For example, if you are surveying interpreter service users, it would not be appropriate to ask them about technical interpreting issues that they may not understand. This point will be further discussed below.

So, if what you are interested in is obtaining people's opinions, then you need to decide whether you would like those people to give you answers to specific closed questions that you have prepared or if you would like them to provide you with in-depth, detailed answers to open-ended questions; or a combination of both. If you want only detailed answers, then interviews or focus group discussions could be better elicitation methods. In a face-to-face interview or focus group discussion, you can elaborate on participants' answers by asking further clarifying questions; you can also obtain information that you had not thought about while designing a questionnaire. This is why it is a good idea to triangulate your data (see Chapter 1) by complementing questionnaires with interviews or focus groups, either before you design a questionnaire or after you have received questionnaire responses. You would conduct preliminary interviews or focus group discussions if the research area is new, and you need to explore the issues in order to be guided on what types of questions are needed in a large-scale questionnaire. However, if the topic has been researched before and many issues are clear to you, you may conduct individual interviews or focus group discussions afterwards to clarify some of the responses you may have received from the questionnaire that you feel need further elaboration.

Large-scale questionnaires are therefore used to elicit large amounts of data that can be analysed predominantly quantitatively, with some level of qualitative analysis. For this reason, the majority of questions tend to be closed questions, in order to restrict the answers people may give and allow for quantitative analysis. The questions must be able to be understood and answered quickly. So if you are interested in exploring complex issues, a self-administered questionnaire may not be the right tool to use, as respondents will not be able to ask you clarifying questions, and either they will abandon the questionnaire or respond arbitrarily.

Exercise 3.1

Determine if a questionnaire is the most appropriate elicitation method for the following research questions:

- Do Arabic interpreters have difficulty understanding people from different Arabic speaking countries?
- Does the passive voice predominate in judges' jury instructions, and does this pose difficulties for interpreters?
- What are the main issues encountered by the police when conducting investigative interviews with interpreters?
- What are the most effective teaching methods used to teach interpreting skills?
- What is the potential impact of interpreters on international negotiations?

After reading the research questions above, read Chapters 1 and 2 again and contemplate the following:

- Are the above questions answerable by research? If not, how can you refine them?
- If so, what would be the best research methods to answer the research questions?
- Can a questionnaire be complemented with other methods to answer any of these questions?

3.4 Questionnaire design

There are several factors to consider when designing a questionnaire apart from the questions themselves. These have to do with the format, structure and visual appeal of the questionnaire. The following are the basic components of a questionnaire:

- Participant Information page
- Questionnaire items
- Open section for comments
- Thank You page

3.4.1 *The participant information page*

All ethical research requires informed consent from the participants, as explained in Chapter 2. An information page will provide potential participants with all the relevant information needed for them to decide whether to spend their time participating in the project or not. In Chapter 2, we provided a list of the typical subheadings of an information page. With questionnaires, participants will not be asked to sign and return a consent form, because usually the researcher will not have direct access to the respondents, especially if the survey is administered on-line. For questionnaires, there needs to be a line at the end of the information page which states that completing the questionnaire will indicate informed consent from participants. If they do not consent to participate, then they will not complete the questionnaire.

As mentioned in Chapter 2, individual universities have their own guidelines for human research ethics requirements, in terms of what information must be included and how participants or respondents can complain if they believe they have been treated unethically. Therefore, before you design any research questionnaire, make sure you check the requirements of your university about any statements they expect to be included on the information page.

Another important ethical requirement that is particular to questionnaires is the amount of time it will take participants to complete the survey. Thirty minutes should be the maximum amount of time required to complete any questionnaire, with the optimum time being from 10 to 15 minutes. After 15 minutes, people may start to resent the time involved in participation, unless they are very interested in the topic, and may abandon the questionnaire, which can skew the results in terms of incomplete responses.

Exercise 3.2

Choose a research question from Exercise 3.1 and devise an information sheet and consent form for it.

3.4.2 *Questionnaire items*

Questionnaires normally elicit three types of information: factual, behavioural and attitudinal. Factual questions elicit demographic information that is relevant to the research aims. These questions may cover information about age, gender, place of residence, qualifications and so on. Make sure that you ask only what is relevant to your research. Eliciting irrelevant information will unnecessarily lengthen the questionnaire and waste valuable time at the commencement, when participants are most keen to respond.

Behavioural questions are those that ask participants about what they do; for example, how often they interpret at conferences, or whether they interpret for friends and family or only professionally. Here again, only questions that are relevant to the aims of the project should be asked.

Attitudinal questions are those that ask participants about their opinions or beliefs; for example, questions that ask respondents about their degree of agreement with certain statements. The order of the questions is very important to maintain interest. A logical coherence between all questions makes the questionnaire easier to follow and to answer.

At the conclusion of your set of questions, it is a good idea to have a question that asks for open comments. This will allow for information that you may not have thought of when designing the questionnaire.

Finally, the concluding page must thank the respondents for taking part in the research project.

The appearance of the questionnaire is also important. Participants will be more inclined to answer a questionnaire that looks clear, attractive and professional than one that looks 'home-made'. There are now many on-line questionnaire packages that can be accessed for free (usually with limited features) or for a subscription fee. Many universities also have their own questionnaire packages. Such questionnaires can be answered on-line, which is the preferred option for many people now, or printed out and distributed to those participants who are unlikely to have access to the internet. A quick search on the internet will produce a list of results for Web-based survey software from which you can choose.

3.4.3 *Content*

As stated above, the content of your questionnaire will be determined by your research aims and questions. One way to ensure that your items match your research aims and questions is to produce a table and plot each aim, question and item in alignment with each other, as seen in Table 3.1 below. If there are aims for which there are no questions, then more questions can be formulated. Alternatively, if there are questions that do not match the aims, then those questions can be deleted. A number of items can be linked to one aim or to multiple aims.

Table 3.1 Matching questionnaire items with each research aim and question

Research aims	Research questions	Questionnaire item
Aim #1	Research question #1	Items # 3, 5, 10, 11
	Research question #2	Items # 1, 4, 12, 20
Aim # 2	Research question #3	Items # 10, 19, 6
	Research question #4	Items # 2, 7, 9, 13
Aim #3	Research question #5	Items # 8, 14, 15
	Research question #6	Items # 16, 17, 18

3.4.4 Question type

Questionnaires are in the main, quantitative instruments, so the responses need to be easily quantifiable. For this reason, most questions ideally should be closed questions. While some open questions are acceptable, if most of your questions are open-ended, then the questionnaire may not be the right elicitation method for your purposes. Closed questions are those that can be answered by choosing an answer from a list of suggested responses, or by checking (ticking) against a range of statements that you agree or disagree with. Such answers can be easily quantified at the time of the analysis and can also be quickly answered by participants. Open questions are those that ask respondents to write an extended answer. These are adequate as extra comments, to cover what the researcher may not have included in the answer options. Many respondents will not want to spend extra time writing narrative answers and will leave those blank.

A questionnaire may have a wide range of question types, depending on the aims of each question. We will list the types of questions below, in relation to each section of the questionnaire.

Section 1: Factual information

The first section will elicit demographic information from the participants. If you are interested in seeing how interpreters' opinions change according to their age group, then you will need a question that asks how old they are. Rather than have an open question where everyone enters their individual age, a list of multiple-choice answers that group ages is more appropriate. These answers must be mutually exclusive, so be careful not to duplicate an age as in: 18–25, 25–35. Similarly, be careful not to omit any age, as in: 18–25, 27–35.

First, you must decide what age groups to list. If you are interested in surveying children who act as interpreters for their parents, then you would include age groups that are under 18. Note that there are very strict regulations about recruiting children into research studies, so check with your university's ethics guidelines about what is acceptable.

However, if you are interested in professional practising interpreters, then you will need to start the age group from age 18. There is no point having a category that is younger because there will be no one in that category. If you look at sample question 1, you will see that each category covers 10 years, except for category 1 (18–25) and category 6 (over 60). This is because those two end categories are likely to be the smallest ones. There will be none under 18, and possibly very few under 21, and there may not be anyone over 60. If that is the case, after receiving all the responses, you can further conflate the categories.

Sample question 1

Please indicate your age:

1 18–25
2 26–35
3 36–45
4 46–55
5 56–65

For example, if the results produced one respondent in category 1, five in category 2, twenty in category 3, nineteen in category 4, two in category 5 and zero in category 6, you may want to reclassify them in the following way:

1 $18 - 35 = 6$
2 $36 - 55 = 39$
3 $56 + = 5$

You can then clearly see that the majority of respondents fall in the new category 2 = 36 – 55. However, when you are analysing the data, you may find differences between age groups 3 and 4, so you can conflate them to describe your sample in a simpler way, but you may still want to keep them separate to see if there are any significant differences between the age groups in the responses provided.

A similar question would be one that asks about years of service. If you are interested in seeing the different opinions of interpreters according to how long they have been working in the field, then a question on how many years of experience they have may also be appropriate, as seen in sample question 2. There may be some link between age group and years of experience, although such a link may not be as prominent in interpreters as it may be in other professions.

Sample question 2

How long have you been practising as a conference interpreter?

   1 Less than 5 years
   2 6–10 years
   3 11–15 years
   4 16–20 years
   5 Over 20 years

With questions such as 1 and 2 above, there is no need to add an 'other' category, because you have covered all possibilities. Respondents must be told to pick only one answer. If the questionnaire is an on-line one, you can customize the questions so that respondents will not be permitted to choose more than one.

However, with a question on interpreter qualifications, the case may be different. You may list the possibilities you know, but there may be other possibilities you will not know which are left open for the respondents to fill in, as in sample question 3.

Sample question 3

What academic qualifications in Interpreting do you hold?

   1 Nil
   2 Undergraduate degree
   3 Post graduate degree
   4 Other (Please specify _____)

In this case, respondents may have more than one qualification, and they should be permitted to tick as many as applicable. Item 4 in sample question 3 is an example of an open-ended question, where respondents are asked to provide information through a text-based response.

Other types of questions that may be appropriate in this first section are state and/or country of residence (depending on whether the survey is national or international), country of origin, gender and so on. The questions will depend on what the researcher wants to find out that is relevant to the study at hand, so there is no set list of required questions.

Section 2: Behavioural questions

This section will ask questions about what interpreters do, such as how often they interpret in certain settings, how they react to certain situations, what they do if they need to ask for clarification and so on. Once again, the content of this section will also depend on the research aims. Below are some sample questions, using different approaches.

Sample question 4 provides a number of settings and four frequencies from which respondents can choose. This is also considered a multiple-choice question.

Sample question 4

State how often you work in the following settings

International settings

Once a week—more than once a month—once a month—less than once a month

Legal settings

Once a week—more than once a month—once a month—less than once a month

Medical settings

Once a week—more than once a month—once a month—less than once a month

Another type of question that is appropriate for behavioural questions is the simple polar interrogative, which elicits either a yes or a no. These should be questions that are mutually exclusive. Often a Yes/No question will lead to an open request to specify or explain, as seen in sample 5.

Sample question 5

Are you a member of AIIC?

Yes ☐ (go to question 6)
No ☐ (go to question 7)

Section 3: Attitudinal questions

There are different ways of asking people about their opinions. One way is to pose an open question and ask them to write down what they wish. This is the least leading type of question because respondents will not be influenced by anything you may tell them. However, they may not be able to respond, either because they have not thought about the issue before and have not formed an opinion, or they may not want to take the time to respond because it would take too much effort to do so. Another way of eliciting their opinions is by presenting them with a list of ready-made opinions in the form of statements and to ask them to choose the one they most agree with. These are probably the most difficult multiple-choice questions to design, because the statements have to be clear and include all possibilities. Sample question 6 is one such question.

Sample 6 question

In your opinion, what best describes accuracy in interpreting?

1 A word-for-word literal translation

2 A free, open translation that keeps the main points

3 A translation that is equivalent in structure and surface meaning

4 A translation that is faithful to the original intent, regardless of the form

Questions such as sample question 6 are problematic for a number of reasons. First, the concept of 'accuracy' is a very complex concept that cannot adequately be described in one short sentence. Secondly, each statement can lead to different understandings depending on the background of the respondent. This means that the answers will not be valid because the question will not have *construct validity* (see Chapter 6). There is also much missing contextual information for the respondents to be able to answer adequately. There is the possibility that the respondent does not agree with any of the statements. You can, of course, add a fifth statement 'none of the above', but if the respondents choose that, you have not been provided with a very useful result. You could also add a sixth option 'other' where respondents can write their own definition, but this may not elicit very thorough and meaningful answers either.

Another way of eliciting people's opinions is by providing a number of statements and asking them to rank them on a scale. These types of questions can elicit more reliable answers, because many respondents may not be completely in favour or against a statement but may feel more or less inclined to agree with certain statements. There are two main types of scale questions: Likert scales and Semantic differential scales, as seen in sample questions 7 and 8.

Sample question 7: Likert scale

Please indicate your level of agreement with the following statements on a scale from 1–5

Pre-service training for medical interpreters is a waste of time

1 —— 2 —— 3 —— 4 —— 5

Strongly agree   Strongly disagree

Sample question 7 uses words only for the two extremes. For most Likert scales, this will be sufficient. It is also possible to specify the meaning of the other numbers, by adding the words: disagree under #2, neutral under #3 and agree under #4. To avoid superficial answers, the polarity of the statement should be switched around, so that the positive is not always on the right and the negative on the left, and vice versa. Question 7 could have a follow-up question as in 7.1:

Sample question 7.1

Pre-service training for medical interpreters is a good idea

1 —— 2 —— 3 —— 4 —— 5

Strongly agree   Strongly disagree

If the respondent achieves a high score for both these questions, then we can surmise that the respondent is in favour of pre-service training. If s/he gets a low mark, then s/he is against training. However, if they get a high mark for 7 and a low mark for 7.1, it may be that they did not read the question carefully, misunderstood the question or just answered at random. This is why it is important to have a number of these types of questions to cross-reference and increase the validity of the responses. It is also important to have a middle number, such as 3 in this case, to indicate neutrality; otherwise, respondents will be forced to take sides.

Semantic differential scales are very similar to Likert scales. However, they are worded differently. Instead of asking respondents to agree or disagree with a statement, they are asked to decide on the value of a proposition on a scale between two opposing descriptors. Sample question 8 is a reformulation of sample 7, using a semantic differential scale. The intermediate values can also have descriptors such as 'useless', 'neutral' and 'useful'.

Sample question 8: semantic differential scale

How useful is pre-service interpreting training for medical interpreters?

Completely useless ——|——|——|—— Very useful

3.4.4.1 The matched guise technique

Although not a question type, the matched guise technique is a method that is associated with semantic differential or Likert questions and is also associated with experimental research. It is a common technique used to elicit responses on language attitudes. Participants are asked to listen to recordings and to evaluate them on a scale on a set of criteria – for example, how credible, how intelligent, how competent they think the speaker is. The recordings are usually identical in content but different in other features. For example, Hale, Bond and Sutton (2011) conducted matched guise experiments to ascertain if interpreter accents made a difference in the evaluations of the witnesses who spoke other languages.

3.4.5 *Question wording*

Writing questions is a difficult task. Research has found that the wording and structure of questions can influence the answers (see Converse and

Presser 1986; Loftus 1979). For example, Converse and Presser (1986) found that asking the same question with either the word 'forbid' or the words 'not allowed' produced very different responses. Similarly, Loftus (1979) found that different terms with the same denotation but different connotations (e.g. smash, collide and hit) also produced different responses from respondents. To avoid such effects, multi-item scales can be used, where a number of items that relate to the same overarching topic are presented in different ways, using different language, to counteract any bias produced by the wording.

Certain structures and terms also can make questions more difficult. When you write questions for questionnaires, the aim is to make them simple and effective. Below are some things to avoid:

1 Questions with a number of difficult concepts or unfamiliar/ technical words
2 Questions that can be ambiguous or too vague
3 Double-barrelled questions
4 Questions with embedded clauses
5 Questions that use the passive voice
6 Leading or loaded questions.

3.4.5.1 Technical terminology or professional jargon in questionnaire items

The level of technical language that is appropriate to be used depends on the target audience. If your audience are professional interpreters, then you can use terms such as 'consecutive interpreting' or 'sight translation' and other terms with which interpreters will be familiar. However, you may not want to use technical linguistic terms, such as 'pragmatic equivalence' or 'ideational, textual and interpersonal functions' that not all interpreters will be able to understand. If your audience are not interpreters, then you cannot assume that they will understand interpreting terms. One example is the way legal practitioners can potentially misunderstand the word 'interpret' as something only lawyers can do when 'interpreting the evidence' or 'interpreting the law', for example. If you want to ask lawyers about interpreting issues, it may be a good idea to start the question with a definition such as 'Interpreting refers to the oral translation of spoken language'. It is often very difficult to simplify the language to cater for a general audience. The more you know about the target population, the better equipped you will be to cater your language to their level of understanding. One way to test whether your questions are understood by the target audience is to test them with a few representatives of that audience before launching the questionnaire. This is known as piloting. We will discuss piloting in more detail later in the chapter.

3.4.5.2 Vague or ambiguous questions

The validity of the instrument will depend on how well all respondents understand the intended meaning of each question. This is why extra care must be taken to ensure that questions are not ambiguous or too vague. For example, if you want to know how often interpreters work in a certain setting, it is better to use specific frames of reference such as 'once a week', rather than 'regularly'. If a word you choose for your question has more than one meaning, it is best to change it for another word. These ambiguities can be detected in the piloting phase.

3.4.5.3 Double-barrelled questions

These are questions that contain more than one concept or more than one question in one single item, as shown in sample question 9:

Sample question 9:

Have you ever been told by a medical practitioner or a lawyer that you should interpret word-for-word or that you shouldn't add or omit anything to your interpretation?

The above example is an exaggerated one to illustrate the point. A respondent may have different answers for what they have experienced from medical practitioners or from lawyers. If you are not really interested in the type of professional, then it is better not to name any at all, and use a generic term such as 'the service provider'. Similarly, the question above may be trying to clarify the meaning of 'word-for-word' by providing the extra piece of information 'not add or omit anything'. However, these are not necessarily the same thing, and they are bound to confuse respondents. To overcome the problem with understanding concepts in many different ways, you can ask a number of different questions that relate to the same point. For example, ask a question about being required to interpret 'word-for-word', another that asks about being required to interpret 'literally', another using the term 'verbatim' and so on.

3.4.5.4 Questions with embedded clauses

As mentioned above, questions in a questionnaire need to be understood quickly by the respondents. If respondents need to read the question twice to understand it, it is not a successful question.

Sample question 10

Have you ever been confronted with ethical dilemmas when you are interpreting at a conference in the booth, in a doctor's surgery or in a courtroom?

Sample question 10 contains a main clause and a dependent clause. If the aim is to ascertain whether interpreters experience ethical dilemmas in different settings, and how often these occur, the above question can be reformulated in the following way:

Sample question 10.1

Please indicate how often you have confronted ethical dilemmas in the following settings:

1 Conference interpreting in the booth
   Never ——|——|——|—— Very often
2 Interpreting in a doctor's surgery
   Never ——|——|——|—— Very often
3 Interpreting in the courtroom
   Never ——|——|——|—— Very often

Although we stated above that the terms 'often' or 'regularly' are very imprecise and should be avoided, they can be used in questions such as number 10, when it is unlikely that the respondent will have a clear indication of the exact number of occurrences of a certain experience.

3.4.5.5 Asking questions in the active voice

Questions in the active voice are always easier to understand than questions in the passive voice. Sample question 9 above uses the passive voice: 'Have you ever been told by a medical practitioner . . .'. This question can be converted into the active voice and into the present tense: 'Do medical practitioners ever tell you . . .'.

3.4.5.6 Leading or loaded questions

You must beware of asking questions that can distort responses in order to support your own opinions or questions that can logically only obtain one answer. For example, it is very unlikely that any respondent would answer No to a question such as sample question 11. This question will not contribute anything to your results.

Sample question 11

Do you believe that interpreters should provide high quality services?

Yes
No

Questions about quality, however, maybe very important to your study, but the way to ask them to ascertain whether the respondents have a real interest in quality or they are only paying lip service to it is by asking different indirect questions that will lead you to a conclusion. The following can be some examples:

Example 3.1: Questions to an interpreting service agency

Do you give preference to interpreters with the highest qualifications?
Do you seek feedback on interpreter performance from those who hire their services?
Do you provide interpreters with feedback on their performance?
Do you provide professional development opportunities to your interpreters?

The questions above are simple yes/no questions to give you an idea of how to ask indirect questions about quality. However, in a questionnaire, you may not want to have too many of these polar interrogatives, as it may lead the respondent to answer them all in the affirmative, because they are positively conducive. In other words, it will be obvious to the respondent that the preferred answer to all of them would be 'yes'. To avoid this, you may want to use multiple choice answers such as in the example below:

Example 3.2: What types of professional development activities do you provide the interpreters you employ?

a None
b Payment to attend activities of their choice
c Short courses by invited facilitators
d Other

Exercise 3.3

Divide your questionnaire into the different sections specified above. Then devise questions for each section using each of the question types outlined above. Once you have written all your questions, test them by ensuring they abide by all the principles you learned in this chapter. Then draw up a table to plot your questions in alignment with your research aims and research question.

3.5 Piloting

Piloting means testing the questionnaire before you launch its final version. You can first pilot it with friends and family and then with a small sample (about 10) of your intended population. In your pilot, you will ask people to check for typographical errors, clarity of the questions, missing questions and how long it took them to complete it. Then you will analyse the responses to see if the answers caused any problems. After the pilot, you will refine your instrument and launch it officially. This piloting phase will help ensure that the questionnaire is a *valid* instrument. In other words, that the questions are understood as intended and that they will elicit the responses that will address your research questions. As Andres states:

> From a survey research perspective, information collected through one or more survey modes is valid or trustworthy to the extent that it (1) produces information that answers the research questions posed by the researcher, (2) accurately describes the sample or population at hand, and, if appropriate, (3) can be extended to individuals beyond the participants of the study (2012, p. 115).

Exercise 3.4

Now choose a few friends and/or family and pilot your questions with them, following the guidelines above.

3.6 Sampling

Before you can administer your questionnaire, you need to decide on your sampling technique. In other words, who you are going to target to answer your questionnaire and how you are going to recruit your participants. This section will discuss the meaning of sampling, the different types of sampling techniques and how to decide on the best one to use for your project.

> The sample is the group of participants whom the researcher actually examines in an empirical investigation and the population is the group of people whom the study is about . . . the sample is a subset of the population that is representative of the whole population (Dörnyei 2007, p. 96).

So, the sample is a fraction of the population that you are researching. Sampling allows for generalizations or good estimates of the whole population based on the sample (a limited number of cases). The level of representativeness of the sample – in other words, how accurately you can claim that the results of your study are representative of the whole population – will depend on the sampling technique adopted. Sampling techniques fall under two broad categories: those normally associated with quantitative research and those normally associated with qualitative research paradigms. You may find it difficult to decide which sampling method to employ. According to Andres (2012, p. 96):

> The best sampling strategy for a given survey project is the one that is best suited to the study. . . . For small-scale research projects, probability sampling is either not necessary, not feasible, and/or not desirable. Also, the tenets of ethics may dictate what can or cannot be done in terms of sampling.

So, there is no rigid rule as to which method you should be using. Nevertheless, you should be able to justify the sampling method you choose. Once again, you need to go back to your research aims and research questions and define your sample accordingly.

One common question from students is 'how many is enough for a sample?' There is no strict rule as to how many respondents are ideal. Once again, this depends on the purpose of the study. If the study is qualitative, it will not be concerned with representativeness, but rather with the detailed analysis of individual answers, so the number of respondents is not important. When it comes to quantitative research, the larger the sample, the less is the likelihood of error. Dörnyei (2007, pp. 99–100) suggests a minimum sample of 100 for a quantitative survey to claim representativeness. Similarly, you may wonder how many completed questionnaires you should be aiming for as a minimum number for your study. While there is no strict rule about response rates either, common sense will tell you that analysing two or three questionnaires will not be adequate. Kumar (2011) suggests that an adequate response rate for surveys is between 20 per cent and 50 per cent.

3.6.1 Probabilistic sampling method

The techniques associated with quantitative research use the Probability method, which means the samples are randomly selected and can be representative of the whole population. Being representative means also being generalizable. When analysed statistically, the standard error (SE) can show the accuracy of the sample: the lower the standard error, the higher the precision of the sample; the bigger the sample, the lower the SE. In a representative sample, every person has an equal chance of being selected and that is why the results can be generalized to the whole population.

There are three main types of probability random sampling techniques: the Simple Random Sampling (SRS) technique, the Stratified Sampling (SS) technique and the Cluster Sampling (CS) technique, as seen in Table 3.2 below. When using any of the probability techniques, it is advisable to use a sample frame, which is a list of the whole population.

For example, say our population comprises Interpreting students of a university for a particular year. Our sample frame will comprise a list of all the students from the particular cohort. This will give us a total number for the chosen population. For this example, we will say that the total population is 100. We then choose the type of sampling technique we would like to apply: SRS, SS or CS. There are three subcategories under the Simple Random Sampling (SRS) technique (see Table 3.2). The first one is the lottery technique, which is adequate for a small population such as this one. We can print out all the names of the students, cut them out into individual strips, put them all in a hat or a box and select the number we want for our sample. If we select a sample of 10 (10%), we can then approach the 10 selected students and administer the questionnaire to them. This means that every student has a 10 per cent chance of being selected (i.e. 10 in 100). If we choose 20, then they would have a 20 per cent chance of being selected and so forth. Whatever percentage we choose must be reported in our results. For such a small population, however, we may not need a sample, as we could conduct a survey of the whole population, which is called a census.

Another method we can use is the systematic method. If we want to survey 10 per cent of a population of 1000 (i.e. 100 in total), we can select every 10th person on our list. This systematic approach will only work if the list is organized alphabetically, for example, and not by language or gender, or any other characteristic. For large populations, we can use the computerized random number method, where the program randomly selects the sample. In this method, you will number your population on your list and then use a computer program (see http://www.random.org/) to generate random numbers. You need to enter the minimum number (1) and the maximum number (in this case 1000). The results I have just generated using the program cited above, for a sample of 10, was: 708, 108, 495, 914, 466, 255, 110, 351, 299, 759. You will then go to those numbers and select the people whose names appear beside those numbers, as your sample.

The SRS technique we used was purely random. In other words, we did not take into consideration any personal characteristics of the population. Let us assume that a population of 1000 interpreters was made up of 500

Table 3.2 Probability sampling techniques

Features relating to these sampling methods	Probability method (Associated with quantitative research)		
	Simple Random Sampling (SRS)	Stratified Sampling (SS)	Cluster Sampling (CS)
Representative of the whole population: generalizable The bigger the sample, the lower is the Standard Error Response rate should always be reported Sampling Frame needed (List of whole population)	Lottery method for small populations (drawing names out of a hat – e.g. 500 members, 50 drawn = 1:10 chance of being selected) Radom number method (generated by computers http://www.random.org/) Systematic method. If 10 per cent sample required, choose every 10th person on the frame. The list needs to be mixed; for example, you cannot have all males first followed by females.	(more accurate than SRS) A combination of randomization and categorization Different groups are formed (strata) which the researcher wants represented in the sample (e.g. trained and untrained interpreters) Then SRS is selected from each group	If population is too large, for example, all Interpreting students in Europe 1st randomly select a group of countries (cluster) 2nd randomly select a sample from each. The higher the number of clusters, the more representative the sample. You can use SRS or SS to choose the clusters

(*Source*: Based on: Bloch 2004; Dörnyei 2007)

Chinese, 100 Japanese, 40 Korean, 60 Spanish, 100 Russian and 200 Arabic interpreters. The SRS technique we used did not guarantee that the sample selected was truly representative of all the different language combinations. Because it was truly random, we could have selected 100 Chinese interpreters and none from any other language, or any other possible random combination. To avoid this situation, we can use the Stratified Sampling technique. We first separate the population into language groups (or strata), and we then apply any of the three SRS techniques to each stratum or group. This means that our population will be sure to have random representation from all the subgroups.

If our population is too large, we may want to use the Cluster Sampling technique. If we are interested in researching the effectiveness of Interpreting teaching methods in Europe, first we should form clusters of the countries in Europe. This can be done according to geographical location or any other criterion. For example, we can have one cluster for Eastern European countries, one cluster for Western European countries, one cluster for Southern European countries and one cluster for Northern European countries. Then we need to randomly select a sample from each cluster, using any of the techniques we mentioned above. To refine our sample, we will need a further step. Once we have the randomly selected countries, then we will need to list the tertiary institutions from those selected countries and again, apply one of the above techniques to select the sample of institutions.

One aspect to keep in mind is that participation in any research project must be completely voluntary, as we explained in Chapter 2. This means, that even if you have devised a very systematic sampling strategy, participants cannot be coerced to participate. For this reason, most samples, especially in Interpreting studies, end up being non-probabilistic, as will be explained in Section 5.2 below.

3.6.2 *Non-probabilistic sampling method*

Qualitative research is normally associated with non-probability sampling methods. Non-probability sampling relies on the judgement of the researcher and is said to be more subjective than probability sampling, although no research study is purely objective, no matter which method is used. Although we cannot claim representativeness with a non-probabilistic sample, if our technique is well-thought out and devised, we can extend our results to other studies. As mentioned above, often a truly random sample will be impossible to achieve. We can also use a mixture of both, probabilistic and non-probabilistic techniques, just as we can mix quantitative and qualitative methods.

There are three main non-probabilistic sampling techniques: quota, network/snowballing and convenience/opportunistic, as shown in Table 3.3 below. Quota sampling is similar to the Stratified sampling technique described above but without the randomness. The researcher decides on the quota of each type of participant from the sampling frame, using his/her knowledge of the population as a whole. For example, if we have a class of 100 students in an Interpreting course with different language groups, where 30 were Chinese, 10 Japanese, 10 Korean, 10 German, 10 French, 10 Spanish and 20 Arabic, we may want to devise quota with the same percentage values (i.e. 30% Chinese, 10% Japanese, 10% Korean, 10% German, etc). If our sample size is 10 per cent of the population, we will then approach 3 Chinese, 1 Japanese, 1 Korean, 1 German, 1 French,

Table 3.3 Non-probability sampling techniques

Features relating to these sampling methods	Non-probability method (Associated with qualitative research)		
	Quota sampling	Network or snowball sampling	Convenience or opportunity sampling
When probability sampling is impossible or undesirable	Similar to Stratified sampling without the randomness	The researcher identifies a group of people with the desired characteristics and asks them to pass it on to others with similar traits	This can be seen as a less structured version of the quota sampling
Non-representative, difficult to generalize to whole population	From the sampling frame, the researcher establishes the proportions of different parameters (e.g. 60% of interpreters are female)		
Limitations of these samples must be reported	This means that 60 per cent of the sample (quota) should be female	Normally obtained through contacts from people who share networks or similar characteristics	The researcher identifies the needed characteristics and asks for volunteers from convenient groups
	The researcher then fills the quota from participants that are accessible to him/ her (e.g. in a sample of 100 interpreters, 60 must be female), but the selection need not be random		
	No way of working out representativeness	Different starting points should be used to avoid getting everyone who shares the same views or experiences	
	Dimensional sampling is a variation of quota sampling, where at least one representative is included for each parameter in the sampling frame		

(*Source*: Based on: Bloch 2004; Dörnyei 2007).

1 Spanish. and 2 Arabic students to participate in the survey. A variation of quota sampling is Dimensional sampling where there needs to be at least one representative from each group. So in the population above, it would be fine to have at least 1 student from each of the language combinations. The problem with this type of sampling is that the researcher may be biased in her/his choice of participants, if they are being handpicked.

The next type of technique is Network or Snowballing sampling. This is a common sampling technique for research into Interpreting. The researcher identifies a professional network with the characteristics needed for the research question, for example, practising interpreters. In Australia, there are a number of ways practising interpreters can be reached: through national professional association e-bulletins (AUSIT or ASLIA) or other similar associations, through the directory published by the national accreditation authority (NAATI), through the different panels they sit on and through the different employers. However, not every practising interpreter is a member of AUSIT or ASLIA, not every practising interpreter is on the NAATI directory and not every practising interpreter is on a panel of interpreters. Similarly, many are on multiple lists and panels. For this reason, those who are contacted are asked to pass on the call for participants to other colleagues they know, which will have a 'snowballing' effect. The researcher will never be sure, however, if the whole population has been reached, and therefore, it cannot be claimed that every interpreter had an equal chance of participating. Similarly, because there is no way of knowing the number of the whole population, a response rate cannot be reported.

The last sampling technique that appears in Table 3.3 is the Convenience or Opportunity technique. This is where the researcher specifies the characteristics respondents need to have in order to participate and asks for volunteers from convenience groups such as colleagues, fellow students, family and friends, etc. There is nothing wrong with convenience samples as long as the respondents fulfil the relevant criteria in order to be qualified to answer the survey questions. For example, if the survey is about students' reactions to different teaching methods, then a sample of students is adequate. However, if the questions are about interpreter working conditions, students who have no professional experience will be of no use at all.

Exercise 3.5

Look at your research question and research aims and decide on the sampling technique you will use to recruit your respondents. What would be the pros and cons of each technique for your purposes?

3.7 Questionnaire administration

Now that you have designed your questionnaire and have devised a sampling technique, you are ready to administer it and start collecting your data. Most questionnaires nowadays are administered via internet survey packages. There are many advantages to administering questionnaires on line:

- They are easy to administer – the software will generate a link which can then be sent to the sample

- They are easy to complete – respondents can click on the link whenever they have 15 minutes to spare to complete the questionnaire in their own time, rather than having to attend a meeting or interview or answering a telephone call

- Respondents can complete the questionnaire using various forms of technology: a computer, an iPad or other tablet or a smartphone. This is particularly suited to interpreters who tend to be mobile, travelling between interpreting assignments, rather than located in an office all day, and therefore more likely to answer the questionnaire if they can access it while they are travelling between jobs

- Participants do not need to post the paper questionnaire back to the researcher – this means there is no delay in receiving the responses and no risk of the questionnaire getting lost in the mail

- Younger generations are much more comfortable using technology and responding in this way, rather than using pen and paper

- They make data collection and data entry very easy – the program automatically collects the responses and provides summary statistics

- It is more cost-effective, as the on-line version removes the need for stationary, printing and postage on the part of the researcher.

There are also disadvantages attached to on-line questionnaires:

- The researcher has less control over who responds to the questionnaire and over how many times the same respondent takes part – although software packages can identify IP addresses, which means the same computer cannot be used twice to respond, any respondent can use multiple computers (or other devices) to participate as many times as they wish. This situation is of course very unlikely with most surveys

- Some participants (especially older ones, or those in remote areas) may not be comfortable using computers or may not have reliable access to the internet. This will exclude some participants leading to a biased sample

- There is a risk that the participant may lose the link. For this reason, a number of reminders need to be sent out to the sample. If the response period is 3 months, then it is advisable to send a reminder at the commencement of each month.

Exercise 3.6

Look for a free on-line questionnaire package and upload your questions. Send it to a pilot group you have decided on following your chosen sampling technique.

3.8 Questionnaire analysis

The analysis of the questionnaire is the exciting part of the research. This is where you read the answers to the questions that you took so much time and effort to design. However, this phase can be really daunting. You are now confronted with a large amount of information, which you have to organize and make sense of. The way you analyse your questionnaire answers will depend on a number of factors: (1) whether your research is qualitative or quantitative, (2) whether your sample is small or large and (3) the types of questions you asked. If you are conducting qualitative research and your sample is small and the questions are simple, you can analyse the responses manually. However, if the sample is large and the questions are complex, you will need to use software to help you. You can use special statistical packages such as SPSS[1] to analyse the quantitative responses, and special qualitative data analysis packages such as nVivo to analyse the open-ended, narrative responses. The choice of package will largely depend on the software your university subscribes to. In order to use these packages, you will need to undergo training. It is beyond the scope of this chapter to teach you how to use those tools. It is also beyond the scope of this book to teach you about statistics. However, under this section, we will briefly describe the types of analyses you can conduct for different types of questions.

3.8.1 Coding your data

We will assume that you have conducted your survey electronically, as per Exercise 3.6 above. This means that the data will be automatically entered and will appear in at least two forms: (1) as a large spreadsheet with all the raw data (responses collected per respondent and per question) and

(2) as individual sheets per question with descriptive statistical analyses. The raw data spreadsheet can be transferred to a program such as SPSS for further statistical analyses, which we will outline below.

3.8.2 *Types of data*

Your questions will generate data that normally fall into two broad categories: Non-parametric (nominal/categorical and ordinal) and Parametric or quantitative (ratio and interval). Nominal data refer to 'names' or categories. For example, a nominal question may be one that asked your respondents to indicate the field where they work as interpreters, such as legal, medical or welfare. These nominal data can later be changed into numbers, or given codes for ease of analysis, such as (1) legal, (2) medical and (3) welfare. Similarly, if you are interested in your respondents' gender, they can only choose 1 of 2 categories, male or female. Normally, male is represented by #1 and female by #2, but there is no hierarchy involved, nor can there be grades or levels of 'maleness' or 'femaleness'. In other words, you cannot have a respondent who is 0.5 male or 1.5 female.

Ordinal data refer to scores 'in order' such as those on a ranking scale, where respondents rank concepts in order of preference or importance or whatever they are asked to do. Semantic scales will produce ordinal data. In such scales, the difference between the rankings or descriptors cannot be said to be precisely equal. If we ask respondents to rate the effectiveness of an Interpreting teaching method on a scale such as the following:

Completely useless —— useless —— neutral —— useful —— very useful

we cannot say that 'completely useless' is half as useful as very useful, or any other exact measurement, as respondents are simply ranking concepts in order. Let us assume that we are comparing two teaching methods: Method 1 and Method 2. First, we need to convert the above descriptors into numbers in the following way: (1) completely useless, (2) useless, (3) neutral, (4) useful and (5) very useful. This is so that we can average out the numbers to get a score that we can compare. For this example, we will say that we have three respondents who answered in the following way:

Method 1: one rated this method as 3 (neutral), one as 4 (useful) and one as 5 (very useful) = average score 4.

Method 2: one rated this method as 1 (completely useless), one as 2 (useless) and one as 3 (neutral) = average score 2.

Although these scores look like quantitative data, they are not. We can say that Method 1 was rated more positively than Method 2, but we cannot say that Method 1 was twice as effective as Method 2, because these figures are superficial and the ratings are not exact.

Quantitative data refer to purely numerical answers, where numbers are exact. There are two types of quantitative data: interval and ratio data. We will not go into the detailed differences between these two. Interval data refer to numbers that have equal intervals between them, where 0 is an arbitrary number, such as dates. Ratio data are similar to interval data with the added characteristic of having a zero with a real value, such as in age.

An example of quantitative data in Interpreting research can be the scores on a multiple-choice test, where each question is weighted equally. We can safely say that a student who achieved a mark of 20/20 performed twice as well as a student who scored 10/20.

3.8.3 Types of statistical analyses

What is important to know when analysing questionnaires is whether the data are nominal or quantitative so as to determine the type of analyses they can lend themselves to, as can be seen on Table 3.4 below:

Table 3.4 Type of analysis according to data type

	Yes	No
Frequency counts and percentages	All types of data	
Median and percentiles	Ordinal, Interval and Ratio	Nominal
Mean (averages), standard deviation, standard error	Quantitative (interval and ratio)	Nominal, Ordinal
Additions or subtractions	Quantitative (interval and ratio)	Nominal, Ordinal

Data can be analysed using both descriptive and inferential statistics. Descriptive statistics include frequencies (simple counts), percentages and means (averages). The online survey packages will provide these as well as graphs and charts. For many studies, especially descriptive, qualitative ones, these will be sufficient analyses.

Exercise 3.7

When you receive the responses to your questionnaire (Exercise 3.6), explore the descriptive statistics provided by the online survey package.

If you want to determine whether your results are significant, then you need to go a step further and use inferential statistics. In the social sciences, significance is determined by the probability value (expressed as p value). A value of 0.05 or less ($p < 0.05$) is considered to indicate significance; the lower the value, the more significant it is believed to be. In other words, if your results are statistically significant, they can be taken seriously and inferences can be made to other populations. This means that there is only 5 per cent or less probability that your results were achieved just by chance. Having said this, not all data can be subjected to significance tests.

Statistics can be very complex, but what you need to know is what tests to use and for what purposes. Those tests are now readily available to you through either SPSS or other similar statistical analysis programmes. Table 3.5 below, adapted from Wray and Bloomer (2006, p. 216), summarizes the purposes for the four most common statistical tests. (For more detailed information about using statistics for language related research, you can refer to Rasinger 2008).

Table 3.5 Data type and relevant statistical test

Data type	Statistical test	Purpose
Quantitative	T-test	To ascertain whether two sets of scores are significantly different
Quantitative	ANOVA (analysis of variance)	To ascertain whether more than two sets of scores are significantly different
Quantitative	Pearson's correlation	To ascertain if there is a correlation between two variables
Nominal	Chi-squared	To ascertain whether the distribution of frequencies is not due to pure chance

Exercise 3.8

Look at your data and separate it into the different types of data (nominal, ordinal or quantitative). Then decide which answers can be analysed with which statistical tools.

Table 3.5 mentions the word correlation, which we have not yet discussed. Correlation refers to any links that there may be between questions. It will be important to find out if one variable affects another. This is done through what is known as cross-tabulation. When you look at the descriptive analyses, you may see for yourself that some answers seem more likely to be given by respondents with certain characteristics. Those characteristics may be independent variables such as age or gender or years of experience. These are called independent variables, because they cannot be affected or changed by other variables. For example, attitudes towards training cannot

Exercise 3.9

Now go through all the answers and decide on possible relationships between questions. The software you have chosen may allow you to do cross-tabulations or links between answers (through filters). Then try to apply statistical tests to determine the p-values. You can do this on Excel, SPSS or on free internet tools, such as http://abstractable.net/biocalc/features/hypothesis-test

change a respondent's age or gender. On the other hand, the respondent's age or gender may influence their attitude towards training. So, if you want to find out whether there is a relationship between age and gender and the dependent variable: attitudes towards Interpreting training, you need to first perform a cross-tabulation and then a Pearson's test to demonstrate if the relationship is statistically significant.

3.9 Review of questionnaire-based research in interpreting

Questionnaire-based research is common in Interpreting research. In a review article of Interpreting research methodology, Liu (2011) provides an excellent overview of Interpreting survey studies using different questionnaire and analysis types that have been published in the journal Interpreting between the years 2004 and 2009.

Now that you have read this chapter and completed all the exercises up until now, we want you to complete a final exercise where you become a reviewer of questionnaire-based studies.

Below we have listed three recent articles that report on the results of questionnaire-based studies. The first two are specifically Interpreting studies conducted by Interpreting scholars. Number 3 is a more general study, conducted by medical scholars, which looks at aspects of Interpreting.

Article 1. Katan, D. (2009). Occupation or profession: A survey of the translators' world. [Article]. *Translation & Interpreting Studies: The Journal of the American Translation & Interpreting Studies Association,* 4(2), 187–209. doi: 10.1075/tis.4.2.04kat.

Article 2. Albl-Mikasa, M. (2010). Global English and English as a Lingua Franca (EFL): Implications for the Interpreting Profession. *Transkom*, 3, (2), 126–48.

Article 3. Papic, O., Malak, Z., Rosenberg, E. (2012). Survey of family physicians' perspectives on management of immigrant patients: Attitudes, barriers, strategies, and training needs. *Patient Education and Counseling*, 86(2), 205–9.

Exercise 3.10: Review three questionnaire-based studies

Steps to the exercise:

1 Search for the journal articles listed above using the skills you learned in Chapter 2.

2 Once you have located the articles, read them carefully and answer the following questions based on what you learned in Chapters 1–3:

    a What were the aims of the study? How achievable were the aims?

    b What were the research questions? How effective were the questions?

    c Were the research questions answered by the study?

    d What paradigm did the study use: Quantitative or Qualitative?

    e How many questions did the questionnaire have?

    f What types of questions did it use?

    g Were the questions clearly formulated?

    h What sampling technique did the study use?

    i What was the population and what was the chosen sample?

    j How was the questionnaire administered?

    k What was the response rate?

    l How representative was the sample?

    m How was the questionnaire analysed?

    n Were statistics used? If so, how appropriately were these used?

    o Comment on the strengths and weaknesses of the research study.

Further reading

Andres, L. (2012). *Designing and doing survey research*. Los Angeles, London, New Delhi: SAGE.

Bloch, A. (2004). Doing social surveys. In C. Seale (ed.), *Researching society and culture*. London: SAGE, pp. 163–78.

Converse, J. M. and Presser, S. (1986). *Survey questions: Handicrafting the standardized questionnaire*. Newbury Park: Sage.

Liu, M. (2011). Methodology in interpreting studies. A methodological review of evidence-based research. In B. Nicodemus and L. Swabey (eds), *Advances in interpreting research. inquiry in action*. Amsterdam and Philadelphia: John Benjamins Publishing Company, pp. 85–119.

Rasinger, S. M. (2008). *Quantitative research in linguistics*. London & New York: Continuum.

Wagner, E. (2010). Survey research. In B. Paltridge and A. Phakiti (eds), *Continuum companion to research methods in applied linguistics*. London: Continuum, pp. 22–38.

Wray, A. and Bloomer, A. (2006). *Projects in linguistics. A practical guide to researching language*. New York: Hodder Arnold.

Note

1 SPSS stands for Statistical Package for the Social Sciences.

CHAPTER FOUR

Ethnographic research on interpreting

This chapter will:

- Define ethnographic research as a qualitative research method
- Discuss ethnographic approaches to research
- Expand on ethnographic approaches to interpreting research
- Provide examples of different ethnographic studies of interpreting
- Suggest practical ways to conduct ethnographic interpreting research
- Pose reflexive questions to the reader
- List further relevant readings

4.1 Introduction

Let us now return to the notion of qualitative research and the detailed approach to investigating research questions as outlined in Section 1.5 of Chapter 1. If you remember, qualitative studies use more general questions that elicit complex answers, and qualitative methods look at the detail, at the specific trends and themes within a particular sample. Qualitative studies tend to be inductive, whereby research is conducted, and a theory evolves from the research data (i.e. the research is data-driven). Qualitative studies tend to adopt the phenomenological research philosophy to analysing human behaviour. According to Lester (1999, p. 1), the purpose of the phenomenological approach is as follows:

> to illuminate the specific, to identify phenomena through how they are perceived by the actors in a situation. In the human sphere this normally translates into gathering 'deep' information and perceptions through inductive, qualitative methods such as interviews, discussions and participant observation, and representing it from the perspective of the research participant(s). Phenomenology is concerned with the study of experience from the perspective of the individual, 'bracketing' taken-for-granted assumptions and usual ways of perceiving.

This chapter focuses particularly on one area of qualitative, phenomeno-logical, research: ethnography.

Exercise 4.1

Before you read this chapter, complete the following tasks:

Go online to Google Scholar or Wikipedia and type in the words: 'ethnography', and 'ethnographic research', then make a note of the definitions.

Go into an on-line journal database (such as Languages, Linguistics and Behaviour abstracts) and type in the same terms: 'ethnography' and 'ethnographic research'. Make a note of the types of titles and abstracts that come up.

4.2 Ethnographic research as a qualitative research method

The roots of ethnography stem originally from the discipline of anthropo-logy (Wilson 1982), where it is still a prominent form of research (Willis and Trondman 2000). Ethnography can be defined as the study of a social group or individual or individuals representative of that group, based on direct recording of the behaviour and 'voices' of the participants by the researcher over a period of time. Ethnography is also widely used by other research disciplines, such as sociology (Blommaert 2005) and in linguistics, by applied linguists, (interactional) sociolinguists and discourse analysts (e.g. Fairclough 1992; Gumperz 1982; Hymes 1974; Rampton 2010; Saville-Troike 1982; Street 2010; Tannen 2004).

According to Nunan (1992, p. 52), ethnography 'contrasts markedly with the experimental method in the assumptions, methods, and attitudes to evidence'.[1] He goes on to say that:

ethnography has suffered somewhat from being applied rather loosely to any research that is not a formal experiment, giving rise, in some quarters, to the suspicion that the tradition and its practitioners lack rigour. However . . . true ethnography demands as much training, skill, and dedication as psychometric research.[2]

Ethnographers seek to uncover the shared norms or cultural conventions governing who can say what in particular situations and attempt to provide a 'thick description' of the cultural and conceptual world in which their subjects live (Geertz 1973). An important dimension of any ethnographic study is the part played by language in context, which makes it an ideal methodology to study Interpreting.

Another central element of ethnography is the role of theory. Ethnographers typically subscribe to a 'data first' grounded theory approach (Glaser and Strauss 1967), whereby a local theory is created (generated) out of the data. This approach is not without controversy as it promotes researchers 'diving into' data without conducting a pre-established theoretical framework (Nunan 1992). A grounded theory approach to research starts with as few preconceptions as possible about what is likely to be found, although researchers may have theoretical constructs, a methodological paradigm or conceptual framework (see Chapter 1) that will influence the researcher's approach. In some forms of qualitative research, the researcher may seek to apply a specific theory. In ethnographic research, however, the goal is more likely to be to interpret (sic) what they see and thus create a local theory from 'the ground' (i.e. the data) up (to the theory).

You may wonder why would we choose an ethnographic approach to research Interpreting? The broad conceptual framework you have in mind, as well as your understanding of language, culture and communication will shape your choice of methodology. If you see Interpreting as occurring within the social context in which it occurs, and believe that the processes and products of Interpreting are influenced by linguistic and cultural factors in context, then ethnography may be the appropriate methodology for your research project.

Traditional ethnographic research is labour-intensive and requires time, energy and resources. However, the rewards of prolonged engagement within a specific community and the richness of data generated via 'fieldwork' make it a methodology worthy of serious consideration by those seeking to engage in qualitative research.

According to Hammersley (1990, pp. 2–3), the key features of a broadly defined ethnographic method include studying people's behaviour in everyday rather than experimental contexts; gathering data from a range of sources, chiefly by observation and/or relatively informal conversation, and collecting data that are not set on pre-set categories or explicit hypotheses but that arise out of a general interest in an issue or problem, which can be explored through immersion in the context being explored (participant observation) or observed at a distance (non-participant observation). For that reason, ethnographic research is typically small in scale and focused on a single setting or group, but can continue for a long period of time. Starfield (2010) states that 'prolonged engagement by the researcher in the research setting is . . . a defining feature of ethnography' (p. 51).

In terms of Interpreting research, the social group or culture could be any of the following:

- Interpreter practitioners
  - Different qualifications/experience
  - Same language group
    - Native L1 users, or L2 late learners
  - Different language groups
    - Spoken or signed language interpreters
  - From 'established'/dominant language groups (e.g. French, Spanish, Chinese)
  - From 'emerging'/less diffuse language groups (e.g. Dinka, Swahili, Hmong)
  - Conference interpreters or community interpreters
  - Medical or court interpreters
- Interpreting students
  - University or technical/community college
  - Same language group
    - Native L1 users, or L2 late learners
  - Different language groups
    - Spoken or signed language interpreters
  - From 'established'/dominant language groups (e.g. French, Spanish, Chinese)
  - From 'emerging'/less diffuse language groups (e.g. Dinka, Swahili, Hmong)
- Interpreting educators
  - Former practitioners, or academics (theoreticians) or mentors
  - University or technical/community college or professional development workshops
  - Same language group
    - Native L1 users, or L2 late learners

  o Different language groups

    – Spoken or signed language interpreters

  o From 'established'/dominant language groups (e.g. French, Spanish, Chinese)

  o From 'emerging'/less diffuse language groups (e.g. Dinka, Swahili, Hmong)

- Minority language client group

- Majority language client group

  o For example, medical practitioner, legal personnel

- Other stakeholders

  o Interpreting service providers

  o Government representatives

Exercise 4.2

Consider what group or culture you might like to investigate within the context of an ethnographic study of interpreting or interpreters. Make a note of the communities that you have access to. Are you an interpreter yourself? What is your status in the interpreting profession? In what contexts do you work? What is your relationship with your clients? Your answers to these questions may influence your decisions and whether you can observe through immersion or at a distance.

4.2.1 *Ethnographic approaches to research*

Ethnographic methods are based on watching and asking, and ethnography is characterized by use of a 'family of methods' (Willis and Trondman 2000). The variety of different methods that can be used include:

- Participant (immersed) or non-participant (distanced) observation, involving interaction with, or discrete observation of, those being studied (fieldwork);

- Formal or informal reflective/retrospective in-depth audio or video-recorded interviews using prompt questions to elicit perceptions on views/ feelings;

- Focus group discussions: as per interviews, but where a small group of people are brought together to have a focused discussion on a particular topic that is guided by a facilitator;

- Desk-top research to collect biographical or demographic of biographical histories and other site-based or archival documentation information through databases and websites;

- Keeping of diaries or field notes to reflect on observations or experiences.

The core component of many ethnographic studies is the use of interviews or focus groups. Heyl (2001) asserts that ethnographic interviews require the researcher to: listen well and with respect; have an ethical engagement with the participants at all stages of the research process; have self-awareness of their own role in the co-construction of meaning; and be aware of how subjects' participation in the research (and developing a short-, medium- or long-term relationship with the researcher) may have an impact on participants, processes and outcomes. These principles also apply to conducting focus groups with small groups of people (ranging from 8 to 10 is the ideal). Interviews and focus groups may also be conducted as standalone methods for data generation (rather than as a complementary method to observations, for example) – this will be discussed further in Section 4.5 of this chapter.

Exercise 4.3

Refer back to your thoughts in relation to Exercise 4.2. Now reflect on the approach(es) you could adopt to engage with data generation for your chosen group to study. Consider the following questions:

- Would you be a participant (immersed) or non-participant (distanced) observer?
- Will you be able to audio or video record the activities being observed?
- Will you conduct interviews or focus groups as stand alone or in relation to observations?
- Is there any other data that you will need to generate?
- Will you be able to organize prolonged engagement with the group?

4.2.2 Validity, reliability and trustworthiness

To ensure validity and reliability of findings, ethnographers rely on triangulation (collation of data from a range of sources, see Chapter 1) and prolonged engagement. Patton (1987) distinguishes four types of triangulation:

1 Data sources – conclusions are developed from more than one set of data, for example, interview transcripts and participant observation field notes;

2   Investigator – multiple investigators are involved in the study;

3   Theory – the same data are analysed using different theories;

4   Methods – more than one data collection method is used, for example, interviews and participant observation.

Starfield (2010, pp. 55–6) expands on this list by referring to the work of Carspecken (1996), stating that ethnographic researchers need to:

1   Use multiple recording devices and multiple observers;

2   Use a flexible observation schedule;

3   Ensure prolonged engagement;

4   Maintain objectivity in fieldwork notes;

5   Use peer de-briefing;

6   Utilize member checking (sharing field notes and interpretations with the people that are being observed).

Prolonged engagement means long periods of time spent in the field until there is a 'saturation of data', that is, that repeated observations and questioning reveal no new information about the categories. Starfield (2010, p. 56) asserts that within a qualitative paradigm, ethnographers are less concerned with 'validity' per se, but rather with the 'trustworthiness' of the data. Thus, 'multiple methods of data collection are seen to contribute to the trustworthiness of the research' (ibid.).

In spite of criteria for maintaining trustworthiness of the data, ethnography acknowledges the subjective role of the researcher. The ethnographic account creates an image of the culture or group being described and interpreted. It is therefore important that an ethnographic report describes the setting, the participants and what they do and say effectively.

Exercise 4.4

Revisit the approaches you identified in Exercise 4.3. Have you factored in the need to triangulate data? How would you go about this? Will you be able to do 'member checking'?

4.2.3 *Data analysis*

Data analysis is recursive, that is, the researcher begins by establishing a set of categories for the data collected, but then refines these categories, making more or deleting some and organizing them in different ways, in order to account for all of the data.

Analysis can be assisted by various data management software tools, such as N-Vivo (formerly known as NUDIST) or ELAN.[3] These tools allow you to tag or annotate extracts of data – field notes, interview extracts, diary extracts, video or audio clips, etc. according to the categories or tiers set-up, which can then be retrieved by the software. Software can also assist by giving a quantitative dimension to qualitative research, which can provide added validity and reliability; for example, conducting a content analysis by counting the number of times a particular word or phrase is uttered. However, it should be noted that this type of quantitative analysis does not have to occur by relying on software. The recursive nature of the analytical method means you may need to return to the field, either for further observation or to ask further questions on specific issues, in order to substantiate findings.

4.2.4 *Participants in ethnographic studies*

As long as the participants are representative of the group and its culture, then there is no fixed criterion for the number of participants. Sometimes, a single *case study* will reveal a lot about a culture, yet several cases can be more revealing and provide a comparative dimension. Larger numbers though will provide more reliable findings (trustworthiness) for the group as a whole.

If using multiple case studies, then a set of criteria is needed for choosing the participants that represent the different aspects of the group or culture. For example, in an interpreting context, if you decide to use three participants, you may select one interpreter who has completed a formal interpreter education programme, one interpreter who is self-taught and has never had any training and an interpreting student. Or you may select participants as representatives of different stakeholders, for example, an interpreter, a minority language client and an interpreting agency.

The number of participants in your study will depend on the scope of your research and on how many people you encounter. For example, if conducting non-participant observations of courtroom interpreting, then the number of participants will be determined by the number of legal personnel, clients and interpreters in a particular court case (e.g. one judge, one prosecuting lawyer, one defence lawyer, one defendant, three witnesses, three interpreters, court clerk, twelve jury members, etc.). If you observe more than one court case, then the number of participants will increase.

In conducting ethnographic research, you do not recruit your participants, you select a community or group and then negotiate and create a relationship with that group (Maxwell 2013), in some cases becoming 'co-researchers' (Holmes et al. 2011) depending on your level of involvement. Details concerning selection of participants for various stages of ethnographic study (i.e. interviews, focus groups) are discussed later in this chapter (see § 4.5).

4.2.5 *Application of findings*

Ethnographers cannot make claims as to the generalizability of their findings, because they focus on one particular group or individual. It is for the ethnographer to interpret (sic) the data, and let others decide to what extent the findings might apply to other groups or contexts. For example, the findings from a study of how interpreters perceive their role in Country A may not necessarily apply to interpreters' perceptions in Country B. For this reason, it is very important that as much detail as possible about the context is provided in the ethnographic account, so that others have a basis for comparison. Ethnographic accounts can also be useful to address social and educational problems in specific contexts, therefore you will often find ethnographic research reports end with specific recommendations for application in practice, policy or pedagogy.

4.3 Contrasting traditional notions of ethnography with ideas of ethnography as qualitative research

For some researchers, ethnography is synonymous with other forms of qualitative research and methods. For example, Miles and Huberman state that '*the terms ethnography, field methods, qualitative inquiry, participant observation, case study, naturalistic methods* and *responsive evaluation* have become practically synonymous' (1994, p. 1, their emphasis). For others, ethnography has very specific procedures and criteria. Johnson (1992, p. 134) is very definite that:

> although other approaches to research may involve similar field techniques, many visits or long stays at the research site, and good descriptive accounts, they are not ethnographies unless they involve holistic study of cultural phenomena and cultural interpretation of behaviour.

In relation to analysis of professional communication, Sarangi (2005) notes that informal ethnography should involve a process of 'thick participation', whereby there is an ongoing commitment to observe and/or interact with a community over a period of time.

In Interpreting studies, it can be seen that ethnographic research has encompassed both of these standpoints. In this chapter, we present examples of qualitative studies of Interpreting that adopt ethnographic principles. First, we provide examples of studies of signed and spoken language interpreting that abide by a more traditional ethnographic approach (§ 4.4), then we give an overview of various qualitative studies that adopt ethnographic principles, but are not ethnographic in the strictest sense. These studies encompass interviews, focus groups, case studies and/or other types of fieldwork but do not feature any prolonged engagement with the group being observed.

Exercise 4.5

Now return to the notes you made for Exercise 4.1.

How would you refine your definition of ethnography based on what you have read so far? Did anything strike you about the titles and abstracts of journal articles that came up when you searched for the term ethnography?

Do you think that ethnography can be applied well in the study of Interpreting?

4.4 Application of traditional ethnographic methods in interpreting research

Interpreting research (especially community interpreting research) is interdisciplinary in nature (Vargas-Urpi 2011). Drawing on sociolinguistics (Wardhaugh 2010), linguistic ethnography (Rampton 2010) or linguistic anthropology (Durranti 2009), the qualitative study of interpreting can be considered as the study of the production and reception of spoken or signed 'texts' in a communicative context, taking into account the role of participants and their co-construction of meaning, the power dynamics and the management of communication. Explorations of interpreting based on sociological constructs (Giddens et al. 2009) seek to observe participant perceptions of their experiences of aspects of interpreting or interpreting-related issues.

The contexts for research are widespread, including medical appointments, classrooms, court cases, conferences or business meetings. There are not many 'authentic' ethnographic studies of Interpreting, and those that exist tend to be focused on medical or legal contexts, as can be seen in Section 4.4.1.

The investigation of interpreters and interpreting from an ethnographic point of view involves the adoption of any of the methods outlined in Section 4.2.1. Spoken and signed language interpreters can be considered as a 'social group', either combined with, or distinct from all the 'actors' in the communities for whom they interpret. For example:

- 'Emerging (minority) language' interpreters, refugee community members, immigration officials;

- Australian Sign Language (Auslan) interpreters, Deaf community members, representatives of public institutions;

- Conference interpreters, conference delegates at that particular conference

- Court interpreters, legal personnel, witnesses, defendants, jurors.

4.4.1 Examples of traditional ethnographic interpreting studies

The examples presented here are those that demonstrate the key features of ethnographic research in terms of prolonged engagement, a triangulation of data from different sources, and in particular observations of interpreters at work, as well as conversations with interpreters about their work.

4.4.1.1 Berk-Seligson (1990)

One of the best-known ethnographic studies was conducted by Susan Berk-Seligson (1990). Over 7 months, she made daily visits to courthouses in the United States and observed the work of Spanish-English interpreters. She tape-recorded 114 hours of courtroom interpreting, plus triangulated her observation notes with interviews with interpreters and attorneys. The focus of her research was on the discourse of the courtroom, on how interpreters dealt with the challenges of interpreting legal discourse and the various participants' perceptions of what was happening. Berk-Seligson frames this study as a sociolinguistic study, as she analyses tokens of interpreted interaction, while taking into account the sociological variables that influence the way that language is used (and interpreted) in the courtroom.

4.4.1.2 Brennan and Brown (1997)

Adopting a combined sociological and linguistic approach to the analysis of signed language interpreting in court, Mary Brennan and Richard Brown (1997) and their research team conducted a major 3-year study to assess the extent of deaf people's access to justice in the United Kingdom. They observed two major court cases involving deaf people and British Sign Language (BSL) interpreters in England and were able to interview some of the various participants, including one of the accused, two defendants and some of the interpreters. They also observed smaller magistrates courts in England and Wales and relied on their observation notes and some interviews. Additionally, they observed various cases in sheriffs' courts in Scotland and were able to videotape one 2-day court case involving three interpreters and two deaf defendants. Across the whole project, in total they interviewed more than 50 BSL interpreters about their experiences of working in court, followed by a questionnaire survey of interpreters (with 107 valid respondents), and interviewed 23 deaf people about their experiences of the legal system (and some interviews were conducted in prison). The focus of their research was on the perspectives of interpreters and deaf people, and the linguistic issues that arose in courtrooms, which were not only bilingual, but also bimodal.

4.4.1.3 Angelelli (2004a)

Drawing on the lenses of social theory, social psychology and linguistic anthropology, Claudia Angelelli (2004a) explored the role of medical interpreters, by drawing on data from over 300 medical encounters in one hospital site in the United States, which she gave the pseudonym California Hope. She conducted the study over 22 months, and data was generated in the following ways: recordings of interpreted events, observation notes, semi-structured interviews with various stakeholders at the hospital and an interpersonal role inventory survey with interpreters. She was more of a participant observer, as she would often walk with the interpreters from one part of the hospital to the next appointment and informally talk with them about their experiences, as well as sitting in and observing interpreted interactions. Her particular interest was to contrast interpreters' perceptions of their role boundaries with what they actually did in practice.

4.4.1.4 Dickinson (2010)

Using a linguistic ethnographic approach in her PhD thesis, Jules Dickinson (2010, also published as Dickinson and Turner 2008) set out to explore the role of signed language interpreters in the workplace. Her key research aims were to determine how primary participants understand the role of signed language interpreters and how this influences the dynamics of everyday interaction. Specific attention was paid to norms of discourse and shared repertoires within a workplace Community of Practice. A detailed description of the interpreting process was generated from her data, enabling a deeper appreciation of workplace dialogue where the signed language interpreter is an active third participant. She generated data through the use of questionnaires, practitioner journals, video-recorded interpreted interaction gathered in workplace settings and video playback interviews. The findings of her study showed that signed language interpreters have a considerable impact on the ways in which members of a Community of Practice interact, specifically in relation to small talk, humorous exchanges and participation in the collaborative floor.

After seeing how Interpreting studies scholars have applied ethnography in their research, revisit your ideas for your own ethnographic study. How have the four studies described above influenced your thinking? Are you interested in adopting a linguistic or sociological framework? Will you be able to have prolonged contact or commit to observations/participation over a period of time? What forms of data collection will you use?

4.5 Other qualitative approaches to interpreting research that incorporate ethnographic principles

In this section, we present examples of research on Interpreting that can be considered qualitative, but some would argue are not technically ethnographic. However, the studies include data collection methods that feature heavily in traditional ethnographic studies. The examples include other forms of participatory inquiry through focus groups or interviews and case studies that explore a single entity or phenomenon bounded by time and an activity.

Interviews and/or focus groups are a popular method of participatory inquiry in qualitative research, used alone or to triangulate data. Both approaches involved in-depth discussion of a particular topic or topics over a short period of time, with individuals or groups that represent the culture or community under investigation. There are advantages and disadvantages to utilizing either interviews or focus groups, which will be explored in this section.

4.5.1 Interviews

Interviews have been used for decades in empirical inquiry across the social sciences as a means of generating data . . . interview research has increased dramatically in recent years, especially qualitative studies that aim to investigate participants' identities, experiences, beliefs, attitudes, and orientations toward a range of phenomena (Talmy 2011, p. 25).

Interviewing is a basic mode of inquiry that allows people to tell their stories. The purpose of interviewing is essentially to gain an understanding into the experience of other people and the meaning they make of that experience. Interviews can be an effective approach to contextualizing observed behaviour; to obtain information that was missed in an observation, or to check the accuracy of something observed (Maxwell 2013). For example, an interpreter could be interviewed after being filmed working in a real-life medical appointment and asked to reflect on the assignment, with the interviewer asking questions about particular decisions made.

Ideas for Interpreting research that could utilize interviews include:

- Experiences of professional interpreters as child language brokers;

- Novice interpreters experiences in their first year of practice after graduation;

- The beliefs of interpreters in developing countries about the status of their profession as compared to developed countries;

- Interpreter educators' beliefs regarding predictive factors for successful interpreting students;

- The work experience of interpreters according to ethnicity, gender or sexuality;

- Attitudes towards new revalidation systems from previously accredited professional interpreters;

- Consumer/client perceptions of the need for interpreters to complete training courses;

- Comparative working experiences of interpreters in different contexts (e.g. legal, medical, education, conference, business).

Talmy (2011) distinguishes two approaches to interviews, which describe the difference between the interview as a 'research instrument' or as 'social practice'. Table 4.1 provides a comparison of the different approaches. These two approaches are worth considering if you are planning to use an interview as part of your research design, as the two approaches situate the researcher differently in terms of the power dynamic between interviewer and interviewee. Nunan (1992), Seidman (2006), Talmy (2011), Maxwell (2013) and others all emphasize the importance of the relationship between interviewer and interviewee, and although the relationship is not necessarily an equal one, steps can be taken to alleviate any hierarchical structure. Participants can be put at ease and invited to talk, rather than 'quizzed' about their thoughts or beliefs. The identity of the interviewer can also have an impact on the outcome of the interviewer (e.g. a researcher who is not an interpreter may be treated with suspicion).

Table 4.1 Two approaches to interviews

	Interview as research instrument	Interview as social practice
Status of interview	Resource for collecting or eliciting information	Participation in social practice, interview as a site for investigation
Status of interview data	Data reports facts, attitudes, beliefs	Data are socially constructed; data represent facts, attitudes, beliefs and are co-constructed between interpreter and interviewee
Voice	Interviews give voice to interviewees	Voice is situationally dependent and discursively co-constructed
Bias	Interviewers must work against contaminating data	Reflexive recognition that data are collaboratively produced so cannot be contaminated
Analytic approaches	Decontextualized content or thematic analysis, summaries of data and/ or uncritical quotation, abridged or verbatim.	Analysis focuses on how meaning is negotiated and knowledge co-constructed.
Analytic focus	Product-oriented, focus on the 'what'	Process-oriented, focus on the 'what' and 'how'

(*Source:* Talmy 2011.)

4.5.1.1 Interview structure

The structure of interviews varies depending on the purpose of the interview and the information sought or stories to be told. At one end of the continuum you can have tightly structured interviews using closed questions that are completed in a fixed timeframe; and at the other end, you can design an unstructured, open-ended anthropological interview which is more like a 'friendly conversation' (Spradley 1979), has no fixed questions or time limits and is guided by the interviewee rather than the researcher. Somewhere in between you have semi-structured interviews, where the interviewer may have a set of prompt questions to guide the discussion and a goal in terms of length of interview. But the interview process is flexible enough to allow the interviewee to express their thoughts and ideas, and build upon and explore the participant's responses to the prompt questions, or drill down into issues raised during the conversation. The semi-structured interview is popular in applied linguistics research as it enables the researcher to strike a balance between having some level of control, as well as having flexibility (Nunan 1992). See Table 4.2 for a comparison of different interview strategies.

Table 4.2 Interview strategies

Type of interview	Required skills
Structured interview	Neutrality; no prompting; no improvization; training to ensure consistency
Semi-structured interview	Some probing: rapport with interviewee; understanding the aims of the project
Open-ended interview	Flexibility; rapport; with interviewee; active listening

(*Source:* Silverman 2006, p. 110; adapted from Noaks and Wincup 2004.)

Seidman (2006) advocates for a three-interview series, so that the interviewer can develop a relationship with the interviewee, get to know them and their life experience and also place their experience in context. This may not always be realistic, however, and a one-off interview can be just as effective if it is planned well, the participant is clearly briefed and you have clear goals for what you want to achieve.

The length of interviews can vary, again according to the topic of discussion. Seidman (2006) recommends 90 minutes per interview, but this may not be necessary. The interview needs to be as long as it needs to be to construct the story to be told, or relate the experiences, beliefs or attitudes of interest to you as the researcher. From the experience of the authors of this book, 30–45 minutes is optimum, as the interview can be engaging and interesting. Much longer than that and the interviewee's interest can start to wane. However, if the interviewee is keen to continue talking, then you may not want to wrap up the interview in order to stick to a timeframe.

4.5.1.2 Interview questions and technique

Interview questions are developed according to the research questions of the study and the goal of the interview. If the interview is being conducted as part of a triangulated study, then questions may be developed to explore earlier data in more depth. For example, after conducting a survey of interpreters through a questionnaire (see Chapter 3), then you could design a follow-up interview with a sample of the survey respondents to elicit more details from them about responses they gave to the survey.

Depending on how structured you want the interview to be, you may devise a list of set questions, prompt questions or topics to be covered. You will need to decide on the question format to be used: open-ended versus closed, direct or indirect, and how the responses are to be collected and analysed.

> Your research questions formulate what you want to understand; your interview questions are what you ask people to gain that understanding. The development of good interview questions . . . requires creativity and insight, rather than a mechanical conversion of the research questions into an interview guide . . . and depends fundamentally on your understanding of the context of the research (Maxwell 2013, p. 101, his emphasis).

Silverman (2006) notes that no special skills are required to conduct qualitative interviews, but the interviewee should not be treated as a 'passive vessel waiting to be tapped' (Silverman 2006, p. 112). Instead, the interview should be collaboratively produced between the interviewer and interviewee, with both people being active participants in the process. Silverman also asserts that no one interviewing style is best: some interviewers may be more passive, others more active; the key to the success of an interview is talk. Seidman's tips for effective interview technique (2006) include the following:

- Listen more, talk less;
- Follow up on what the participant says;
- Ask questions when you do not understand;
- Explore, do not probe;
- Ask real questions;
- Avoid leading questions; ask open-ended questions;
- Follow up, don't interrupt;
- Ask participants to reconstruct, not remember;
- Share your own experiences sparingly;
- Avoid reinforcing your participant's responses;
- Explore laughter;
- Follow your hunches; and
- Tolerate silence.

Silverman (2006) outlines six types of knowledge that can be addressed through interviews: (i) facts that relate to the background of the interviewee; (ii) interviewee beliefs about the topic of the interview; (iii) feelings and motives, elicited through open-ended questions; (iv) interviewee perceptions about actions or behaviours; (v) interviewee recounts of present or past behaviour; and (vi) conscious reasons for responses to knowledge types i–v. Table 4.3 outlines the knowledge types that could be elicited through an interview with a medical interpreter in relation to the research question: 'What are the challenges for medical interpreters?'.

Table 4.3 Example of knowledge types in an interpreter interview

Knowledge type	Question(s)
Facts	How long have you been working as a medical interpreter? What qualifications do you have? Have you ever had specialist medical interpreter training?
Beliefs	Do you believe that there are any challenges in medical interpreting?
Feelings and motives	How do you feel when a doctor addresses you directly?
Perceptions of actions or behaviours	If an interpreter does not relay faithfully everything that is said in a doctor-patient consultation – do you think there are any justifiable reasons for this behaviour?
Recount of present or past behaviour	Can you recount an example from your own interpreting experience where you have asked the doctor to explain something that you know the patient has not understood.
Conscious reasons	Which tenets in your Interpreter Code of Ethics guide you in your decision-making for the examples we have discussed today?

Exercise 4.7

Following on from your ethnographic research ideas, make notes on the following:

– Will you incorporate interviews into your research design?
– What type of interview structure will you use?
– What knowledge types do you need to elicit during your interview?

4.5.1.3 Interview process

As discussed in Chapter 3 with regard to questionnaires, in order to ensure that your interviews will be successful, it is important to pilot the interview questions with a small sample of people beforehand. This will give you the opportunity to check whether your questions are eliciting the kind of data you want, and whether your interview approach is suitable for the topic under discussion.

Recruitment of participants: It is ideal to recruit a representative sample of the group or community involved in the research study, although this can be difficult in a small-scale study. If part of a triangulated study, you may have the contact details for participants involved in another phase of data collection that you can contact directly. Otherwise, you can send out invitations or calls for expressions of interest via membership groups, professional associations, service providers or educational institutions. According to Seidman (2006), there are two criteria that you can use to determine if you have enough participants: (1) Sufficiency: are there sufficient numbers to reflect the range of participants from the population being interviewed; and (2) Saturation: When you get to a point in your interviews that you are beginning to hear the same information. Some researchers determine a target number before they commence data collection, and others take a 'snowballing' approach to recruiting new participants through interviewee contacts (see Chapter 3 about sampling techniques). Either is suitable depending on your networks and the research goals.

Elements of the interview: In setting up the interview space, give careful consideration to the positioning. Walker (1985, cited in Nunan 1992) suggests that sitting beside, rather than in front of, your interviewee can be more effective as it makes the participant feel less confronted. This only works for interviews conducted in a spoken language, however, as signers need to sit opposite one another to be able to see the signed utterances. Before the interview begins, make sure you have allowed enough time to explain the nature of the research and the purpose of the interview and give the interviewee the opportunity to ask any questions for clarification. This is the time to go through the information sheet, clarify how the interview will be recorded and analysed, explain how the interviewee's anonymity will be retained and ask the participant to sign the consent form agreeing to participate in the interview (see Chapter 2). Once you begin the interview, keep an eye on the time and the technology.

Recording the interview: It is advisable to record the interview as that frees you up from taking copious notes, and you can concentrate on interacting with the participant. But taking some notes can be worthwhile, as they can enhance the subsequent transcribing and analysis tasks. Nunan (1992) observes that there are strengths and weaknesses in recording as compared to note-taking, depending on the nature of the interview, time and technology available, how much data you want to capture and the importance of being able to reanalyse (i.e. playback) after the event. Historically spoken, language researchers have relied on audio recordings, and signed language researchers on video recordings because of the nature of the languages involved. However, with improvements in the cost and quality of video technology, and the fact that cameras are now much smaller and can be less obtrusive, many researchers now recommend using video cameras for recording (regardless of the language being used), as many interactive elements of an interview can be picked up when reviewing a video recording, which cannot be identified through sound alone. If you are using some form of technology to record, make sure that it is running throughout the interview, as there is nothing worse than completing an excellent interview and discovering that the recording stopped half way through.

Exercise 4.8

In relation to your own interviews, consider the following:

 – How will you recruit participants?
 – How will you record the interviews?

4.5.1.4 Interview analysis

The analysis of the interview data can draw on the same principles as outlined in Section 4.2.3. Typically, a researcher transcribes the interview and uses the text-based version for manual analysis, or analysis in a data management program such as N-Vivo. According to Seidman (2006, p. 116): 'a detailed and careful transcript that re-creates the verbal and non-verbal material of the interview can be of great benefit to a researcher who may be studying the transcript months after the interview occurred'.

Transcribing interviews can be time-consuming and costly, and depending on the goal of the interview, needs to include all elements of the interaction to represent the talk as closely as possible. Below is an example from an interview conducted in spoken English with a signed language interpreter in Sydney, as part of study of video remote interpreting in court (Napier 2013). You can see in the transcript that the pauses, repetitions, hesitations and use of signs are all transcribed so that the researcher has captured all elements of the way that the interviewer and interviewee spoke to one another.

The process of data analysis can involve content analysis (Krippendorff 2004), thematic analysis (Silverman 2006) or a more detailed discourse analysis (Gee 2011). More detail can be seen about discourse analytical approaches in Chapter 5. Essentially the goal is to analyse the data to identify interesting themes or patterns that can be compared across the interviewees.

With the advent of software such as ELAN, it is now possible for researchers to annotate interview data using the tiers in ELAN, without necessarily transcribing the full interview. A screen grab of an interview annotation template from a real study can be seen in Figure 4.1. The study involved a series of 1-hour face-to-face interviews conducted in Australian Sign Language (Auslan) with 72 deaf people throughout Australia, to discuss

---

Example 4.1: Transcript of interview

Int: Er . . . coz when I had to ask for a repeat I think had he been in person I could have got what I needed quickly without stopping everything . . . yeah. . . . I actually had to stop something. Erm where as before, I can't remember . . . oh about paying me (signs PAY-ME) I wasn't sure what he meant and I could've just done that (signs PAY-ME INTERACTION with quizzical facial expression) without anybody knowing almost.

RA: The first time I think it was something to do, erm, with his address?

Int: Ah yes Fairfield.

RA: But you clarified really quickly and it didn't seem to be a problem or anything.

Int: Yeah but I think because I had that wait wait wait and he was still going on, but see he was reading from the script.

RA: And he wasn't looking at you as well.

Int: But had he had his eye on me all the time I could have stopped that there and then without having to go (signs GO-BACK). So yeah, so that was an issue.

RA: So it's possible but it's not the same as if you were face-to-face.

Int: I think you can get it done more subtly if you're in person.

Legend: Int: Interpreter, RA: Research Assistant.

---

issues concerning access to healthcare information and health literacy (Napier and Kidd, in press; Napier and Sabolcec 2012). Tiers 1 and 2 were created for guide and full Auslan to English translations; Tier 3 was created for thematic analysis; and Tier 4 was used for observational comments about the points made by the interviewee. The analysis then followed three stages:

1 The interviewer and interviewee comments were translated into English.

2 A thematic analysis was conducted of the data to identify overarching themes.

3 A content analysis was conducted to pull out representative quotes to elucidate various themes.

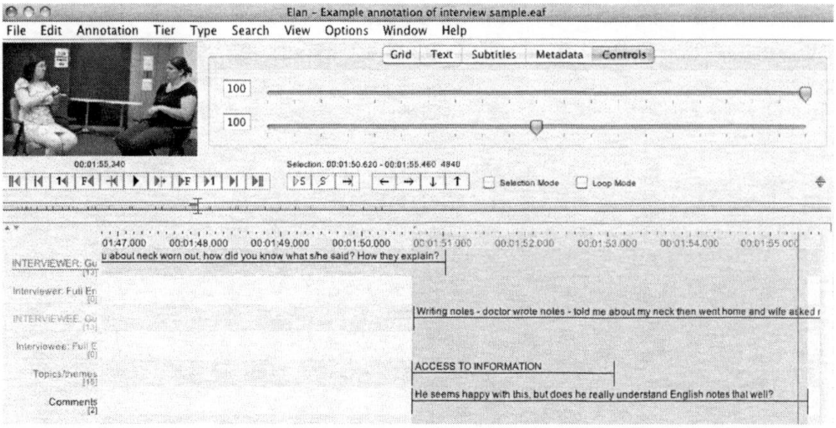

FIGURE 4.1 *Example of interview data ELAN annotation tiers*

4.5.2 Focus groups

Interviews can take place just as effectively in a group context and are often referred to as 'focus groups' or 'group interviews'. Focus groups can adopt the same interview techniques, procedures and analytical approaches as discussed in Section 4.5.1 and are typically run as open-ended group discussions with a focus on a particular topic. The discussion can last anywhere between 1–2 hours and is guided by the researcher as the facilitator.

> The more common versions [of focus groups] have a substantial degree of flexibility and are effectively some form of hybrid with characteristics of a discussion as well as of an interview. Even though general topics, and sometimes specific questions, are presented by the researcher, the traditional interview format of alternate question and answer is both difficult to maintain and eliminates the group interaction which can be a particular strength of the group interview (Robson 2011, p. 293).

Focus groups are becoming more popular as they generate a lot of data and are relatively easy to organize. Like individual interviews, focus groups can be used as part of a mixed methods study to triangulate the data. However, there are advantages and disadvantages to using focus groups. Table 4.4 provides a comparison of the advantages of focus group interviews relative to individual interviews (from Fern 1983; citing Hess 1968).

4.5.2.1 Focus group participants, process and analysis

We recommend that you refer back to Sections 4.5.1.3 and 4.5.1.4 in relation to the interview process and analysis, as all the guidelines also apply to using focus groups, although there are some variations that should be taken into consideration.

Table 4.4 Advantages of focus group interviews

Participant interaction advantages	Researcher advantages
Synergy: Combined effort of the group can produce wider range of information and ideas than a series of interviews	*Serendipity:* Ideas that had not previously occurred to participants can arise as triggered by discussion. Group interview enables exploration of the idea to its full significance
Snowballing: Chain of responses can be triggered throughout group members	*Specialization:* Group interview can be more cost-effective due to specialist knowledge of facilitator and participants
Stimulation: Participants quickly warm up and want to contribute their ideas, stimulating discussion builds	*Specific scrutiny:* Closer scrutiny can occur as more people can be present as observers
Security: Group members feel safe in sharing their ideas when they realize their views are mirrored by others	*Structure:* More control is possible with regard to the topics covered, as the facilitator can revisit topics if covered in insufficient depth
Spontaneity: Individual's responses can be more spontaneous and less conventional as they only speak when they feel strongly about the topic, as it is easier not to say anything at all in a group context	*Speed:* More data can be collected from interview participants at the same time

Various researchers recommend that focus groups should have an optimum size of 6–10, or 8–12 (Robson 2011). We suggest a group of 8–10 to be optimum. The make-up of the group could include people that are strangers or have a level of familiarity through work or social networks. The choice that you make about the composition of the group should be thought through carefully, to ensure that the dynamics of the group interaction will not have a negative impact on the data collection process. For example, in discussing the requirement for compulsory interpreter training, bringing together a group of interpreters who are friends, and that all either have, or do not have, Interpreting qualifications, will likely bias the discussion.

Focus group interviews are facilitated by a moderator (or facilitator), whose role it is to regulate the discussion and encourage participation so that the group runs effectively. Prompt questions can be used to guide the discussion, and for the moderator to monitor the progress of the discussion so that the key topics are covered in enough depth. Robson (2011) also recommends having a second researcher present to assist with the logistics of running the focus group (e.g. recording, taking notes, etc.) so the moderator can concentrate on the facilitation role.

Initially, the moderator should explain the purpose of the group interview, ask participants to sign the consent form and then allow all participants to introduce themselves and why they have agreed to participate, and what they feel they can contribute to the topic under discussion (i.e. what expertise/ experience do they bring?).

Focus groups can be recorded using audio or video recorders, with transcription of discussion and analysis of the text. The transcription of focus groups, however, may need to include overlapping talk among participants, and researchers need to ensure that anonymity is preserved through the allocation of participant codes or pseudonyms. Example 4.2 illustrates an extract from a focus group transcript, taken from a study that involved

---

Example 4.2: Extract from focus group transcript

Focus Group 1

(HEARING)

Attending: HF1 = Facilitator, H1.1 = [name], H1.2 = [name], H1.3 = [name], H1.4 = [name]

HF1 We're rolling. So H1.1 –

H1.1 I'll start. My name's H1.1. I work at [omitted]. I'm an audiologist. But my background is speech pathology and audiology and I did a lot of work in [name of area] with the deaf community and sign language. So I'm not a conventional audiologist in a lot of ways and have done some interpreting in [name of area] for 10 years with sign language users. But, [here] I do not have [the sign language] skills to speak of and I've been here for 8 years now and so rapidly losing my [home sign language] so, um, that's sort of my background . . . but small amount of experience of interpreting, really working- there was no training in [name of area] as an interpreter I was untrained interpreting people I knew very well and worked with and so have more to say I suppose about working with interpreters mostly.

H1.2 My name's [name] I'm currently at [name of university] finishing a Doctorate in – in during that Doctorate work I've been using sign language interpreters. The thesis is focused on the written English – developing written English language skills in deaf writers so I've been using interpreters through TAFE in doing that research. Also through [name of institution] I've [X] years I was senior head teacher in charge of the [name of department]. During that time my Auslan skills – different stages became quite good, but the Auslan teachers all managed to have ways and means to communicate with me, all the deaf teachers signed so didn't always have to use my Auslan skills, so I haven't been practising as much but over the years in my teaching roles – I've often used interpreters because many of the students in the class have – first language has been signed English and [sign language] in the classes. So they've been a bit of mixture in those classes. So over those, so probably for 20 years I've used Auslan interpreters in classes, in classrooms . . . at [name of university]. I've had tutoring experience one on one and used Auslan interpreters in that experience as well.

H1.4 My name is [name] and I am the Manager of Administration at [name of organization]. I'm not obviously a signer. I know a little bit of sign language. We have about 10 deaf staff in [my organization] and everything you do is always bilingual, so bilingual workplace I use sign every day to the best of my ability but yeah we use interpreters all the time.

H1.3 And I'm [name]. I work here at [name of university] as a disability advisor and my role is mainly with students and prior to having someone here who having performed the role of assisting students who are deaf or have a hearing impairment, I worked fairly closely with interpreters in assisting students who are deaf, through interviews I've had with the students and interactions when making presentations at conferences where deaf people were present so yes, I have had a fairly close working relationship for some time back. I don't have any sign language skills.

HF1 Lovely broad range thank you very much. So yeah if we want to just start a very general conversation maybe start at the top. Something that you like about interpreters and then we can just casually work our way through the list that would be great, so you don't like or benefits of working with an interpreter.

six focus groups, two with each stakeholder group: deaf people, signed language interpreters and non-deaf (hearing) professionals; to discuss their experiences of interpreters and interpreting in Australia and to determine whether consumer and practitioner attitudes towards interpreting were the same (Napier 2011c; Napier and Rohan 2007). You can see from the transcript how the moderator initiates the introductions and then segues into the discussion itself (participants had previously been provided with a list of prompt questions).

Example 4.3: Transcription extract revealing group interview turn taking

1 H1.2 What I particularly like, is that the most – many interpreters, not most but many interpreters that I have worked with have also been? encoders which has meant that I they can give a great link to the community so not only have you got the language but you've also got that other additional emphasis on the cultural background and a depth of understanding beyond just any surface understanding of what's being said. It's been particularly helpful and useful for myself.

2 H1.1 What I think the most – I mean to say what I would like the most about interpreters would be then that you then don't have to worry about the communications aspect as being have you actually made yourself clear understood because that obviously detracts from sometimes the content of what you're trying to get. Trying to provide a quality service, this is in a service-providing context. There's a certain amount of being able to feel that what you're giving is some of what you've been looking for. Without an interpreter you're never quite sure if you've made yourself actually understood.

3 H1.4 And I like I don't like . . . ? work . . . thing . . . about some people communicate work and the interesting thing is that you see the interpreter – when you're having an interpreter for a meeting or a conversation whatever and they're certain topics discussed that you can't just translate literally then you actually see the interpreter stepping back and explaining the concept rather than just interpreting it. So you see there's less a whole other comprehension with the time and the need, the people that need the interpreting.

4 H1.3 I like working with an interpreter I guess it's very important, because of my own disability – I have vision impairment, it means that you can ensure that the person that you're working with does understand what you're communicating to them and similarly they hopefully will have some confidence that through the interpreter you're understanding what they're trying to get across so it's a two way communicating facility which I'm really appreciative of interpreters being available for that you just – you wouldn't get from any other source, technology it's just can't be that spontaneous as an interactive interpreter can be.

5 H1.1 But then there is – I mean going on to the next thing of what you least like, again in that service-providing context there is a problem that there is another person there which often, you know, may not be a problem if it's a lecture or a classroom or something but you know a small case, particularly an audiology clinic where the room is very small, we have students, we have interpreters, and sometimes because you're talking about is highly emotional or technical you don't actually know that actually the converse can be true what I said earlier, liking about them, you don't know if people are saying actually people what they really want to say because there is another person there. So you have – it's really like you know a paradox – what is good about it is what is bad about it. But that's not to say we wouldn't use them for that reason that's just the –

6 All Hm.

7 H1.2 I've had great and happy experiences with all my interpreters and really enjoyed their um – the input I've always had dynamic experiences really. I don't – I've never found any opportunities where I haven't fully used the interpreters, sometimes there's been situations where interpreters have struggled with the language content you know and that's been very hard because you know to get the meaning across but that's not their fault, it's the concept that – you know to try and interpret it has been very difficult but that's not a negative that's a positive. Really I don't have any negatives to say.

8 H1.3 I wouldn't call it a negative I guess it's just a matter of getting used to working with them. Um, just how much information is interpreter as distinct from how much one takes for granted that a person gets, or understands or doesn't understand. It took me oh a few experiences, I guess in working with an interpreter on a one-to-one basis to realise that. So even like things like you were talking to the students through an interpreter and your telephone rang the interpreter would voice and sign 'the phone's ringing' to the person, I thought 'Ooh-ah'. It's just not something you would think about! Or she's got a grim tone in her voice or something like that and you think hang on. But of course they're giving the person the level of information that we take for granted I guess in an audal sense as well visually. Yeah it's not – not liking it – I didn't like it at first but if you sit back and think what the role of the interpreter is then it's natural that they're going to do that and you just have to become used to that and it does, in a way moderate your own behaviour too.

9 H1.4 Hm. I can't think of a negative – I work with interpreters all the time. The only thing I can think of is the flipside of the coin, and I mentioned it before that and it's mainly happening the – ? . . . . interpreters they don't always realise that the English level of the person..? that person may or may not be a par with the rest of the ?crew in a setting. So in conversational workshop or conference can be interpreted like . . .?? 11:55 in the past but the concept behind it's not a question of interpreting it's a question of comprehension and I guess that just requires experience from the interpreter and a little bit of understanding and . . .? culture and the client's and the person . . .

(Continued)

Exercise 4.3 (Continued)

But it's kind of frustrating when you're watching it happen and you see difficulties when you have the interpreters there and that person or those people are ..? question mark. So it's not – it – I guess it's just part of sitting back and going a step further.

10 H1.1 Because it's also interesting because I don't only use sign language interpreters I also use spoken language interpreters and probably because I have a little bit of experience with sign language and it is visual it's not ..? but spoken language interpreters there can long discussions and then they just say yes. And I'm sure the same thing's happening with explaining that concept but it somehow seems to be more obvious in spoken language interaction

11 H1.4 Yeah but it's a question of a deaf person may not have the English language skills so that-

12 H1.1 I know that – same with the person – with spoken language-

13 H1.4 Yeah hm.

14 H1.1 I think sometimes you think it's only we think it's only sign language interpreters you have to explain context things but with spoken language interpreters it's often the same and you think it's because they're not interpreting for you what's being said but I think what they're doing is explaining the concept as well. Which can be quite disempowering for the other person, you know. Doesn't quite know what's going on and it's easier to see the concept being explained I think if you know a little bit about sign language than it is when you're spoken language because you really don't know what they're saying.

15 H1.2 So when you say spoken language, how does that work?

16 H1.1 Well say they are – people who come into services who are not Australian.

17 H1.2 Oh I see.

18 H1.1 And who speak other languages . . .

19 H1.2 Alright so they're hearing persons?

20 H1.1 Yeah.

21 H1.2 OK

22 H1.1 Or they . . . hearing . . . deaf people .. oh yeah coming in like they're not sign language users.

23 H1.2 OK.?

24 What was the next question?

25 H1.1 So what are the benefits of working . . . what do you like most,

what do you like the least. And then the next one is the benefits, which is probably similar to the first one.

26   H1.4 Hm

27   H1.3 I guess the critical point in there is, the benefits are to – you've got increased confidence of facilitating a two-way interchange between the person who's deaf and the person who doesn't use sign language.

28   H1.2 That's right. Too many . . . ?

29   HF1 Um, and so while you were talking about your experiences before, was there- I guess probably more positive aspects, is there a particular interpreting assignment that you liked the best? Like, did something spring to mind as you were making those comments? I'm just jumping down [the list of prompt questions] a bit but trying to follow on from what you were just talking about?

30   H1.3 Um, yes I think – I think um the best experience I had and I know you can't always have this, is when I've had email communication with the student, there's one student that comes to mind and I've had a telephone conversation with the interpreter prior to the interaction between 2 or us, there's 3 of us and the interpreter and the client and myself in this case, had a handle about the context for the interaction in the first place, so you're not coming in cold to it. Whereas if you're meeting up with a person who's deaf plus an interpreter for the first time, it's often – found it difficult to initiate small talk. I kept it – I felt that I had to keep it very focused on something that I knew people had some familiarity with. They're the interactions I like best. More rewarding though as I say that's a very contrived environment and you can't always have that but that was my most positive experience, the topic was certainly not foreign to . . .?

31   H1.4 Can you repeat your question? Sorry.

32   HF1 It's – what has been your best interpreting experience-

33   H1.4 Oh –

34   HF1 – so far. So I just wondered before, when you were talking about what you liked about interpreters, was there one or a few standout experiences that you remember?

35   H1.4 I have mostly good ones, I can only think of one bad one

36   HF1 You can only think of one bad one?

37   H1.4 Yes everyone else had been good.

38   HF1 We'll jump to that next then.

39   H1.4 I'm also probably spoiled because it's like a daily thing it's bilingual language it's like the office environment so yeah.

When the discussion begins, you can see from Example 4.2 that once the first participant has made a contribution, there are several turns between participants before the facilitator takes a turn again (turn 29). At that point, the facilitator links to a comment made by one of the participants and attempts to steer the conversation in a slightly different direction. There are then several turns between the facilitator and some of the participants to clarify the next point of discussion (turns 30–9). Thus you can see how the process of the group interview differs from that of the individual interview and how the interviewer needs to be mindful of the role they play.

Focus groups have been used by many interpreter researchers to complement other forms of data collection or as the primary methodological approach. For example, in attempting to define 'entry to practice competencies' for American Sign Language interpreters, Witter-Merithew and Johnson (2005) conducted individual interviews and focus groups with stakeholders, including interpreters, interpreter educators, interpreting students, deaf people, employers and policy makers. Hale (2007) also held a focus group discussion with interpreter educators who had taught in Australia and Spain to discuss the main challenges they faced as community interpreter educators.

Exercise 4.9

Revisit your interview plan. Do you think there would be any benefit to your collecting data in a focus group instead. Or perhaps to complement the interviews?

4.5.3 Case studies

The final form of qualitative participatory inquiry that we will consider is the use of case studies. Smart (2008) argues that a case study should be distinguished from ethnography, as a case study does not necessarily explore the culture of a group or involve a significant enough amount of time; or provide a 'thick' enough description (as per Geertz 1973). However, it is also acknowledged that the critical feature of ethnography – to contextualize problems in the wider context – also applies to case studies, and that in-depth investigations of a single case can be considered as neo-ethnographic (Stenhouse 1975). Case studies can be explanatory, exploratory or descriptive (Stake 1995). Explanatory case studies present data bearing on cause-and-effect relationships; exploratory case studies attempt to define the questions and hypotheses of a subsequent study, and descriptive case studies present complete descriptions of phenomena within their context. Nunan (1992) notes that there is a range of definitions of case studies in the literature on language research, but that it is a suitable research methodology for the in-depth analysis of a single instance and a legitimate form of inquiry. He cites Denny (1978) in stating that 'while an ethnography is a complete account of a particular culture, case studies examine a facet or particular aspect of the culture of subculture under investigation' (in Nunan 1992, p. 77).

In the examples we provide here, it can be seen that the case studies often do provide a very thick description of the interpreting process or product, and the case studies are snapshots taken by interpreter researchers as part of their on-going work in a given context.

4.5.3.1 Examples of interpreting case studies

- Roy (1989, 1992, 1993, 1996, 2000) analysed a case study of an American Sign Language interpreter mediating a meeting between a deaf PhD student and a university professor. She provided a rich discourse analytic description of the turn-taking and communication management within the interaction.[4]

- Wadensjö's body of work (1998; 2001b; 2002; 2004) presents a series of case studies of detailed discourse analyses of Swedish interpreters working in medical, mental health and legal contexts. Her work focuses on how interpreters are active participants in interpreter-mediated interaction who co-construct meaning with the other interlocutors.

- In her case study, Jacobsen (2008) analysed the politeness strategies used by a Danish courtroom interpreter in order to save face and mitigate face threatening acts for herself or her client.

- Napier et al. (2008) present a case study of a deaf professional working with two signed language interpreters, and they document the cues and signals used by all three of them in order to cooperate to ensure the smooth delivery of the deaf presenter's Auslan utterances into spoken English in a formal seminar presentation.

Each of these case studies provides what Geertz (1973) would term a 'thick' description of the interpreter working in that context. Although there may not have been prolonged contact with a social group, many case studies feature analysis of authentic data (i.e. real interpreting assignments) that are triangulated with interviews and investigate an aspect of interpreting in-depth.

Exercise 4.10

Find a published article that features the discussion and analysis of a case study of interpreting (a different one from those outlined above). Write a critique of the case study in relation to the ethnographic principles discussed in this chapter.

- Does the case study provide a 'thick description' of the context?
- How does the author present their interpretation of the findings of their case study?
- Has the author drawn on a theoretical framework for the study?
- Do you think the case study can be considered as an ethnographic study?

4.5.3.2 Case studies as interpreter action research

Another use of case studies is when interpreters engage in *action research* on their own practice, as 'practisearchers' (Gile 1990; Shlesinger 2009). Drawing on the principles of action research (Burns 2010; Scott 1999) to engage in cyclical, reflective analysis of a key problem, interpreters can record themselves working in authentic assignments and present critical case study analyses of their own practice; also termed 'interpreter fieldwork research' (Napier 2005a, 2011b). This approach could be considered as a form of autoethnography (Starfield 2010): a blend of autobiography and ethnography. This has been particularly popular in signed language interpreting studies, for example, a special edition of the journal Deaf Worlds features five articles from British Sign Language (BSL)/English interpreter practisearchers who conducted analyses of their interpreting work in translating for a deaf professional (Cragg 2002), telephone interpreting

Exercise 4.11

Think about how you could conduct a case study of interpreting, in order to pilot any ethnographic principles: either an autoethnographic analysis of your own interpreting practice, or the neo-ethnographic analysis of another single interpreter's work. The key is that it needs to rely on interpreting happening in an authentic setting. So consider the following questions:

- Who do you know that you could approach?
- What contexts could you legitimately access to record an interpreter working?
- What would you be interested in analysing?

Write a brief research proposal to conduct a traditional ethnographic study of interpreting (refer back to the template in Chapter 2) using mixed (triangulated) methods of qualitative data collection.

You need to outline the group or community that you have chosen and why, your research question, how you will develop a relationship with the participants, how you will collect the data and over what period of time and how you will analyse the data.

In particular think about what would be innovative about your proposed study. What new knowledge would it contribute to the field?

(Dickinson 2002), making lexical choices when interpreting from BSL into spoken English (Hema 2002) and ethical choices when interpreting in a classroom (Hull 2002). Other examples are Leeson and Foley-Cave's (2007) linguistic case study of Irish Sign Language/English interpreting for university lectures and two linguistic case studies of theatre interpreting, with an argument that it is a hybrid between interpreting and translation (Banna 2004; Turner and Pollitt 2002).

4.6 Conclusion

In this chapter, we have given you an overview of ethnographic research and the various methodological approaches to conducting ethnographic research. In particular, we have outlined a range of Interpreting research studies that have adopted ethnographic principles. The methods of interviews and focus groups can be used to complement other research approaches as discussed in Chapters 3, 5, 6 and 7.

Further reading

Angelelli, C. (2004). *Medical interpreting and cross-cultural communication*. London: Cambridge University Press.

Berk-Seligson, S. (1990). *The bilingual courtroom: Court interpreters in the judicial process*. Chicago: University of Chicago Press.

Maxwell, J. A. (2013). *Qualitative research design: An interactive approach* (3rd edn). Thousand Oaks, CA, USA: Sage Publications.

Nunan, D. (1992). *Research methods in language learning*. Cambridge: Cambridge University Press.

Robson, C. (2011). *Real world research: A resource for users of social research methods in applied settings*. Chichester, West Sussex: Wiley Blackwell.

Seidman, I. (2006). *Interviewing as Qualitative research: A guide for researchers in education and the social sciences*. New York: Teachers College Press.
Silverman, D. (2006). *Interpreting qualitative data* (3rd edn). London: Sage.

Notes

1   See Chapter 6 for a discussion and overview of experimental methods in interpreting research.

2   Psychometric research is defined as 'research carried out by the collection of data through an experiment, and the analysis of that data through the use of inferential statistics' (Nunan 1992, p. 231).

3   An N-Vivo software licence must be purchased (many universities subscribe for staff and students) and relies on the input of formatted transcribed text, using 'nodes' for content or thematic analysis – see http://www.qsrinternational. com/products_nvivo.aspx. It is available in several languages. ELAN is free to download from the Max Planck Institute of Psycholinguistics, Netherlands, and provides researchers with the capabilities to annotate up to four video or audio files in the same file using tiers for different levels of analysis – see http://www.lat-mpi.eu/tools/elan/. It is user-friendly with all languages that have a written form. Both software tools can export data directly into Excel spreadsheets. See Wittenburg et al. (2006) for more information.

4   See Chapter 5 for a detailed discussion of Discourse Analytical approaches to studying interpreting.

CHAPTER FIVE

Discourse analysis in interpreting research

This chapter will discuss:

- Definitions of discourse analysis
- Basics of discourse analytical research (design, data collection, data analysis)
- Specific features of discourse analytical methods in Interpreting
- Discussion of corpus studies as data collection technique for this method
- Exercises and practical advice
- Further reading

5.1 Introduction

Discourse analysis (DA) has been the main research methodology in dialogue interpreting research (see for e.g. Berk-Seligson 1990; Cambridge 1999; Davidson 2000; Roy 2000; Tebble 1999; Wadensjö 2001a). Pöchhacker (2004, p. 79) called it the 'dialogic discourse-based interaction paradigm'. Because of this, this chapter will deal mainly with DA as a method to analyse dialogue interpreting. However, DA can be used to analyse monologic types of interpreting as well, such as long consecutive or simultaneous interpreting. It can also be used to analyse a discussion or an interview about interpreting, rather than an interpreted interaction or text. In Chapter 4, we introduced you to ethnographic qualitative methods, and already dealt with the use of DA to analyse interviews and focus group discussions about interpreting, so we will not cover that type of DA in this chapter.

This chapter will provide you with an overview of what discourse analysis is and how it can be applied to Interpreting research. Although Interpreting research draws from the many different established research methodologies, it also tends to introduce innovative variations that are particular only to Interpreting studies. The methods used, therefore, tend to be eclectic and usually do not rigidly adhere to a specific paradigm. As the discipline is emerging, this trend is likely to continue, with more innovative methods evolving as new research into Interpreting is carried out.

5.2 What is discourse?

First, we need to understand what the word 'discourse' means. This term can mean different things to different analysts. Discourse has sometimes been described in contrast to text, where discourse refers to oral language and text to written language, so the analysis of written language would be called 'text analysis' and the analysis of oral language would be called 'discourse analysis'. However, the two are also often used interchangeably, so that both terms 'discourse' and 'text' can refer to both oral and written language. According to Johnstone '. . . "discourse" usually means actual instances of communicative action in the medium of language . . .' (Johnstone 2009, p. 2). Another way to describe discourse is to refer to it as language in use and in context, as opposed to artificially constructed sentences. This definition of discourse has informed the fields of Pragmatics and Speech Act Theory, Interactional Sociolinguistics, Conversation Analysis and the Ethnography of language, among others (see Hale 2007 for a description of these different types of discourse analysis.)

Another way of looking at discourse is as a general concept that goes beyond the utterances of the speakers; as a way of perceiving and interpreting the world around us and determining how we act and speak in turn. When we speak, we create and reveal our own 'discourse' or ideologies or belief systems. Johnstone states that '. . . people's generalizations about language are made on the basis of the discourse they participate in and the result of it (people apply what they already know in creating and interpreting new discourse)' (2009, p. 3). So we understand what we hear based on what we already know, on what we have experienced and on what we believe; and all new interactions or linguistic and social transactions continue to contribute to shape and modify our discourse. As Johnstone further explains

> . . . describing how language and thought, language and culture, or discourse and society are interrelated has been one of the major goals for theorists of language throughout the past century. The consensus

among discourse analysts is that discourse is both shaped by and helps to shape the human lifeworld, or the world as we experience it (p. 33).

When we deal with interpreted discourse, we are confronted with at least two discourses, the source language discourse and the target language discourse, which encompass the many cross-cultural and cross-linguistic differences inherent in each. We can also argue that the interpreter creates a third discourse. Our analysis of interpreted discourse will greatly depend on our background knowledge of the cultures, the languages, the settings, the context and the participants involved as well as on our theoretical stance. The more we know about all of these aspects, the better equipped we will be to conduct an analysis. This means that we are really using 'our' own discourse to analyse the discourse of others.

5.3 What is discourse analysis?

The term 'discourse analysis' (DA) can be confusing because it has been used by many to mean different things (Wooffitt 2005). It can be used to describe a method of data collection, a method of data analysis and one or many different theoretical or ideological positions. As Gee and Handford explain:

> Some forms are closely tied to linguistics and tie their claims closely to facts about grammar and about the way different grammatical structures function in different contexts of use. Other forms are less closely tied to linguistics or grammar and focus on the development of themes or images across the sentences of utterances in an oral or written text. Some forms of discourse analysis are primarily interested in description and explanation. Others are also interested in tying language to politically, socially, or culturally contentious issues and in intervening in these issues in some way. These latter forms of discourse analysis are often called "critical discourse analysis" (2012, p. 5)

In its simplest definition then, discourse analysis is the systematic analysis of language in use, through the application of a variety of different methods, theories and approaches. Stubbs (1983) speaks of three main characteristics of discourse analysis: the data to be analysed must be authentic, the units of language to be analysed must be above the sentence level and the analysis of the language needs to take context into account. A more current definition of discourse analysis is given by Gee and Handford:

> Discourse analysis is the study of language in use. It is the study of the meanings we give language and the actions we carry out when we

use language in specific contexts. Discourse analysis is also sometimes defined as the study of language above the level of the sentence, of the ways sentences combine to create meaning, coherence, and accomplish purposes (2012, p. 1).

Bax, however, argues that the need for the unit of language to be above the sentence is not necessarily valid, as discourse can be text of any size, written, spoken or signed as long as it is authentic and taken in context (2011).

So if you decide to use DA as a research method, you must choose how you want to use it. Whatever you decide, however, must be systematic and made clear and transparent in your methodology. Before you embark on any type discourse analysis, we recommend you read the seminal publications in the field. We list some of them in Table 5.1 below. Once you have read those, then you will need to read the publications that are specifically on discourse analytical research in Interpreting. We will ask you throughout this chapter to read specific references in connection with the different exercises.

Table 5.1 Seminal references on discourse analysis

Austin, J. (1962). *How to do things with words*. Oxford: Oxford University Press.

Schegloff, E. and Sacks, H. (1973). Opening up closings. *Semiotica*, 8, 289–327.

Jefferson, G. (1974). Error correction as an interactional resource. *Language in Society*, 2, 181–99.

Sacks, H. Schegloff, E. and Jefferson, G. (1974). A simplest systematics for the organisation of turn-taking for conversation. *Language and Communication*, 50, 696–736.

Grice, P. (1975). Logic and conversation. In P. Cole and J. Morgan (eds), *Syntax and semantics*, Vol. 3. New York: Academic Press, pp. 41–58.

Goffman, E. (1981). *Forms of talk*. Oxford: Basil Blackwell.

Coulthard, M. (1985). *An introduction to discourse analysis*. London: Longman.

Brown, P. and Levinson, S. (1987/1992). *Politeness: Some universals in language usage*. Cambridge: Cambridge University Press.

5.4 Conducting discourse analysis

Because there are so many different forms of discourse analysis, it is impossible to provide one single set of guidelines or one single method to conduct DA research. According to Titscher et al., it is '. . . more a question of a research strategy than of a single method of text analysis' (2000, p. 55). Bax (2011) agrees that discourse analysis should not be seen as '. . . a set of "hard-and-fast" rules or methods which can lead us step-by-step into the analysis of every text we wish to examine' and suggests that DA should be considered more as a 'craft skill' (p. 95). So we hope that you will not be disappointed after you finish reading this chapter, because we were not able to give you one set of clear-cut steps to conducting discourse analysis. The nature of DA makes such a task impossible.

We believe that before you can start to analyse interpreted discourse, you should be able to analyse monolingual discourse. The next section will therefore deal with monolingual discourse.

5.4.1 *Analysing monolingual discourse*

In their book 'An introduction to forensic linguistics: Language in evidence', Coulthard and Johnson present an example of how to analyse a forensic text (2007). In it, they state that when analysing a text, linguists '. . . draw on diverse interpretative tools, methods and theories. . . . Often it is an eclectic selection of tools and a developmental approach to methodology that is necessary' (p. 14).

We can say that there are essentially two main approaches to DA: the top-down approach and the bottom-up approach. The top-down approach is a deductive-type approach (see Chapter 1), where the researcher has determined the structures or characteristics of the discourse that s/he wants to find. For example, the researcher may want to find out how frequently the discourse marker 'so' is used in a particular text and how it is rendered by the interpreter into a particular language. The researcher may be attempting to prove or disprove the results of a previous study (or a hypothesis). The bottom-up approach allows the data to tell the researcher what to analyse, without any preconceived ideas. This is a type of inductive approach (see Chapter 1). Both approaches can of course be used to complement each other. The researcher may start with an inductive approach to identify patterns, particular tendencies and special features of a text first. This can be done with a single case study or using a corpus-based approach (see § 5.8 below). Then those identified patterns and features can be used to determine what to look for and analyse in a different text or set of texts.

Coulthard and Johnson suggest that a first step in the analysis of a text is to '. . . consider how it is similar and what distinguishes it from other texts in other contexts and which theories and methods are most appropriate to analyse it' (2007, p. 14). In other words, the analyst needs to find features that can be used to describe the particular discourse under study. For example, discourse analysis into courtroom interactions has found that court hearings are similar to other dialogic interactions in that they consist of questions and answers. However, they differ from most other dialogic interactions such as conversations or even other institutional encounters like a doctor-patient consultation in many ways. One such difference is that courtroom questions are rarely genuine questions because they do not aim to elicit new information. Their purpose is to present a version of the facts, already known to the questioner, that is either favourable or unfavourable, depending on whether it is examination-in-chief/direct examination or cross-examination. Because of this, the language used, the types of questions used and the intonation of the questions, are among other things, all very particular features that distinguish courtroom discourse from other types of discourse (see Hale 2004, for a detailed discussion on courtroom discourse). In order for an analyst to arrive at conclusions based on a description of the discourse, s/he must be conversant with the setting and the aims of that speech community. This is because discourse is made up of features that relate to linguistic, contextual and cultural aspects. This is why the more the analyst knows about these three aspects, the better equipped s/he will be to produce a reliable analysis of the discourse and to draw valid conclusions. Such knowledge is gained through a thorough review of the literature as a starting point, as well as through other factors such as background knowledge, observation and personal experience. This is something for you to keep in mind when embarking on a DA study of Interpreting. You may be a practising interpreter yourself, in which case, you will have a wealth of knowledge about the context, situation and activity under analysis from your own personal experience. If you are not an interpreter, then you will need to conduct some preliminary ethnographic research first by undertaking a period of fieldwork where you become acquainted with the setting and the research activity through observation and interviews (see Chapter 4).

Exercise 5.1

Read Chapter 1 'Approaching a forensic text' from Coulthard, M. and Johnson, A. (2007).

Analyse the transcript provided below using the guidelines offered by Coulthard and Johnson (2007).

Excerpt of a court transcript: Cross-examination of a detective senior constable of police (adapted from a NSW Local Court hearing)

1   Q - Detective, I think you said that at 5.30 a.m. or thereabouts on 30th May, you interviewed the complainant, is that the case?

2   A - That's correct Sir.

3   Q - Did you take notes of the interview?

4   A - Yes, Sir, I did.

5   Q - Do you have those notes?

6 A - Sir they can be produced, yes.

7 Q - Where were they taken?

8 A - They are in my notebook. They were just brief notes, to, if I recollect, of what happened.

9 Q - All right. And you have looked at those notes?

10 A - Yes Sir.

11 XXXX

12 Q - And you had a conversation with him.

13 A - That's correct.

14 Q - Yes. Now what time was that?

15 A - It would have been in the afternoon.

16 Q - Well, can you estimate the time?

17 A - Approximately 1.30.

18 Q - And that is some seven, eight, nine hours plus, after the alleged assault?

19 A - That's correct, yes.

20 Q - Now, I think you said that you took him to the police station where you had a further conversation and you asked him to comment on the allegation?

21 A - That's correct.

22 Q - That he assaulted X?

23 A - That's correct.

24 Q - And I think he said to you, did he not, words to the effect 'nothing, I don't want to say anything I was over there, I was there that's all I'm saying, we went to a party and whatever happened I had some', did he say those words to you?

25 A - No, he said 'I did it'.

26 Q - But did you take a note of that?

27 A - No Sir, I did not.

28 Q - When did you write that conversation, or note that conversation down in any form, detective?

29 A - On the day I made the statement, Sir, on 8th of July.

30 Q - So you have made no note between 30th May and 8th July in respect to the conversation you had with Y?

(Continued)

Exercise 5.1 (Continued)

31 A - No Sir.

32 Q - See, I put it to you that what he was talking about there, was Indian Hemp.

33 A - He may have indicated that Sir, because it was alleged to have been at the flat, yes.

34 Q - So when you say he said the words 'I did it', your recollection is that he was talking about Indian Hemp or the use of it?

35 XXXXX

36 Q - Now, you said that when he responded he used the words 'she's a slut'.

37 A - That's correct.

38 Q - See, I put to you that he never said the words 'she's a slut'.

39 A - He did.

40 Q - Did you make a note of that?

41 A - No, I did not Sir, no.

42 Q - See, did you ever make that suggestion that the woman was a slut at all, to either of the defendants?

43 A - I did not Sir.

44 Q - Now, you say later you had a conversation with the defendant.

45 A - That's correct

46 Q - Did you gain the impression that Mr Z had been at that location for there to four hours?

47 A - No, I did not Sir. He was, as far as I recall, he was drinking lemon squash. I have no idea how long he had been there.

48 Q - Well, you do not know whether he was, if he was drinking lemon squash, whether he was toning his alcohol intake down from having been there, or having consumed alcohol earlier that day?

49 A - I've no idea, no.

50 Q - So you do not know how long he had been at the pub before you located him there?

51 A - I do not.

52 Q - See, when you introduced yourself and put the allegation to him or put to him that you wanted to question him about an incident, did he not respond 'fair enough, I'll come with you but I'm not saying anything without a solicitor present'.

53 A - No, he just said, 'fair enough'.

54 Q - Well, could he have said at that point, could he have said 'look, I'm not saying anything with the presence of a solicitor'?

55 A - No, he didn't say that to my recollection, Sir, no.

56 Q - Well, did you ever, you say he never said it to you, I put to you that he did say it to you.

57 A - I can't recall him saying that to me Sir, no.

58 Q - Did you make a note of that conversation that you had with him?

59 A - No, I did not, Sir.

60 Q - When did you first notate that conversation that you had with Z on 30th May?

61 A - On 8th July when I made the statement.

62 Q - And would it be reasonable to say Detective, that you had been involved in a number of investigations since, between 30th May and 8th July?

63 A - Yes, that's correct.

64 Q - I suppose you could not number the investigations you have been involved in since then or between those dates at least?

65 A - No, not sexual assault matters, no.

66 Q - Or general matters?

67 A - No, I could not.

68 Q - You see, could not your recollection there be lacking in that regard in view of the fact that you made no notation of the conversation on the 30th, no contemporaneous notation on 30th May, in fact made no notation of the conversation at all until 8th July, to be fair?

69 A - That's possible, yes.

70 Q - So it is possible, is it not, that Z said to you 'I'm not saying anything without a solicitor at all'?

71 A - Sir, to my recollection he never mentioned a solicitor at all.

72 Q - Well, but that does not, that's to your recollection, but could it have been the case that in fact he did mention that and you have now forgotten it, I mean, that is possible, is it not?

73 A - It is possible.

Another way of approaching your text is by looking at language from a hierarchical perspective and choosing to analyse different levels of discourse. Merten (1983, cited in Titscher et al. 2000, pp. 61–2) offers the following typology:

Table 5.2 Approaching a text from different levels

Level	Object analysed
Syntactic	Letter, syllables, words, sentences and their structures
Syntactic-semantic	Influence of the syntactic structures on formation of meaning
Semantic	Meanings of words and sentences
Syntactic-pragmatic	Relationship between syntax and textual effect
Semantic-pragmatic	Relationship between effect and words or sentences
Pragmatic	Pragmatic structures used to affect reception

5.4.2 Sample analysis of a text

Below we offer another way of analysing the same transcript provided for Exercise 5.1. The first step is to read through the transcript and look for patterns and characteristic features that stand out or 'jump out' of the page as you read it. You can use your knowledge of the research into courtroom discourse to specifically look for features that previous research has identified, and you can also find extra features that either nobody has yet identified or that are singular to your data. A simple way of determining whether certain features are prominent or not is by doing a quantification of them, which is what we have done below.

From this basic quantitative analysis we can draw some conclusions:

1   The word length of the questions is longer than that of the answers. Your knowledge of the discourse of the courtroom will tell you that this is because we are dealing with cross-examination where the cross-examiner is presenting a version of the facts that is different from that of the witness and is simply putting that version to the witness for comment. This results in the lawyer presenting most of the information, with the witness simply agreeing or disagreeing.

2   The types of questions used also confirm the point we made in number 1. The majority of the questions are leading questions. These are questions that give more information than what they ask and are normally presented as polar interrogatives or declarative questions.

Table 5.3 Quantitative analysis

Questions by lawyer	Answers by witness
Word length of questions: 686	Word length of answers: 233
Number of tags in questions: 3	Number of tags in answers: 0
Number of declarative questions: 10	Number of answers that disagree with question: 10
Number of polar interrogatives: 21	Number of answers that agree with question: 13
Number of Wh questions: 3	
Number of modal interrogatives: 1	
Number of discourse markers in questions: 20	Number of discourse markers in answers: 0
Use of politeness markers in questions: 0	Use of politeness markers in answers: 13
Modality in questions: 8	Modality in answers: 4

(Source: Total number of words of question and answer sequence: 919.)

> We see from our quantitative analysis that 31 questions fall into this category and only 4 questions fall into the category of open questions (in the form of Wh or modal interrogatives). These two findings corroborate previous research results about the discourse of cross-examination.

3   Another interesting fact is that the power imbalance is shown not only in the fact that questions are asked by the lawyer 100 per cent of the time, but also in the occurrence of politeness markers. The witness uses politeness markers 13 times, whereas the lawyer never does.

Another way of analysing this text is by doing a content analysis and finding its thematic structure. The analysed text consists of five sequences:

Sequence 1: establishing facts about taking notes of an incident

Sequence 2: casting doubt on accuracy of witness statement – lapse of time between taking notes and event

Sequence 3: casting doubt on witness testimony regarding the use of offensive words by defendant

Sequence 4: casting doubt on credibility of witness regarding facts

Sequence 5: casting doubt on police recollection/dereliction of duty

The above sequences are consistent with the aim of cross-examination, which is to discredit the witness' testimony by casting doubt on the evidence. Now we can analyse the discourse by looking at each of the sequences and describing how language is used strategically to achieve these aims.

One interesting pattern that appears prominently from sequence 2 onwards is the cross-examiner's use of discourse markers and tag questions. Almost every question is prefaced with a discourse markers: 'now', 'well', 'so' and 'see'. Previous research has found specific uses of these discourse markers in conversation (see Schiffrin 1985, 1987), in the context of the courtroom (see Hale 2004), and in the context of a signed lecture (Roy 1989). Once again, these results corroborate previous findings.

Another interesting finding is found in sequence 5. Here the cross-examiner uses modality to change the witness' answer from a definitive 'no' to a possible 'yes':

52. Q -Well, *could* he have said at that point, *could* he have said . . . (see segments 52–72 of the transcript).

This is a strategy that has been described by others with regard to courtroom discourse (see Gibbons 2003).

The above discussion has been limited to the basic methods used and to the description of the findings. Such a discussion needs to be complemented with a review of the literature and with conclusions that are relevant to the aims and research questions of a particular research project.

5.5 Conducting discourse analysis for interpreting research

We stated at the beginning of this chapter that DA has been a popular research methodology with Interpreting researchers, but especially for those interested in community/dialogue interpreting. Research into conference interpreting, both of long consecutive (CI) or simultaneous interpreting (SI), has tended to use experimental methods (see Chapter 6), although there are more recent studies of CI and SI that use corpus-based discourse analysis (e.g. Sergio and Falbo 2012; Setton 2002). DA lends itself very well to the study of triadic interpreted interactions because interpreter-mediated events are oral in nature and are influenced by context and participants. Interpreting cannot be conducted or analysed out of context, and dialogue interpreting is conducted in a participatory framework, where each turn affects the other. For these reasons, most Interpreting scholars who have used discourse analytical methods have been inspired by DA research into English monolingual oral interactions. For example, many have been influenced by the early work of analysts such as Schegloff and Sacks (1973), Gumperz (1981), Brown and Yule (1983), Coulthard (1985), Brown and Levinson (1987) and others, who in turn were inspired by the work of theorists such as Austin (1962), Grice (1975) or Goffman (1981). Such early work has provided frameworks of analysis into features of oral interaction such as turn taking, footing, expressions of politeness, use of discourse markers, to name a few, predominantly within the broad field of Pragmatics. Interpreted interaction is of course much more complex than monolingual interaction. For this reason, Interpreting scholars have adapted and innovated on research methods to suit the particular needs of this new field of enquiry. Mason (2000, 2004) provides an excellent overview of the main DA methods and the main theoretical approaches adopted in *Dialogue Interpreting research*, which we recommend as further reading below.

Interpreting researchers have also been influenced by the results of DA into institutional settings, such as legal discourse (Drew 1992; Gibbons 1990) (Coulthard 2004), medical discourse (Ainsworth-Vaughn 2001; Cicourel 1999; Cordella 2004) and business discourse (Bargiela-Chiappini et al. 2007). The results of these studies have generally been instrumental in the understanding of the discourse practices of the settings in which interpreting is carried out (e.g. Angelelli 2004a; Berk-Seligson 2002; Hale 2004; Metzger 1999).

Most authors will indicate at the outset of their article or chapter, or in their methodology section, which approach they have used to analyse their data. Gavioli and Baraldi (2011), for example, conducted a discourse analytical study of interpreter-mediated interaction in health and legal settings. When explaining their approach, they state that:

Exercise 5.2

Look for the following references using the skills learned in Chapter 2 and identify the theoretical frameworks and methodological influences for each of the cited studies:

1 Mason, I. and Stewart, M. (2001). Interactional pragmatics, face and the dialogue interpreter. In I. Mason (ed.), *Triadic Exchanges. Studies in Dialogue Interpreting*. Manchester: St. Jerome, pp. 51–70.

2 Hale, S. (2002). How faithfully do Court Interpreters render the style of non-English speaking witnesses's testimonies? A data based study of Spanish-English bilingual proceedings. *Discourse Studies*, 4(1), 25–47.

3 Pöllabauer, S. (2004). Interpreting in asylum hearings: Issues of role, responsibility and power. *Interpreting*, 6(2), 143–80.

4 Napier, J. (2007). Cooperation in interpreter-mediated monologic talk. *Discourse and Communication*, 1(4), 407–32.

Given the complexity of interpreter-mediated interaction, our data lend themselves to being studied from a perspective that combines different approaches, integrating research in the field of Interpreting studies, interaction research and work on interlinguistic and intercultural communication. Following studies in Conversation Analysis (Sacks 1974) we look at the ways in which participants co-construct understanding through a coordinated system of turn-taking (p. 206).

5.5.1 *Approaching interpreted text using discourse analysis*

When conducting DA into interpreting, we can broadly look at our text in the following ways:

1 *As separate sets of discourse, which can be analysed independently* – For example, if we choose an interpreted hearing as our data source, we can do a discourse analysis of the English questions, a discourse analysis of the answers in the other language and a discourse analysis of the interpreted renditions into both languages. This approach would be a descriptive approach, where patterns and specific characteristics are found and used to devise a profile of each of these separate discourses: original English questions, original answers in a language other than English, interpreted questions and interpreted answers. The identified characteristics could include lexical and grammatical features as well features that go beyond the syntax level, such as stylistic and register related features. The same approach could be used to analyse other types of interpreted talk, such as the simultaneous interpretation of conference presentations in a particular setting, for example. We can analyse a corpus of source language speeches and a corpus of the interpreted versions of those speeches into different languages and then compare the two.

2 *As one interrelated discourse* – with this approach, we would look at the way each participant's turn, including the interpreter's, affects the other, even when we are dealing with two different languages. This approach would concentrate on features relating to the interaction, such as turn taking between participants, overlapping speech and the interpreter's ability to manage or coordinate the triadic speech event.

3 *As translated text* that can be analysed against the source text in order to compare the original with the interpreted text. The issues to be considered here could include: translation difficulties and interpreters' strategies to overcome them, issues of accuracy,

equivalence, semantic and pragmatic meaning, illocutionary point and effect, cross-linguistic and cross-cultural differences.

4   *As a combination of all of the above.*

Your research aims and research questions will determine how you approach your text. Let us look at some potential research questions and see how you could approach them.

Sample research question 1

- You are interested in seeing whether lawyers' questions differ at all when the case is being interpreted.

- Your research question can be: *Do lawyers' courtroom questions differ when the case is being interpreted? If so, how?*

- For this research question, your text could be a set (or a number of sets) of questions in English.

- For this question you would be adopting approach number 1 above.

- Your underlying aim would be to see if lawyers accommodate for interpreters in order to get their message across.

- Your theoretical framework would be based on what you have read about the influence of interpreters on bilingual interactions. You may have a 'hypothesis'[1] that states that 'no matter how good an interpreter is, a bilingual case can never be the same as a monolingual case', and you may want to prove or disprove this hypothesis by seeing if there are any differences in the English questions when an interpreter is involved.

- There may be a number of variations to your methodology, including:

  o 1 monolingual hearing and 1 bilingual hearing – based on your literature review on courtroom questions in English, you can categorize the questions in the monolingual case and in the bilingual case, quantify them and compare the two cases. You can also look at how the questions are influenced by the answers in both cases and see if there are similarities. Your analysis would be mostly qualitative and interpretative even if you use some quantification.

  o You could analyse a couple of bilingual cases with different interpreters and compare them to themselves and to what has already been found by other researchers about monolingual questioning styles. Your analysis would be mostly qualitative and interpretative.

  o You could rely on corpora of monolingual and bilingual cases (if there are any available in your language combination), or create your own, with different interpreters and different language combinations. You could then use quantitative methods to analyse the data (see Section 5.8 below).

Sample research question 2

- You are interested in the way interpreters coordinate the flow of bilingual interactions, especially when there are multiple parties in the room.

- Your research question could be: *How do interpreters manage multi party interactions with different participating speakers?*

- For this question you would be adopting approach 2 above.

- Your aim would be to describe how interpreters coordinate turns and to see whether they are successful at achieving smooth communication between different parties.

- Again, your theoretical framework would be established by reading the literature about the topic.

- Your hypothesis may be that interpreters need to step out of their 'interpreter' role during the dialogue to take on the 'coordinator' role to manage the interaction.

- There may be a number of variations to your methodology, including:

  o You may want to analyse an authentic business negotiation with an interpreter (if you are permitted to video tape the interaction)

  o You may want to analyse different multi-party interpreted interactions and then compare them (for e.g. a medical consultation with a patient and his/her family who also contribute to the discourse, a business negotiation and a parent-teacher interview with both parents)

  o It may be too difficult to access authentic interpreted interactions. One way to overcome this difficulty is to reproduce (simulate) an interaction and have a professional interpreter interpret live. This way, your data will still be authentic, because it is the interpreter's behaviour you are mostly interested in. (See Major and Napier 2012, for a discussion of the benefits of use simulated role-plays for Interpreting research).

Sample research question 3

- You are interested in the way interpreters interpret educational terms into a particular language.

- Your research question could be: *How do interpreters interpret educational terms relating to secondary schooling?*

- For this question you would be adopting approach 3 above.

- Your aim would be to ascertain the different ways certain educational terms that may not have direct equivalents in your particular language, are interpreted by interpreters in parent-teacher interviews, and to see what strategies interpreters use to overcome any translational challenges.

- Again, your theoretical framework would be established by reading the literature about issues relating to lack of equivalence at word-level and about achieving pragmatic accuracy.

- Your hypothesis may be that when confronted with terms that do not have direct equivalents in the target language, interpreters use the term in English and provide an explanation in the other language.

- For your methodology, you may audio record a number of parent-teacher interviews with interpreters of the same language combination, or simulate a parent-teacher interview (as per example 2) containing all the terms you want the interpreters to interpret and invite a number of interpreters in the same language combination to interpret without any preparation.

Exercise 5.3

Read the articles that you found for Exercise 5.1 again and determine which of the approaches above each of the researchers adopted. Remember that a combination of all approaches is also possible.

5.5.2 *Sample methodologies from published Interpreting research*

Below, we cite three different studies that use DA as a research method. We will look at their methodology sections and describe their approaches to the analysis of their chosen data under the subheadings of: Aims, Setting, Data and Method.

Study 1: Martinsen, B. and Dubslaff, F. (2010). The cooperative courtroom. A case study of interpreting gone wrong. *Interpreting*, 12(1), 21–59.

Aim of the study: '. . . to investigate the influence the interpreter exerts on the interaction' (pp. 22–3)

Setting: A Danish district court sitting

Data: A 90-minute trial with a Danish-French interpreter. This constitutes one interpreted event with one interpreter (a case study). The interpreting was conducted in the short consecutive mode.

Method: A combination of methods was used, including field observation, survey and discourse analysis of transcribed audio-recordings of the interpreted proceedings. To minimize the subjectivity of the researcher in transcribing the discourse, the researchers consulted the participants about their intentions and reactions. Only certain segments of the proceedings that related to the aims of the project were analysed and presented in the findings as numbered excerpts.

Study 2: Krystallidou, D. K. (2012). On mediating agents' moves and how they might affect patient-centredness in mediated medical consultations. *Linguisticaantverpiensia*, 11, 75–94.

Aim of the study: '. . . to shed some light on indicators that might potentially challenge patient-centredness . . . within a mediated medical encounter' (p. 75)

Setting: Urban hospital in Belgium

Data: Selected instances of interpreted doctor-patient consultations from a corpus of 19 transcribed video-recorded interpreted consultations and 27 audio-recorded interviews with medical practitioners and interpreters. The interpreting was conducted in the short consecutive mode.

Method: The researcher selected segments that were relevant to the research aims. The data were coded using an existing model of content analysis. 'Meaning units' were identified and the data were organized in themes. The data were analysed for both verbal and non-verbal cues, which aided or detracted from patient-centredness.

Study 3: Dal Fovo, E. (2012). Topical coherence in television interpreting: Question/answer rendition. In F. S. Sergio and C. Falbo (eds), *Breaking ground in corpus-based interpreting studies*. Bern: Peter Lang, pp. 187–209.

Aim of the study: To analyse the way questions and answers in American presidential debates are interpreted by interpreters working as a team 'in terms of topic reconstruction and topical coherence' (p. 187)

Setting: Media interpreting (simultaneous interpreting in booths)

Data: Set of American presidential debates televised in Italy between 1988 and 2004 and interpreted simultaneously into Italian by professional interpreters. The segments were selected from a large corpus of Italian Television Interpreting data. The data were in the form of written transcripts.

Method: 1. Classification of question types in the source language; 2. Classification of the interpreted versions of the questions identified in 1; 3. Analysis of the changes that occurred in the interpretation; 4. Analysis of coherence achieved in the interpretation. The data were analysed quantitatively and qualitatively.

5.5.3 *Steps to conducting DA in Interpreting research*

We provided a basic description of the methods used by three groups of researchers to analyse interpreted data. We recommend that you read those references in detail to gain a better understanding of the methodology used, including the theoretical frameworks adopted by each of the studies. As evidenced by the cited studies, and as we expressed at the commencement of the chapter, there is no rigid way of conducting discourse analysis. Nevertheless, below we offer some basic guidelines to get you started.

1 Decide on the setting or domain you would like the discourse to come from – for example: medical, legal, business, education, conference.

2 Decide on the genre – for example: doctor-patient consultation, multi-party negotiation, hearing or trial, police interrogation, parent-teacher interview, media interview.

3 Decide on the mode of interpreting – for example: face-to-face interpreting, telephone interpreting, interpreting via video conference, simultaneous or consecutive interpreting.

4 Decide on the data to be analysed – for example: audio or video recordings of authentic interpreted interactions or interpreted speech; audio or video recordings of simulated interpreted interactions or interpreted speech; transcriptions of interpreted interactions or interpreted speech (these could be also part of a publicly available corpus).

5 Decide on the approach to be taken – for example: will you take a bottom-up or a top-down approach? Will you take approaches 1, 2 or 3 above (see point 5.5.1) or a combination of all three?

6 Decide on the theoretical framework – for example: will you follow a specific theoretical framework such as conversation analysis or critical discourse analysis or systemic functional linguistics? Or will you adopt a more eclectic approach drawing on different theories and methods?

7 Decide on what will be analysed – for example: will you take a grammatical approach and identify the way certain parts of speech

or different syntactic structures are used in different contexts by different participants? Or will you take a more pragmatic approach and analyse, for example, the way politeness is interpreted or issues of alignment and footing? Or will you take more of a critical discourse analysis approach and analyse issues of power as expressed through the distribution of turns, the way speech overlaps or the forcefulness of the language used by different participants?

Most of the points above will be decided based on your research questions and on your theoretical framework and methodological approach which you will determine while doing your literature review. The data you analyse may also be determined by how easily you can access such data.

Exercise 5.4

Now read: Wadensjö, C. (2001). Approaching interpreting through discourse analysis. In D. Gile, H. Dam, F. Dubslaff, B. Martinsen and A. Schjoldager (eds), *Getting started in interpreting research. Methodological reflections, personal accounts and advice for beginners.* Amsterdam and Philadelphia: John Benjamins, pp. 185–98.

Analyse the transcript of an interpreted interaction that appears below applying the approach suggested by Wadensjö.

After you have undertaken your basic analysis of the transcript provided, read Cambridge's article and see how she analysed it. Then compare your approach with hers.

Transcript taken from: Cambridge, J. (1999). Information loss in bilingual medical interviews through an untrained interpreters. The Translator, 5(2), 201–19.

D - So, you said about exams soon

M -¿Tienesexámenesahora?

(Do you have exams now?)

P - Yeah. Uhuh.

M - ¿Ahora, en junio?

(Now, in June?)

P - Yeah.

M - Now, in June, so they're about to happen.

D - Quite soon? Okay. How do you think you will feel after the exams?

M - ¿Cómocreesque vas a encontrartedespués de los exámenes?

(How do you think you'll feel after the exams?)

P - Pueseso (.) Si lasapruebo, bien.

(Oh, that. If I pass, fine)

M -¿Y si no, seráunadesgracia? (laughs)

(And if not, will it be a disaster?)

P - Bueno, si no, yaveré

(Well, if not, I'll find out)

M - Uh, he thinks he's going to feel much better if he pass exams of course. Otherwise he will have to reorganize his life and think over what he is going to do.

D - I feel that you are quite worried, but I don't sense that you're unhappy or depressed. Do you, d'you feel like crying?

M - Em, eh, entiende, creequeestáspreocupadopero mmm, de momento no vequeestásinfeliz o queestásdeprimido, que mm si a veceslloras o quehayaunasensación en timismo de angustia o depresión. ¿Túcrees, esotepasa?

(Um, er, he understands, he thinks you're worried, but mmm, at the moment he doesn't see you as unhappy or depressed, mmm do you cry sometimes or do you feel inside yourself that you're anxious or depressed. Do you think that happens?)

P - Que me/ mmn hombre de eso me dangana ¿no? Porque lo típico de esoessaber ¿porqué me tienequepasar a mí?

(I Mm, oh I do feel like it, you know? Because the thing is I think why does this have to happen to me?)

M → He sometimes, he doesn't reckon it's too serious, he feels depressed because he feels how, why this has to happen to me? And when things are difficult around and when it's a bad moment to be suffering ehhm, but/

D - Right.

M → Only occasionally. He is not unhappy continuously.

(Cambridge 1999: 210–11)

5.6 The data we analyse

We have mentioned above that a crucial aspect of DA is that the discourse to be analysed must be naturally occurring. This is in contrast to experimental studies that construct data to test specific hypotheses (see Chapter 6). This is true in particular of Conversation Analysis (Clayman and Gill 2012).

For Interpreting research, there is more flexibility. The data can be drawn from the following:

1 Authentic bilingual encounters in different settings – for example, a medical consultation between an English-speaking medical practitioner and a non-English-speaking patient with the assistance of a professional interpreter. The data used by Martinsen and Dubslaff (2010), Krystallidou (2012) and Dal Fovo (2012) we cited above all used authentic interpreted data.

2 Simulated bilingual encounters – for example, a simulated medical encounter where the roles of doctor and patient are played by actors who do not speak each other's language, but where the interpreter interprets the interaction as if it were in an authentic situation. The interpretation is therefore, still naturally occurring. The study by Cambridge (1999) we cited above uses simulated interpreted interactions.

The type of data you decide to use will depend, again, on your research question and on the availability of the data. If you will be taking an inductive approach, then the first type of data will be more adequate, because you will not have any input in what is generated. Many Interpreting researchers have been able to access naturally occurring data from courts, tribunals, medical consultations and other interpreted interaction. However, such data are always difficult to obtain. You need to consider ethics approval (see Chapter 2), which may be difficult to obtain from certain institutions, such as hospitals. It may also be difficult to obtain consent from the participants themselves (e.g. doctor, patient and interpreter). Using publicly available corpora will avoid the difficulties of obtaining the data.

If you will be taking a deductive approach, where you want to test certain hypotheses, then the second way of generating the data will be more appropriate. This is because you can construct a script that contains the features you want to test and force the interpreter (or even a number of different interpreters) to deal with those features. The interpreter will not have access to the script, so the interpretation will be the same as if the interaction were a real one. The only problem with this approach is that the actors need to be very good at adapting the script to the turns that will inevitably be affected by the interpreter's intervention, in the case of a triadic interaction. (See, e.g. Napier's 2011 analysis of video remote signed language interpreting in court using scripts for five different case studies).

The data that you analyse can be in three different forms: audio recordings, audio-visual recordings and written transcripts. Whether it is an authentic interaction or a simulated one, you will need permission from the participants to record the communicative event. You will, of course, need to have adequate recording equipment in order to produce good quality recordings. Some participants will not agree to recording but will agree to observation. In that case, the researcher/observer can be present and take notes. However, this is not a very effective way of collecting data for discourse analysis, as the notes cannot be full, accurate representations of authentic speech.

If you audio or video record your own data, then you will have to transcribe it before you can analyse it. Our next section will deal with transcriptions in general, but in particular transcriptions of audio recordings. When you use video recordings, visual cues, position of the interlocutors and other physical conditions may be important for your research and will need to be annotated as comments that complement the transcription of the audio. For signed language interpreting, you will inevitably need to rely on both – audio recordings for the spoken language segments and video recordings for the signed language segments.

5.7 Transcriptions

As Johnstone states, '. . . there is no single generally accepted way to represent speech on the page' (2009, p. 23). Once again, the way you transcribe audio or audio-visual material will depend on your research question/s and on what you would like to analyse. This in itself makes your data and your analysis subjective. The way you view your data will differ from the way the same data are viewed by someone else. So, even with naturally occurring speech, you will have an influence on how it is presented when you decide what and how to transcribe it. Ochs discusses the difficulties of transcriptions and highlights the myth of the 'untouched' or 'unadulterated' data. Ochs mentions that transcription is a selective process which converts the naturally occurring data into the 'researcher's data' (1979) Conversation Analysis normally uses the transcription system developed by Gail Jefferson (1974), which uses standard orthography, but is complemented by very detailed additional symbols to indicate features of interaction such as pauses, silences, overlapping speech, pitch and so on. Other discourse analysts and critical discourse analysts use less detailed transcriptions (see e.g. the transcripts provided above, or the transcription used by Coulthard and Johnson in the chapter we asked you to read).

Below we provide some guidelines on how to transcribe, based on the transcription conventions suggested by Jefferson (1974). You can choose to use as many or as few of these as suit your purposes. Alternatively, you may decide to create your own transcription conventions. Whatever you decide to use, you must make it clear to the reader. It is always a good idea to include a key of the transcription conventions you used at the end of your paper.

Table 5.4 Transcribing oral speech

- Decide whether your unit of analysis will be a short exchange or a long one. If it is a short one, then number each exchange. If it is a long one, then number each line. This is for ease of reference when you do your analysis.

- You may decide to include the following in your transcription: Turn taking (latching, overlapping), pauses, non-verbal communication (e.g. head nods if it is a video recording), hesitations, pitch, emphasis, volume, speed, intonation.

- You may want to annotate different pronunciation, coughing, sneezing, yawning, etc. for example, D: I don't like him ((coughs)).

- If transcribing audio-visual data, decide how you will transcribe signs. Will you focus only on giving a gloss (e.g. GIVE) or will you describe parameters of the signs, including hand shape, movement, location and orientation? Will you delineate specifically when fingerspelling is used (e.g. G-I-V-E), or when signs are repeated or incomplete? See Johnston and Schembri (2007) for detailed discussion of signed language transcription norms.

- Give each speaker an initial – for example, P: (for patient) I: (for interpreter)

- Use = to indicate latching – for example,

  (1)   W: We had eighteen of =
          R: Yeah
          W: = them here.

- Use [ ] to indicate overlapping speech – for example,

  (2)   W: [[Take if y -
          E: [[I mean
          (Two people start to speak at once)

  (3)   R: So we didn't have to [wait long
          T: [no we didn't
          (overlapping speech)

- Use brackets for pauses and in-breaths, with the length of the pause in seconds – for example,

  (4)   K: He was (0.6) hhh - no I s'pose not

- Stretched out words – for example,

  (5)   S: we~ well it was (.) enor: : : : mous

- Unclear speech – for example,

  (6)   P: He was just about to (indecipherable) or (???) or (*****)

- Falling Intonation - ↓

- Rising intonation - ↑

- Emphasis – <u>underline</u>

- Exclamation - !

- Applause – Audience xxxXXXXXxxx

- Loudness – Capital letters

- Quiet – °quiet°

- Missing sound –

- To draw the reader's attention to a line – for example,

  → (7)   K: Wh~ ↓ what!

(*Source*: Adapted from Jefferson 1974.)

Exercise 5.5

Using the transcription conventions provided in Table 5.4, read the following text aloud as the speakers would have said it:

H: Mummy <u>look</u> ↑ there's FIVE!

R: don- (.) make so much (.) [noise°

H: [((whispered)) Mum[there's =

R: [°yes I know°

H: = five! Isn't there ↓

5.7.1 *Transcribing interpreted discourse*

When you transcribe interpreted discourse, you will be dealing with at least two languages. When you report the results of your study, you need to translate the segments that are not in the language of the publication or thesis. This can turn your transcription into a tri-lingual text if neither of the two languages of the interaction is the language of the publication or thesis. An extra layer of complexity is thus created, leading to a methodological dilemma. It is always better for the researcher to be conversant with all the languages that are being analysed. This way, the translation of the segments will be done by the researcher him/herself and become part of the analysis. If the researcher does not master one of the languages, then the services of a translator/interpreter need to be obtained. It is crucial that this person be highly competent and trained. It is also essential for the researcher to work closely with the translator/interpreter (see § 1.6.1 in Chapter 1 about collaborating with interpreters in conducting research). As you know, there are different ways of translating a text, and the choices made by the translator can lead to different ways of interpreting the data. The translator will need to be briefed by the researcher about what approach to translation s/he must use. For example, a literal, word-for-word approach, a semantic approach or a pragmatic approach with annotations (see Hale 2004, on a discussion about these three approaches). Even when the researcher translates the segments him/herself, it is important to describe the approach taken for the benefit of the reader. This is a complex issue in Interpreting research that has not received much, if any attention and which in essence deserves its own research to ascertain the impact of different translations on the analysis and on the research results.

Below we provide an example of a segment of a transcription of an Italian-German interpreted interaction, which is published in an English language journal, to illustrate the way the researcher used the transcription conventions and translated the Italian and German segments into English in italics.

Sample transcription from Pittarello (2012, p. 123)

41 D   alloraadesso do un'occhiata
         so I will now have a look

42 I   mhm ↑ (.) der Arztwirdihnjetztuntersuchen
         the doctor will examine him now

5.7.2 *Transcription equipment and software*

In order to transcribe effectively and efficiently, you will need some transcribing equipment. In the days of tape recorders, there were special transcribing machines that you could buy. Now the recordings will be digital, so you can undertake your transcription using your computer and a special transcribing software. You can now download transcribing software from the internet either for free or for a fee (e.g. InqScribe). You can use a pedal to control the segments that you will hear and transcribe when you are focussing on audio data. Other software, such as ELAN (see Chapter 4), can be used with audio or video data and enables you to create tiers for each layer of transcription that you want to use (see Wittenburg et al. 2006). ELAN also allows you to do frequency counts of different analysis categories and to export the data into an Excel spreadsheet. Whichever software you use, it is important that you can slow down the text so you can capture all the nuances in the transcription.

Exercise 5.6

Find transcribing software that you can download to your computer.

Watch and listen to the interview between a nurse and a patient that can be found on: http://www.youtube.com/watch?v=oMaTcGjOPsU& feature=related

Using the transcription conventions above, transcribe the interview.

You will need to go over your transcription many times to ensure it is accurate.

Time yourself and use this as a guide for your future transcriptions.

Alternatively, if you are interested in transcribing signed language discourse, you can view video samples of conversational discourse in British Sign Language (BSL) or Australian Sign Language (Auslan) through the freely available BSL corpus: http://www.bslcorpusproject.org/data/ or the Auslan corpus: http://elar.soas.ac.uk/deposit/johnston2012auslan

One other practical point to keep in mind is that it will take you approximately 2 to 3 hours to transcribe 1 hour of speech, depending on how detailed your transcriptions are. For transcription of signed language data, however, the estimation is 20 hours for every 1 hour of video footage, depending on the level of detail.

5.7.3 *Corpus-based discourse analysis*

A corpus is a body of text that is stored electronically. It can comprise transcriptions of every day conversations, institutional discourse, court hearings, etc. Some examples of English language corpora are:

- CANBEC (Cambridge and Nottingham Corpus of Business English)

- LLC (London-Lund Corpus)

- HKCSE (Hong Kong Corpus of Spoken English

- CANCODE (Cambridge and Nottingham Corpus of Discourse in English)

- NHCC (Nottingham Health Communication Corpus) – a one million word corpus of different health communication contexts – both written and spoken – doctor-patient and non-physician communication (nurses, mental health workers, chaplains, midwives and chemists) (Flowerdew 2012).

Corpus-based discourse analysis uses technology to analyse large collections of specifically defined texts. As Sergio and Falbo comment: 'Corpus linguistics aims first and foremost at giving an account of language in its various manifestations, capitalising on information technology potential, particularly as regards the organisation of a considerable quantity of data' (2012, p. 11).

Corpus linguistics is generally considered a methodology, rather than a theory (although some argue it can also be considered a theory). Different approaches can be taken: one can be to find patterns through the use of quantitative methods; the other can be to validate or refute what DA has found through more traditional methods. We stated in this chapter that DA is generally qualitative. We also stated that quantitative methods can be used to complement discourse analytical methods. The use of corpus linguistics as a method is one way of achieving this goal. Whereas once there was a philosophical divide between Discourse Analysis and Corpus Linguistics (CL), now linguists are using CL to complement DA and vice versa (see discussion in Flowerdew 2012). When we use corpora, instead of analysing one transcript of a speech event for a particular feature, we have access to hundreds of them.

Biber (2012), who has conducted corpus-based research into register in English, describes the essential characteristics of corpus-based analysis in the following way:

> It is empirical, analysing the actual patterns of use in natural texts; it utilizes a large and principled collection of natural texts, known as a 'corpus', as the basis for analysis; it makes extensive use of computers for analysis, using both automatic and interactive techniques; it depends on both quantitative and qualitative analytical techniques (p. 194).

Corpora are tagged (marked or coded) for specific features to make them searchable.

Some common corpus searches include:

- Word frequency – if you want to know which are the most frequently used words in a particular genre

- Word meanings – if you want to determine the most common usage of a certain word that can have multiple meanings

- Co-occurrences of words – if you want to know in what contexts certain words or phrases occur. You can choose a key word which will generate all surrounding words for a line, a sentence or a paragraph

- Collocations – if you want to know how words collocate together

---

Exercise 5.7

Below we list some free on-line corpora and text analysis tools:

http://www.devoted.to/corpora
http://sara.natcorp.ox.ac.uk/cgi-bin/saraWeb?qy = bail&mysubmit = Go
http://www-rcf.usc.edu/~billmann/diversity/DDivers-site.htm
http://view.byu.edu/
http://www.webcorp.org.uk/guide/

Explore the sites listed above and try using one of the tools
Type in the word 'Interpreter' in one of the tools and see what results you get

---

5.7.4 Interpreting corpora

There are now some very good corpora of translated and interpreted discourse. According to Sergio and Falbo:

The main reason behind the use of corpora. . . is identifying typical phenomena of translation and interpretation as a whole and on a wide scale, in a more or less overt attempt to confirm or disavow results from 50 years ago, resulting from the analysis of rather limited corpora or case studies (2012, p. 10).

Many interpreting studies have relied on very small data sets, from a single case-study of one interpreter (e.g. Martinsen and Dubslaff 2010 above), to larger corpora of a set of interpreted events (e.g. Dal Fovo 2012 above). You may be wondering how much data is enough for a discourse analytical study of interpreting. There is really no simple answer for this question. Qualitative research is not interested in representativeness, so small data sets are very adequate to be analysed in great 'qualitative' detail. What you need to bear in mind is that you cannot claim representativeness when reporting your results. Mason (2000) explains this very aptly below:

What matters is not the scale of the study but that the resulting generalizations are commensurate with the supporting evidence. Valid findings may range from the relatively weak claim that 'X happened' (on some occasions), through the stronger claim that 'X happens' (from time to time), as evinced by qualitative analysis, to the very strong claim that 'X frequently or typically happens' on the basis of a quantitative study. All such generalizations will be worth making, provided that they are not stronger than the evidence adduced in support of them. Beyond this, the difficulty remains of seeking to add explanation to description. However frequently a particular interpreter move is attested, it can never be stated with certainty that the move can be attributed to a particular cause. What we can do is show regularities of behaviours and co-occurrence of various features (pp. 229–30).

Corpus-based quantitative interpreting studies can therefore complement small-scale qualitative studies, to make more representative claims, and Shlesinger (1998) has long since called for greater corpus-based approaches to interpreting studies.

When you use a corpus created by someone else, you must bear in mind that others have done some of the discourse analysis work for you already. They have chosen the texts and they have chosen how to transcribe them. As it is impossible to include every single feature of spoken discourse in a transcription, the creators of the corpus must select the features that they consider to be important depending on the context and type of discourse (see Russo et al. 2012 for a discussion on the methodology used to create a corpus of interpretations of European Parliamentary sittings).

Falbo (2001, cited in Sergio and Falbo 2012) presents a set of criteria for the development of an interpretation profile that can be used in creating corpora. An interpreted event can be described by looking at five macro-factors, each of which has subcategories:

1 Interpreter
  a Professional
  b Student
  c Ad hoc
2 Situational context
  a Real situation
    i court setting
    ii medical setting, etc.
  b Simulated situation
3 Mode
  a Consecutive
  b Simultaneous
4 Language and directionality
  a English, Chinese, etc.
  b Bidirectional or unidirectional
5 Type of interaction
  a Doctor-patient consultation
  b Media interview, etc.

A corpus with the above factors defined becomes a very useful tool of analysis.

In the edited volume by Sergio and Falbo (2012), which we recommend as further reading, three Interpretation corpora are described:

- EPIC – The European Parliament Interpreting Corpus, which consists of audio-video recordings and transcriptions of interpretations of Parliament sittings in 2004 in Italian, English and Spanish. This corpus is freely available on-line http://catalog.elra.info/product_info.php?products_id=1145(see Russo et al. 2012).

- DIRSI – Directionality in Simultaneous Interpreting Corpus, which is a bilingual Italian-English corpus of recordings and transcripts of international medical conferences (see Bendazzoli 2012).

- Corpus of Italian Court hearings – a corpus of interpreted proceedings used for a PhD research project (see Biagini 2012).

Exercise 5.8

Explore one of the interpreting corpora listed above.
Devise a research question using the chosen corpus.

You will not find corpora for all languages and all interpreter settings, so you may want to create your own corpus. A simple corpus is a compilation of transcriptions in digital form, which you can tag yourself for the features that you would like to analyse so that they can be searchable.

Exercise 5.9

Collect a set of recordings of monolingual or interpreted interaction. Read Russo et al. (2012) and follow their steps to create your own corpus.

5.7.5 Conclusion

In this chapter, we have provided you with an overview of the main issues surrounding Discourse Analysis as a research method. We have stressed the fact that Discourse Analysis is very diverse and that the approach you choose to take will depend greatly on three factors: 1. your theoretical framework, 2. your research aims and questions and 3. your data. We have also discussed the use of corpora to conduct quantitative discourse analysis, and we have provided you with a long list of references that will provide you with detailed information on DA theoretical frameworks and research methods.

Further reading

Bargiela-Chiappini, F. (2009). *Handbook of business discourse (Find full ref)*
Coulthard, M. and Johnson, A. (2007). *An introduction to forensic linguistics: Language in evidence*. London & New York: Routledge.
— (eds) (2010). *The Routledge handbook of forensic linguistics*. London & New York: Routledge.
Drew, P., Raymond, G. and Weinberg, D. (eds) (2006). *Talk and interaction in social research methods*. London, Thousand Oaks, New Delhi: Sage Publications.
Gee, J. P. and M. Handford (eds) (2012). *The Routledge handbook of discourse analysis*. New York: Routledge.

Jaworski, A. and Coupland, N. (eds) (1999). *The discourse reader*. London and New York: Routledge.

Mason, I. (2000). Models and methods in dialogue interpreting research. In M. Olohan (ed.), *Intercultural fault lines. Research models in translation studies I. Textual and cognitive aspects*. Manchester: St. Jerome Publishing, pp. 215–32.

— (2004). Conduits, mediators, spokespersons: Investigating translator/interpreter behaviour. In C. Schäffner (ed.), *Translation research and interpreting research. Traditions, gaps and synergies*. Clevedon/Buffalo/Toronto: Multilingual Matters, pp. 88–97.

Roy, C. B. (2000). *Interpreting as a discourse process*. Oxford: Oxford University Press.

Sergio, F. S. and Falbo, C. (eds) (2012). *Breaking ground in corpus-based interpreting studies*. Bern: Peter Lang.

Schiffrin, D. (1994). *Approaches to discourse*. Oxford and Cambridge, MA: Blackwell.

Wadensjö, C. (2001). Approaching interpreting through discourse analysis. In D. Gile, H. Dam, F. Dubslaff, B. Martinsen and A. Schjoldager (eds), *Getting started in interpreting research. Methodological reflections, personal accounts and advice for beginners*. Amsterdam and Philadelphia: John Benjamins, pp. 185–98.

Note

1   In Chapter 1, we explained that the term 'hypothesis' is a term that belongs to experimental research. However, many researchers also use it in qualitative, non-experimental paradigms as a concept or idea that the researcher would like to investigate.

CHAPTER SIX

Experimental methods in interpreting research

This chapter will:

- Define experimental research as a quantitative research method and the basic principles of sound experimental design
- Discuss when and why experimental research could be used, and what it can analyse
- Describe different types of experimental interpreting research and typical research designs
- Provide a critical review of sample experimental studies
- Suggest practical ways to conduct experimental interpreting research
- Pose reflexive questions to the reader
- List further relevant readings

6.1 Introduction

At this stage of considering how to conduct Interpreting research, we have thus far focused on different approaches to research that draw on various disciplines, but predominantly from the social sciences, namely sociology, anthropology and linguistics. This chapter focuses on a methodological approach that is more closely aligned with the disciplines of science and psychology and employs a quantitative approach to research. One popular image of research is that of the 'mad scientist' conducting formal experiments in laboratory-like conditions. Therefore, people might assume that it is not possible to conduct scientific, experimental research on Interpreting, as we cannot literally view our work through a microscope or in isolation from the ecological factors that have an impact on the nature of interpreting work (Moser-Mercer 2011). However, this is not the case, as we can metaphorically analyse Interpreting practice through a microscope by designing research projects that adhere to experimental conditions, but that do not necessarily take place in a laboratory. Daniel Gile (1990, 1994; 1998) and Barbara Moser-Mercer (1994) have long been calling for the need for experimental studies in Interpreting, and we have certainly seen an increase over the last 20 years, although this methodological approach is typically more common in the study of simultaneous, conference interpreting, rather than dialogic, community interpreting. Experimental methodology is often used in language research (Nunan 1992), and thus is suitable for Interpreting research.

6.2 Experimental research as a quantitative research method

Experimental research is a way of determining the effect of something on something else. Typically, a researcher begins with the idea to investigate why something happens and manipulates at least one factor (variable), and/or controls others, to determine the effect on some other variable. In contrast to qualitative inductive research, experimental research is deductive, whereby theory underpins research, and studies are designed to test theoretical standpoints (see Chapter 1).

> The traditional model of science, which largely shapes the notion of scientific methods and has also provided inspiration for research on Interpreting, is based on a deductive movement from theory to data: a research problem is defined within a particular theoretical framework and formulated as a hypothesis; by defining all relevant variables and specifying measurable (quantitative) indicators, the hypothesis is operationalized; using an appropriate methodological procedure, the hypothesis is tested against the data and either upheld or rejected, thus lending empirical support to the underlying theory or necessitating its modification (Pöchhacker 2004, p. 62).

The quantitative notion of experimental research is the fact that variables can be measured or counted. In Chapter 3, we discussed another form of quantitative research in the form of survey questionnaires, which leads to either descriptive or correlational (inferential) statistical analysis of results. In descriptive statistics, the characteristics of a sample of individuals or phenomena are presented, as opposed to correlational statistics that investigate the relationship between the variables. Results from experimental studies can also be presented through descriptive or correlational statistics.

By identifying, isolating and eliminating or introducing a range of variables, it is possible to ascertain the extent of impact on the 'thing' being investigated. For example, if someone develops a rash, then the variables that would be investigated could include food, medication, new products (e.g. shampoo or face cream) or plants. The person with the rash would eliminate these items from their daily life one at a time to see if there is any noticeable change to the rash, in order to identify what is causing the allergic reaction. In the reverse, testing can also occur under controlled conditions in a clinical environment. If, for instance, it is suspected that the rash is due to an egg allergy, then the person in question would undergo an 'egg intervention', where parts of the egg are gradually introduced over a period of time and any reactions are noted:

1   Touch of egg yolk on the arm

2   Touch of egg white on the arm

3   Taste of egg yolk on the lips

4   Taste of egg white on the lips

5   Swallow a small amount of egg yolk

6   Swallow a small amount of egg white

7   Swallow a larger amount of whole egg (yolk and white combined)

If the reaction becomes serious at any point, then the intervention stops. Therefore, experimental research replicates these kinds of conditions, whereby variables are eliminated or introduced to determine the effect.

True experimental research involves the random assignment of participants to different groups and comparison between a control group and an experimental group. The control group participates in the study with no 'treatment', that is, no variables are manipulated. The experimental group, however, undergoes some kind of treatment, whereby they are required to engage in some kind of activity that will change something. The most common example would be a test of new medicines, where a control group would be given placebo tablets, and the experimental group would be given the actual medicine being trialled.

Let us consider an example in relation to the analysis of interpreting. If we want to know whether focussing an interpreter's attention on one aspect

Exercise 6.1

Think about your own daily life (non-interpreting) – can you think of a time when you have had to identify variables that have impacted on something else? How did determine the effect of one thing on another? How did you rule out the various factors?

For example: On two consecutive Saturday afternoons Jane felt nauseous. What factors could have contributed? What had happened that day? Was she pregnant? Had she had too much alcohol the night before? Did she have a stomach bug? Did she have food poisoning? Had she eaten something that didn't agree with her?

She was able to eliminate the variables:

- she definitely was not pregnant
- in both weeks she had not had any alcohol the night before
- she had not come into contact with anyone else that had a stomach upset recently and the symptoms would have been on-going rather than 7 days apart
- she had eaten the same as her friends at every meal, so it was unlikely to be food poisoning as no one else was sick
- she doesn't have any food allergies that she is aware of

So what was different?

She realized that over the course of the morning on both Saturdays she had drunk 4 cups of strong coffee, which was 3 or 4 more than she would usually drink in a whole day. She surmised that she had consumed too much coffee, as the high level of caffeine made her nauseous, so after that she was careful not to drink more than 1 or 2 cups of coffee a day. She never experienced the nausea again.

of their interpreting output (e.g. their accent) has an effect on the accuracy of their interpretation product, then an experimental study can be designed to isolate the accent variable and analyse its effect, involving a study with different stages, as seen in Table 6.1.

In sum, experimental research involves the manipulation of at least one variable (the independent variable), in this example accent, while keeping other variables constant and determining the effect of the manipulation on some other variable (dependent variable), in this case the interpretation accuracy.

Table 6.1 Different stages of an experimental study

Stage	Example
Pre-experiment	Selection of two groups of interpreters, who are matched on a range of variables. These variables could include: native language, working language pairs, interpreting qualifications and training, professional accreditation (certification), years of interpreting experience, age, gender, etc.
Pre-test	All the interpreters would be required to complete an interpretation of the same source text, which would be analysed and scored for accuracy in terms of source > target language interpretation output.
Treatment session	The experimental group (Group A) would receive focused attention on their accent (e.g. by completing a questionnaire on their attitudes to different spoken accents, including their own), before undertaking a similar interpreting task as in the pre-test; while the control group (Group B) would undertake the same interpreting task but would not have the 'treatment', that is, complete the questionnaire.
Post-test	Measures any changes in the interpretation product of Group A by applying the same accuracy scores as used in the pre-test, and contrasting post-test scores with Group B.
Presentation of results	This can be done either through descriptive or correlational statistics. Descriptive statistics would involve just presenting the characteristics, for example, 50 per cent of Group A produced an interpretation with a lower rate of accuracy; more male than female interpreters appeared to have been distracted by becoming more self-aware of their own accent. Correlational statistics would involve presenting any significant relationships between the variables, that is, whether there was any relationship between the native language, working language pairs, interpreting qualifications and training, professional accreditation (certification), years of interpreting experience, age, gender, etc. and the interpretation accuracy score, between the experimental and the control group.

Exercise 6.2

In relation to the example above – what variables do you think would be the most important to consider? How would you recruit interpreters who might be appropriate participants for the study?

6.3 Basic principles of sound Experimental design

When we carry out experimental research, there are basic principles that ensure the sound nature of any experimental design:

1 Development of a specific and precise research question, possibly followed by a series of sub-questions. The research question follows on from a deductive theoretical standpoint and is generally based on a previously unanswered question.

2 Statement of explicit variables, that is, what is being varied and what is being measured. These variables must relate directly to the construct(s) being investigated.

3 Randomly select a group of participants who are then arbitrarily allocated to various treatment conditions and/or control groups. The treatment must be described explicitly and related back to the research question(s).

4 Effects of the treatment are analysed and presented through statistical means.

5 Interpretation of results from the experimental group is counterbalanced with results from the control group, in order to determine accuracy of findings.

Exercise 6.3

In relation to point (1) above, write two different research questions for a study of Interpreting that could be answered using an experimental approach. Remember that experimental studies are deductive – based on a theory or theories, and on answering an as yet unanswered question.

6.3.1 *Research questions*

Research questions must be stated explicitly and be related to previous literature (see Chapter 1). Consider the following two examples:

1 *Should videoconference facilities be used to provide interpreting services?*

This question is problematic as it is not researchable. The question is too vague and use of the word 'should' implies some sort of right or wrong, which cannot therefore be empirically evaluated.

It is crucial that experimental research present answerable questions. In considering whether a question is answerable, the key is to ensure that a question is feasible and can be investigated in the time allocated and within the confines of the budget available. This means that initial research questions often have to be scaled back to avoid levels of complexity that are too cumbersome. PhD students in particular often find that within the scope of a 3–4 year study, their initial research questions are considerably narrowed down to be achievable and answerable within the period of their candidature.

2 *Does extended length of interpreting time impact on the production of omissions in simultaneous interpreting?*

This research question is explicitly stated and related back to existing literature as Moser-Mercer et al. (1998) investigated the effects of fatigue on the quality of conference interpreters' output and the coping strategies that were used. They found that as interpreters became more tired, they made more errors and were only able to detect their mistakes once they had reached such a point of fatigue that they could no longer mentally process the source language message. Several other researchers (e.g. Barik 1975; Cokely 1992; Kopczynski 1980; Napier 2002) have explored the impact of omissions on the interpreting product, but not all have made connections between the production of omissions and cognitive load brought on by extended interpreting time.

However, the question still needs more elaboration of specific variables that are to be tested. Given that experimental research ideally should compare variables, then the question can be made more explicit. The ideal question could be something such as:

Do interpreters that simultaneously interpret for an extended length of time produce more omissions than interpreters who interpret for shorter periods of time?

It is important that the question relate to existing research literature, and ethical considerations also need to be given as to whether a question can be tested and is answerable. The first question above is dubious, and it would be too difficult to design a study to answer this broad question, given the range of variables that would need to be identified and tested.

If there are several variables to be tested, then it is possible to construct a primary research question, and a series of sub-questions, such as:

1 *Do interpreters that simultaneously interpret for an extended length of time produce more omissions than interpreters who interpret for shorter periods of time?*

   a *How many omissions are produced by interpreters who interpret for 20-minutes?*

   b *How many omissions are produced by interpreters who interpret for 40-minutes?*

Exercise 6.4

Review the research questions you wrote in Exercise 6.3 above. Are they feasible and answerable? Do they relate to existing literature? Are they explicit enough? Do you need to break the questions down into sub-questions?
Re-write your research questions to make them more explicit.

6.3.2 *Hypotheses*

In experimental research, in addition to research questions, there are also hypotheses. Hypotheses are predictions based on the research question(s). In relation to the first research question above, based on a review of the literature, the researcher might suggest the following hypothesis:

Interpreters who simultaneously interpret for an extended length of time produce more omissions than interpreters who interpret for shorter periods of time.

Furthermore, the researcher could be even more explicit with the hypothesis, as follows:

Interpreters who simultaneously interpret for an extended length of time produce more omissions than interpreters who interpret for shorter periods of time, due to cognitive overload and fatigue.

These types of hypotheses would be expressed as null hypotheses, which state that there are no differences between or among groups. The primary goal of the research project would be to reject the null hypothesis. The null hypothesis would be stated as:

Interpreters who simultaneously interpret for an extended length of time DO NOT produce more omissions than interpreters who interpret for shorter periods of time.

Exercise 6.5

Now that you have finalized your research questions that could be investigated through an experimental study, select one of the studies and set of research questions to focus on and think about your hypotheses.

Do you have a sense of what you are trying to prove or disprove with the question(s)?

If you have developed a question based on observations of your own practice, do you have a hypothesis about what you expect the outcomes of the study to be?

Write down your hypotheses for this study.

6.3.3 *Variables*

Variables are characteristics of a class of objects that vary, and any experimental research design must make the variables explicit (see Chapter 3). To return to research question (a) above, there are a number of variables that need to be explicitly identified and outlined in order to conduct the research, such as:

- Time periods for interpreting: how long is extended?
- Qualifications of the interpreters in the experiment
- Experience of interpreters in the experiment
- Definition of omissions
- Omission types to be analysed
- Experimental conditions for interpreting simultaneously. In a booth or whispered.

When conducting and reporting experimental research, it is essential that researchers are clear on how the terms are defined. For instance, in the analysis of interpreting omissions, it would be vital for the research to define what s/he means by 'omissions'. Earlier studies of interpreting omissions have tended to focus on omissions as errors, whereas more recent studies have considered a range of omission types, and that some omissions may be produced very deliberately and strategically by interpreters, and may not necessarily be detrimental to the overall message, and even help achieve a pragmatically accurate rendition.

As mentioned earlier, in experimental research, there are two primary variables of concern: independent variables and dependent variables. Independent variables are the object of investigation. They are the variables that are being investigated in order to determine their effect on something else. In the above example, the length of interpreting time is the independent variable, and 'omissions' is the dependent variable. Dependent variables are those that are being affected by the independent variable. So by changing, the time variable in interpreting (independent), such as getting one group to interpret for a maximum of 20 minutes and another group to interpret for 40 minutes, the omission variable may change. That is, the rate and types of omissions produced would be affected by the length of time the interpreter was interpreting for.

In addition, there are also extraneous variables that are independent variables that the researcher has not controlled for, which can interfere with the results of a study. Referring back to the same example above, another independent variable could be familiarity of the topic of the source text to be interpreted. The interpreter participants' level of familiarity with the topic could influence how easily they get fatigued, and how many erroneous omissions they produce.

Exercise 6.6

Following on from Exercise 6.5, identify all the variables that need to be tested in your study. What are the independent and dependent variables?

6.3.4 Random assignment

A particular identifying feature of experimental research is the random assignment of participants to one group or another. Random assignment means that each participant has an equal chance of being assigned to any of the conditions of the study (i.e. to the experimental group or the control group). This type of randomization is not always possible, depending on the size of the population being studied and the variables being explored.

In the above research question on interpreting time and omissions, one key variable to test would be the experience of interpreters in dealing with this pressure. Therefore, participants could be randomly assigned to the experimental group (40-minutes interpreting) and the control group

(20-minutes interpreting). The experimental group is given the longer period of interpreting as this is the non-standard length of time for simultaneous conference interpreting.

The intention of randomization is to eliminate the possibility that extraneous variables will impact on the research design. The randomization of interpreter participants in the above example would mean that there would be an equal chance of having interpreters in both groups that have some familiarity with the topic of the source text.

In some contexts, random assignment of individuals is not possible due to constraints of the context that already exist. This is referred to as quasi-experimental research because not all of the variables can be completely controlled. Aspects of each group may be the same and testing takes place under the same conditions, but there are some variables that are different. See Section 6.7 for an example of quasi-experiments. The differing characteristics between pre-experiments, quasi-experiments and true experiments can be seen in Table 6.2 (adapted from Nunan 1992, p. 46).

Table 6.2 Different types of experiments

Type	Characteristics
Pre-experiment	May have pre- and post-tests, but lacks a control group
Quasi-experiment	Has both pre- and post-tests and experimental and control groups, but no random assignment of subjects
True experiment	Has both pre- and post-tests, experimental and control groups, and random assignment of subjects

Exercise 6.7

Can you randomly assign participants for your own experimental study? What would be the advantages and disadvantages?

6.3.5 *Interpretation of results*

The interpretation of experimental results is conducted initially through statistical analyses. An overview of different types of statistical analysis has been given in Chapter 3 with the discussion of survey questionnaires. In general, for most Interpreting research, the significance level (p value) is generally set at 0.05. This means that when we interpret statistical results, there is a 95 per cent chance that the results are due to the experimental treatment and only 5 per cent due to chance alone. Some researchers will talk about results approaching significance when the statistical analysis is somewhere around 0.05. In different disciplines where the consequences of a chance finding are greater (e.g. life-altering medical treatment), higher significance levels are required.

Thus it can be considered that the α level is a generally accepted guide used by researchers in any particular discipline. When accepting or rejecting a hypothesis, we should try to avoid any errors in interpretation of the results.

There are two predominant error types:

- Type I (α error)
- Type II (β error)

A Type I error occurs when a (null) hypothesis has been rejected when it should have been proved, and Type II refers to the acceptance of a (null) hypothesis when it should have been rejected. Both of these error types are minimized through the rigorous use of statistics.

As part of the process of interpretation of results, researchers need to have a reasonable degree of confidence that extraneous factors did not influence their research outcomes. There are ways to minimize the possibility of extraneous variable interference. One way to do this has already been discussed – through randomization. The other is to test for the variable and eliminate participants that demonstrate that characteristic. In the case of the interpreting experiment we have discussed above, this would mean eliciting from the participants whether they have any prior knowledge of the source text topic and eliminating them from the groups. Alternatively, that variable could be included in the research design and tested for level of influence.

Another variation on including the variable into the design would be to match participants so that one has a particular characteristic and another does not. If, for example, in our interpreting study we look at the variable of interpreter qualification and consider how someone with formal training might cope differently from another interpreter with no formal interpreter training, then both groups (experimental and control) would be balanced with participants with or without formal Interpreting qualifications.

6.4 Reliability and validity

Any research, but particularly quantitative experimental research, needs to be reliable and valid. Anybody should be able to read the results of a study with confidence that the findings are trustworthy. Reliability and validity checks are techniques used to ensure the quality of research.

6.4.1 Reliability

When data are obtained from a data gathering instrument or technique, we need to know what faith we can put in the data as truly indicating the person's performance or behaviour (Burns 1997, p. 259).

Reliability refers to consistency in scoring across the data and in use of research instruments (such as analytical and coding tools). Thus, in relation to our hypothesis on interpreting omissions, it is necessary to have an appropriate and accurate measurement of what we mean by an omission, but also of cognitive overload and fatigue if those variables are to be measured.

Often variables cannot be measured directly. In these instances, a working definition is created that allows us to identify the variable in question with something that is understandable and measurable, otherwise known as operationalization. Once a variable has been operationalized, it is easier to work with and can save the researcher (or research team) a lot of time and effort. This process of operationalization ensures that the study design reflects what it ought to and can be applied more broadly outside of the population being studied.

In relation to interpreting omissions, Napier (2002, p. 121) adopted the following operational definition of an omission:

> When information transmitted in the source language with one or more lexical items does not appear in the target language, and therefore potentially alters the meaning.

There is much debate in the Interpreting Studies literature concerning the measurement of accuracy, and there is still no agreement as to how omissions should be evaluated. However, it is generally agreed that omissions should not be counted as a word for word direct interpreting error. That is, if a word uttered in the source text is not exactly reproduced in the target utterance. Rather, it is accepted that a faithful interpretation conveys meaning and sense (Seleskovitch 1978), so any analysis of interpreting omissions needs to have a clear construct of what it means to observe an 'omission' in the coding instrument. In this way, any researcher should be able to pick up the instrument and apply it and produce reliable coding across the data set that is comparable. Although there is no agreement on the measurement of interpreting omissions, there are many taxonomies that exist that can be replicated, adapted or combined, examples of which can be seen in Table 6.3. By drawing on the existing research, this provides further likelihood of reliability in the research design.

In order to ensure reliability and appropriate measurement of constructs, Interpreting researchers will often use inter-rater reliability measures. This

Table 6.3 Examples of omission taxonomies

Researcher(s) and year	Omission categories
Barik (1975)	Skipping (single lexical item)
	Comprehension (larger unit of meaning as a result of an inability to comprehend the source language message)
	Delay (larger unit of meaning due to lagging too far behind the speaker)
	Compounding (conjoining elements from different clauses or sentences)
Kopczynski (1980)	Obligatory omission
	Optional omission
Cokely (1992)	Morphological omission
	Lexical omission
	Cohesive omission
Wadenjsö (1998)	Reduced renditions
	Non-renditions
	Zero renditions
Napier (2002)	Conscious strategic
	Conscious intentional
	Conscious unintentional
	Conscious receptive
	Unconscious

process enables researchers to check how judgments are made about the data and involve more than one rater (as opposed to intra-rater reliability, where only one researcher's coding is used). By asking more than one rater to use the same measurement tool, the consistency of rater results across a dataset indicates that the raters are measuring the constructs in the same way. This can be referred to as a 'test-retest' method (Burns 1997), whereby the scores of the researcher are compared with the scores of another person who reviews the same data independently. The reliability check would incorporate exactly the same coding procedure as conducted by the original researcher.

In the example of Napier's study of interpreting omissions (2002), a rater used the operational definition of the concept of an omission originally used by the researcher (see above) to code the omission types produced by a random sample of the interpreter participants. The rater was asked to mark on a transcript any omissions that were noted, following the same procedure initially adopted by the researcher. The numbers and types of omissions found per subject were then compared with the number originally noted by the researcher. An ideal reliability target should produce an agreement of 80 per cent, or preferably more (Burns 1997).

6.4.2 *Validity*

Validity refers to the correctness and appropriateness of the interpretation of study results. Many of the constructs presented in the preceding sections of this chapter ensure validity by providing a mechanism to trust that the research design gives consideration to all variables (or as many as possible) that may impact on the research results.

There are different types of validity that need to be taken into consideration when ascertaining the trustworthiness of research design:

6.4.2.1 Content validity

Is the measurement of the phenomena about which we want information representative? For example, the study under discussion is an investigation of simultaneous interpreting and omissions, but the findings cannot be generalized to say that we fully understand omissions in all forms of interpreting. Suffice to say, if we want to clearly state that we have investigated interpreting omissions, we need to ensure that the instruments include a representative range of descriptions/definitions of various possible omission types.

6.4.2.2 Face validity

Closely related to the notion of content validity, face validity helps us to consider the consumers of the research. We need to ask the question whether the instrument is readily recognizable as measuring what is claimed to measure. For example, the construct of interpreting omissions can be measured in different ways, but there are certain instruments (as outlined above) that are well accepted as measuring this construct. Thus, face validity refers to the familiarity of the instrument and how easy it is to convince others that content validity exists. If testing interpreting omissions with a newly developed instrument, there may be a perception by some stakeholders (e.g. interpreter practitioners, educators) that the instrument is not valid. If the participants do not perceive a connection between the research activity and their practice, they may be less likely to take the experiment seriously.

6.4.2.3 Construct validity

This type of validity refers to the extent to which the research adequately captures the concept in question. In Interpreting Studies research, construct validity is a concern because much of what we investigate is not easily quantifiable and not directly measurable (as with much of other linguistic and language studies). Often researchers are dealing with constructs like accuracy, language proficiency and performance, which are concepts that are not easy to pin down. How can we measure these constructs so that we can compare individuals on a common scale? If the constructs are not directly measureable, their validity may be called into question. One way to enhance construct validity is to have multiple measures. Thus, if we were to measure interpreters' language proficiency, we could utilize measures that reflect oral use, written use, extent of vocabulary knowledge, etc. These multiple measures could then be used as an aggregate to give greater confidence in the researcher's ability to differentiate individuals along a scale of proficiency.

6.4.2.4 Criterion-related validity

This type of validity refers to the relationship that a given measure has with another well-established measure. For example, if a researcher develops a measure for interpreting omissions, it will have criterion-related validity if it measures interpreters' output in much the same way as another well-established instrument.

6.4.2.5 Predictive validity

This form of validity deals with how well the measure being used predicts performance on some other measure. Therefore, if a test measures working memory capacity in interpreters, it has predictive validity if it accurately predicts performance in terms of directionality in interpreting practice.

6.4.2.6 Internal validity

Related to the notion of reflectiveness, this form of validity means that a researcher needs to consider whether the results of a study truly reflect what s/he believes they reflect. That is, are the dependent and independent variables sufficiently related to one another? Is there a cause-and-effect relationship? Does the cause precede the effect? Are observed changes attributable to the experimental intervention? To establish a cause-effect relationship you need to meet three criteria: (1) temporal precedence (does the effect happen after the cause?); (2) covariation (if x then y or if not x then not y); and (3) no other possible causes or explanations for the effect. A researcher must control for all other possible factors that could possibly explain the outcome of any study. To refer back once again to the study of interpreting omissions – by accounting for the variable of familiarity with the topic, this ensures internal validity. Before conducting any research study, researchers need to think through the research design very carefully to ensure that any threats to internal validity are minimized or eliminated. Finding a relationship does not guarantee that it is causal. To establish internal validity, all other plausible explanations need to be ruled out. This can be done by using a two-group design.

In critiquing Napier's (2002) study of interpreting omissions, this could be considered as a one-group pre-test design (see Table 6.1 in § 6.2 above), with weak internal validity as there was no control group. Although the interpreter participants were identified and matched through a pre-experiment survey and could be divided into groups: native versus non-native signers, those with formal interpreting qualifications versus those without, those with university interpreting experience versus those without, or those familiar with the lecture topic versus those who were not; there was no treatment or post-test stages of the experiment, so we could not determine whether another group who did not receive the intervention would be affected in the same way. The pre-test involved ten Australian Sign Language interpreters interpreting the same university lecture text under the same experimental conditions, that is, they followed exactly the same procedure. Thus, technically, the whole study could actually be considered as a pre-experiment (see Table 6.2 above).

However, this was a necessary test design to develop the omission categories for analysis, as the categories were data-driven. That is, Napier developed her omission taxonomy based on the immediate post-interpreting task qualitative retrospective recall interviews with the interpreter participants, and what they reported as their level of consciousness about the omissions they were making and why. The use of qualitative data is often crucial for the interpretation of quantitative study results (cf. Nunan 1992), and in this case, Napier was able to make sense of the omissions produced by talking to the interpreters about their conscious interpreting process.

The internal validity of Napier's study could have been greatly improved by making it a true experiment, through the addition of a control group and some kind of treatment stage, as seen in Table 6.4.

6.4.2.7 External validity

The extent to which a study can be considered generalizable demonstrates its external validity. There are three threats to external validity: people, place

Table 6.4 Suggested improvements to Napier's study

Stage	Design	Previous/new
1 Pre-experiment	Selection of ten interpreters, matched on a range of variables: native/non-native Auslan users, general level of education (i.e. university qualification?), interpreting qualifications and training, professional accreditation (certification), years of interpreting experience, age, gender, university interpreting experience, familiarity with the selected lecture topics.	Previous
2 Pre-test	All participants interpret the same university lecture source text under the same conditions, with varying levels of familiarity with the topic (Text 1), then participate in a post-task retrospective interview to identify omission categories. Data analysed and scored for omission types in relation to variables identified in pre-experiment. Omission taxonomy established.	Previous
3 Treatment session	Ten interpreters split into two matched groups – all interpreters are familiar with the topic of lecture Text 2. The experimental group (Group A) are given a transcript of Text 2 to read (focused attention), before undertaking a similar interpreting task as in the pre-test (i.e. interpreting university lecture Text 2 under the same conditions); while the control group (Group B) would interpret Text 2 without having received any preparation.	New
4 Post-test	Measures any changes in the interpretation product of Group A by applying the same omission taxonomy as developed from the pre-test, and contrasting post-test scores with Group B.	New
5 Presentation of results	Presentation of pre-test results using descriptive statistics.	Previous
	Presentation of post-test results using descriptive statistics (if numbers were larger it would be worth considering correlational statistics to measure significance of variables).	New

and time. In order to ensure external validity, you need to be sure that the study would achieve similar results with a different population in a different place and at a different time. In an experimental study, it is more useful if we can apply the results from our study participants to a broader population, especially if results can be applied to interpreters of different languages in various contexts. Thus, if a study is designed to investigate the interpreting omissions of Australian Sign Language interpreters in university lectures (cf. Napier 2002), then it needs to be considered how much the results can be applied to the following constructs:

- Signed language interpreters in other countries working in university lectures (cf. Leeson and Foley-Cave 2007)
- Australian Sign Language interpreters working in other contexts
- Signed language interpreters working in other contexts
- Spoken language interpreters working in other contexts

To use another example, Wadensjö (1998) developed a taxonomy of renditions that represent (among other things) omission types (reduced, zero, non-renditions). She conducted analyses on interpreter-mediated communication in various contexts applying the same taxonomy, including police interviews, therapeutic encounters and medical consultations, and documented the patterns of renditions in interpreter utterances for interpreters working between Swedish and Russian. Wadensjö's taxonomy has been applied by other researchers investigating interpreter-mediated communication in medical encounters with spoken language interpreters (Amato 2007; Cirillo 2012) and signed language interpreters (Major and Napier 2012). Although all of these studies have adopted a qualitative discourse analytical approach (see Chapter 5), by using the same taxonomy to code the interpreter utterances, the researchers could be assured of the external validity of their studies, as the assessment instrument had been used before. Although each of these studies identified slightly different patterns of rendition types produced by interpreters working with different languages, they were all able to confirm that all the interpreters involved in the various studies did produce the same types of renditions that demonstrated a level of interpreting omission. The use of an existing taxonomy also provided criterion-related validity (see § 6.4.2.4 above).

In experimental research, external validity can be increased with appropriate sampling procedures (see Chapter 3), ideally using a random sample so that each member of the population being studied has an equal and independent chance of being selected. In reality though with Interpreting research, this is not always possible or practical, so non-random sampling is more likely to be used by calling for volunteers to participate in a study. Even if using non-random sampling, the goal would be to have a sufficiently large enough sample so that true differences between the control and experimental groups could be more probable. Small sample sizes mean that the results may be questionable, as differences between groups may be coincidental. That is, the larger the group, the more likely you are to identify a representational pattern. In order to avoid drawing uncertain conclusions, various statistical packages are available to test the significance of results (see Chapter 3).

As true random sampling is not always possible in Interpreting research, it is important for researchers to fully and accurately describe the population studied as well as provide details about the materials, methods and procedures. In doing so, any study can be replicated by others, which means that the population base of the original study is indirectly broadened through the testing of the same phenomena with other populations. Thus, for example, if Napier's (2002) study of interpreting omissions produced by Australian Sign Language interpreters in university lectures was replicated by other signed language interpreter researchers in other countries, using the same (non-random) sampling technique, materials, method and procedure, then it could be argued that the results could be generalized to signed language interpreters working in university lectures in any country.

Exercise 6.8

Give consideration to the reliability and validity of your proposed experimental research design. Is there anything you have overlooked? Would it be possible for your study to be replicated by other researchers?

6.5 Typical experimental interpreting research designs

In her review of Interpreting research studies published in the journal 'Interpreting', Liu (2011) gives an excellent overview of the types of experimental research designs utilized to conduct empirical research on Interpreting, which include:

6.5.1 Natural groups design

The selection (rather than manipulation) of independent variables, such as interpreting qualifications. For example, in Australia, an experiment could be designed to select interpreters with the different types of qualifications that are attainable in Australia:

- Community college (TAFE)[1] Diploma in Interpreting
- TAFE Advanced Diploma in Interpreting

- University Undergraduate degree in Translation and Interpreting
- University Postgraduate Certificate in Community Interpreting
- University Postgraduate Diploma in Translation and Interpreting
- University Master degree in Translation and Interpreting
- University Master degree in Conference Interpreting

Liu provides a word of caution however in the use of natural groups design, stating that:

> Unlike experiments in which variables are manipulated and controlled, results of a natural groups design have to be interpreted carefully to draw causal inferences. It is likely that groups of individuals are different in many ways besides the variable used to classify them. . . . Therefore, the differences observed among groups of individuals can be confounded (2011).

In other words, such studies cannot claim to have internal or external validity.

6.5.2 *One-variable design*

This refers to the manipulation of only one independent variable, such as interpreting mode (consecutive, simultaneous), language modality (spoken or signed) or use of first or third person.

6.5.3 *Factorial design*

This design involves two or more independent treatment variables (factors), which are tested for effect on one dependent variable, as separate variables and also in interaction with one another; for example, years of interpreting experience, gender, working language pair. This type of design should ideally be used with a large sample size to ensure that significance can be determined after the control of certain variables.

6.5.4 **Quasi-experiments**

This technique is used when it is not possible to randomly assign participants to experimental or control groups (see § 6.3.4).

6.5.5 *Pre-experiments*

This is also known as a 'one-shot case study' (Liu 2011), in which there is no differentiation between an experimental group and a control group and no type of treatment or manipulation. (See earlier discussion of Napier's study of interpreting omissions in § 6.4.2.6).

Exercise 6.9

Consider which category above your experimental design would fall into.

6.6 Experimental interpreting research: What and why

Alvstad et al. (2011) suggest that experimental research designs are well-suited to analysing process, product and expertise in interpreting, and Pöchhacker (2005) provides a detailed overview of the shift in methodological approaches in investigating interpreting processes. Furthermore, the following major issues can be (and have been) analysed using some form of experimental design, often with a combined focus on process and product (see Pöchhacker 2010a; 2011b for more detail). The majority of experimental designs have concentrated on simultaneous, rather than consecutive or community interpreting, although there are some exceptions (e.g. Berk-Seligson 2002; Hale 2004; Hale et al. 2011).

6.6.1 Language processing and simultaneity

Interpreting researchers have shown interest in investigating the linguistic aspects of interpreting as a bilingual process, including the comparison of natural ad hoc (untrained) and formally trained professional interpreters, working languages and direction. Additionally, other psycholinguistic analyses have focused on cognitive and information processes, cognitive load and brain function involved in comprehension and production while interpreting. A range of experimental Interpreting research has also analysed the various simultaneous processes involved in interpreting, including listening and speaking and input and output (also known as ear-voice span or timelag). See, for example, Isham and Lane (1994), Hyönää et al. (1995), Massaro and Shlesinger (1997) and Englund Dimitrova and Hyltenstam (2000).

6.6.2 Memory and attention

Various studies have explored the relationship between working memory, short-term memory, long-term memory and/or attentional resources in simultaneous interpreting, with the measurement of interpreting performance as the dependent variable. The work of Chincotta and Underwood (1998),

Christoffels et al. (2006), van Dijk et al. (2012), Wang and Napier (2013) and Wang (2013a) are good illustrations of this type of research.

6.6.3 *Strategies*

There is an emerging body of research that has focussed on the strategies or 'tactics' used by interpreters while 'on task', for example, their use of omissions (Bartlomiejczyk 2006; Napier 2004) and/or additions (Barik 1994; Siple 1996), anticipation (Adamowicz 1989; van Besien 1999), inferencing (Chernov 2004) and compression strategies (Finton 2005).

6.6.4 *Quality*

Various experimental Interpreting research projects have focus on the quality or effectiveness of interpretations, through the evaluation of the interpreting product. These include the analysis of source-target language lexical or semantic correspondence, delivery features, representation of source language affect, consumer/client comprehension or judgement of efficacy and/or professionalism (see Pöchhacker 2001; Shlesinger et al. 1997). Kalina (2005) provides a comprehensive framework for the analysis of interpreting quality, based on her observation of a range of variables across different conferences.

The existence of a range of experimental designs that explore Interpreting in the above categories provides the opportunity for researchers and research students to replicate and build upon existing studies, contrast findings to increase our knowledge about interpreting processes and products and explore the generalizability of results. It should be remembered, however, that as stated by Setton (2006) 'Experimental methods do not lend themselves easily to exploring the use of context in ordinary utterance interpretation, let alone in as complex and fast-moving an activity as [simultaneous interpreting]'. Therefore, although experimental research can be designed well to represent what happens in the real world, the interpreting process and/or product being analysed within an experiment will feature an interpretation removed from context. Thus researchers may need to consider triangulating experimental data with other forms of qualitative research data (interviews, focus groups, authentic or simulated discourse analyses) to verify the accuracy and applicability of their findings (see Hale 2004, for the triangulation of results using discourse analysis, experiments and questionnaires).

Exercise 6.10

What are you proposing to investigate with your experiment and why? Finalize the research design for your experiment, in light of what you have read in this chapter.

6.7 Sample experimental studies in interpreting research

Below is a list of topics of more recently published Interpreting research that utilize an experimental approach:

- Investigation of cognitive processes mediating performance in simultaneous spoken language interpreting (Ivanova 2000)

- Lexical retrieval and memory in simultaneous spoken language interpreting (Christoffels et al. 2003)

- Language skills in spoken and signed language interpreting students (Shaw et al. 2004)

- Psychological testing of personality in signed language interpreters (Seal 2004)

- Language choice in note-taking in consecutive interpreting (Szabó 2006)

- Analysis of prosodic utterance boundaries in signed language interpretation (Nicodemus 2009)

- Aptitude for interpreting (Timarová and Salaets 2011)

- Quasi-experimental studies of signed language interpreting in court (Napier 2011a; Russell 2002)

- Cognitive abilities and signed language interpreting – aptitude and personality as a predictor of performance (Macnamara et al. 2011)

- Interpreter accent and witness credibility (Hale et al. 2011)

6.8 Conclusion

This chapter has discussed how to take a quantitative, experimental approach to studying Interpreting, either by investigating the process or product of interpreting. A critique of one particular experimental interpreting study has laid out the various stages of designing and implementing an experimental project, and thus how to make the research design as robust as possible. In summary, a range of examples of experimental interpreting projects have been given, which may inspire you to conduct your own research adopting this approach.

Further reading

Alvstad, A. Hild and E. Tiselius (eds) (2011). *Methods and strategies of process research*. Amsterdam: John Benjamins.

Englund Dimitrova, B. and Hyltenstam, K. (eds) (2000). *Language processing and simultaneous interpreting: Interdisciplinary perspectives*. Amsterdam: John Benjamins.

Gass, S. (2010). Experimental research. In B. Paltridge and A. Phakiti (eds), *Continuum companion to research methods in applied linguistics*. London: Continuum, pp. 7–21.

Liu, M. (2011). Methodology in interpreting studies: A methodological review of evidence-based research. In B. Nicodemus and L. Swabey (eds), *Advances in interpreting research*. Amsterdam: John Benjamins, pp. 85–120.

Shlesinger, M. and Pöchhacker, F. (eds) (2011). *Aptitude for interpreting: Special issue of interpreting 13(1)*. Amsterdam: John Benjamins.

Tirkkonen-Condit, S. and Jääskeläinen, R. (eds) (2000). *Tapping and mapping the processes of translation and interpreting*. Amsterdam: John Benjamins.

Note

1   Australia's community colleges are referred to as Technical and Further Education Colleges (TAFEs).

CHAPTER SEVEN

Research on interpreting education and assessment

This chapter will:

- Introduce key principles in adult learning and teaching
- Define specific features and methodologies of educational research
- Give an overview of different approaches to research into interpreting education and assessment
- Provide a critical review of a sample of research studies in conference and community interpreting education and spoken and signed language interpreter education and assessment
- Suggest practical ways to conduct interpreting education research
- Pose reflexive questions to the reader
- List further relevant readings

7.1 Introduction

You may be wondering why we have decided to include a separate chapter on conducting research on interpreter education and assessment. Historically, as with Gile's observation of previous accounts of interpreting being based on personal observations rather than empirical analysis, discussions of interpreter education, training and assessment have typically been based on the intuitions and experience of translator and interpreter educators (1998). Daniel Gile, in fact, wrote a book on how best to educate and train interpreters based on his extensive experience (1995; updated 2009). Conferences have been organized that have been dedicated to the exchange of knowledge and information about interpreter education (e.g. the Conference of Interpreter and Translator Educators Association of Australia; the Conference of Interpreter Trainers in the USA); and several publications have resulted from such education-focussed conferences, that feature descriptions of translation and interpreter training programmes, their curricula, delivery methods, assessment tasks and teaching activities (Buogucki 2010; Dollerup and Appel 1996; Dollerup and Loddegaard 1991, 1994; Sewell and Higgins 1996), and many of them have posed questions as to how to improve interpreter training and how to make it more consistent.

However, with the growing number of research studies and publications in Interpreting studies, this has led to a call for more empirical evidence of how to educate, train and assess translators and interpreters and for a greater dialogue between research and practice (Angelelli and Jacobson 2009; Pöchhacker 2010c). As stated by Pöchhacker (2010c):

> For all the steep rise in the number of university-level interpreter training programs worldwide, we know very little about what actually transpires in the interpreting classroom (p. 4).

Many interpreter educators would disagree with this sentiment, as the body of experience and expertise presented in the above named publications demonstrates that those who teach, do in fact, know what happens in the translation or interpreting classroom.[1] Nevertheless, we are now witnessing a growing body of research on translation and interpreting pedagogy that is providing evidence for effective approaches to education and assessment that enables translator and interpreter educators to replicate teaching and assessment methodologies.

The research is providing translator and interpreter educators and researchers with frameworks to focus on more systematic and critical forms of enquiry in relation to teaching and assessment. Educational researchers have long since focussed their interests on how to teach and what students learn, and featured their research in journals such as Higher Education, the Journal of Further and Higher Education, Journal of Learning Development in Higher Education, Adult Education Quarterly, New Directions for Adult and Continuing Education and Studies in the Education of Adults. However, the paradigm shift towards more translator and interpreter education research follows closely a trend in higher education generally to encourage more scholarship of learning and teaching (Hutchings and Shulman 1999), whereby academics employ various research methods to analyse questions about learning and teaching across a range of disciplines, in distance education, in assessment and so on. Scholarship projects are supported by specific funding bodies, such as the Australian Learning and Teaching Council; and there is now a dedicated journal (Journal of the Scholarship of Teaching and Learning). For example, academics who teach professional courses such as accountancy, nursing, veterinary science and others are examining their pedagogies through the lens of educational scholarship (e.g. Kern 2001; Malone and Spieth 2012; Nardi and Kremer 2003). Typing 'teaching scholarship' in Google will lead you to a plethora of university websites that feature the learning and teaching scholarship projects, policies or practices in their institution.

Therefore, the 'translation' of teaching scholarship into our discipline has led to a demand for more robust scholarship of translator and interpreter education, and this is evidenced by two specific discipline-related teaching journals that feature research from our discipline: the Interpreter and Translator Trainer (ITT – published by St. Jerome) and the International Journal of Interpreter Education (IJIE – published by the Conference of Interpreter Trainers).

Thus, we felt that it was worthwhile to feature a chapter that focuses specifically on research that is conducted in relation to interpreting pedagogy. All the research methods outlined in previous chapters can be applied to the investigation of interpreter education and assessment, but in this chapter we will give you specific examples and suggestions for research in this area. We will be concentrating only on interpreter education research. Examples of references for research on translation pedagogy can be seen in the ITT journal and other journals such as Meta, The Translator and the International Journal of Translation and Interpreting Research.

Before we give an overview of the kinds of research conducted on interpreter education and assessment, we will first focus briefly on general principles of adult learning and teaching from a theoretical point of view and specific features of educational research. Again, it is not within the scope of this chapter to give a detailed overview of educational theory, so we have given suggested readings at the end of the chapter.

7.2 Adult education theory

Adult education theory has evolved over the years. Knowles et al. (2005) are an advocates of an andragogical approach to adult education. They define andragogy as 'the art and science of helping adults learn', adopting a process-based, rather than content-based approach to teaching and learning. Although there are theoretical and evidence-based discussions of effective teaching (e.g. Bain 2004), there has been a shift from teacher-focussed to student-centred learning and teaching theories.

Two particular theoretical approaches in educational research can be considered in light of the research approaches discussed in Chapter 1 of this book. The first, 'critical theory', is critical in the sense that it challenges both the positivist and interpretivist research traditions, as discussed by Barnett (1994) and Scott (1995). While the main approach of critical theory is to critique ideology, educational research undertaken in the critical theorist tradition is not confined to unmasking or consciousness-raising. It also has to involve informed, committed action, that is, not to just find out about the world but change it in the name of justice and democracy. The problem with critical theory, according to Usher (1996) is 'its self-proclaimed commitment to emancipation as a universal value', wherein it also retains positivism's polar opposites (e.g. emancipation-oppression).

Alternatively, the 'post-structuralist' educational research tradition challenges the view that there is a determinate world that can be definitively known and explained (Lee 1992). There are three commonalities that distinguish the features of post-structuralism: (i) emphasis on situated local narratives, (ii) deconstruction of apparent binary opposites and (iii) knowledge generation as a practice of textual production. These three commonalities problematize the epistemological and ontological assumptions that underpin positivism, interpretivism and critical theory. Another important aspect of post-structuralist research is reflexivity, which means that when researchers undertake social research, their activities become part of what is being researched. From this perspective, educational researchers do not hide their presence but rather will locate themselves within the research, which makes their presence a legitimate and productive part of the study (Usher 1996).

Other theories focus on the process of learning and teaching, rather than on conducting educational research. A constructivist approach to learning highlights the importance of reference to the student's own experience and embodies the notion of active learning, wherein the main interest is in the process by which the learner reaches an understanding of the structure of the learning tasks (Larochelle and Bednarz 1998). Constructivism (also known as social constructivism) encompasses the notion of problem-based learning (Boud and Feletti 1997), which has been an approach long applied in medical education (Engel 1992). Social constructivism is an approach that is becoming popular in translator education (Kiraly 2000; Varney 2009).

Other popular theories focus on collaborative or cooperative learning principles. The notion of collaborative learning supports an active learning approach, by allowing students to work together where they can be immersed in challenging tasks. By recognizing that learners are diverse, variable collaborative learning asks are designed for students which require them to explore or apply the new concepts they have been introduced to, in a search for understanding, deriving meaning and consolidating their learning (Leigh Smith and MacGregor 1992). Likewise, cooperative learning promotes students working together to accomplish shared learning goals (Johnson and Johnson 1994). Problem-based learning is a framework that underpins, and is central to, constructivist and collaborative learning theories (Savery and Duffy 1996) and encourages students to work together to analyse scenarios and engage in problem-solving. For a comprehensive overview of adult learning theory, see Jarvis (2004).

Exercise 7.1

Think about your own experience as an interpreting student.

- What educational principles do you think were/are used in your programme?
- Was/is the programme teaching teacher-centred or student-centred?
- Think about one of your favourite activities – what was the goal? What were the outcomes?
- Were you asked to complete student evaluations? Were you asked about what you learned, or about what you were taught?

AND/OR:

Think about your own experience as an interpreter educator.

- What do you like about teaching?
- What is your teaching philosophy?
- Think about one of your favourite activities to teach – what is the goal?
- Do you teach using a particular educational theoretical framework?
- How do you evaluate your teaching and students' learning?
- How often do you adapt your lesson plans/activities?
- Do you consider yourself to be a reflective teacher?

7.3 The role of educational research

Educational research has many roles in the eyes of both researchers and those who have an interest in the results of research. This diversity arises from differences in views about the nature of educational research and differences in the sources of research questions. The differences in views create differences in expectations and differences in judgments about whether the expectations are fulfilled (McGaw et al. 1992, p. 55).

McGaw et al. (1992) provide an excellent critique of educational research, asking questions concerning the level of interaction between research and practice, whether research should evolve from curiosity and a desire to develop greater understanding, from a need to inform practice through application of new knowledge gleaned from research or from a combination of the two.

A range of educational research using qualitative, quantitative and action research approaches have given rise to a greater understanding of the nature of educational problems, and studies using a combination of methodological approaches have been particularly beneficial (Cohen et al. 2011; McGaw et al. 1992). However, in order for research to have an impact on educational policy and practice, there are general features of research design and implementation that are required for links to be established. McGaw et al. (1992) suggest that educational research must be proactive and realistic, must function within a wider research agenda, must recognize and interact with the audience for the research and be of high quality.

Interpreter educators are becoming more mindful of the role of Interpreting research, and the need to link research to education and practice, both in terms of doing research on interpreting for interpreter educators, and also doing research on interpreter education (Pöchhacker 2010b). This emerging consciousness of the need for scholarship is evidenced by the two new journals mentioned earlier, and also a book series on interpreter education based on research, published by Gallaudet University Press (series editor: Cynthia Roy).

As an under-researched sub-field of Interpreting studies, the possibilities for interpreter education research are huge. Drawing on adult educational theory, and research in literature on teaching professional and vocational programmes in further and higher education, there is potential to explore any of the following areas (to name but a few):

- Teaching effectiveness

- Student learning styles

- Programme entry testing

- Formative and summative assessment methods

Exercise 7.2

What are you interested in exploring in terms of interpreting education or assessment?

- Curriculum?
- Teaching approaches?
- Particular teaching activities?
- Student aptitude or outcomes?
- Use of technology?

Draft a research question and potential sub-questions based on your interest in conducting interpreting education research.

Refer back to Chapter 1 and think about the goals of the study – what are you looking to prove, demonstrate or investigate? Why are you interested in doing this research? What educational and interpreting studies theories could you draw upon?

- Curriculum development
- Educational change
- Teaching and curriculum innovation

As with Section 7.2, here we have only highlighted specific features of educational research in order to contextualize how interpreting education research fits within a broader framework of educational research. The suggested readings at the end of the chapter will guide you more in this area.

7.4 Educational research methodologies

Educational research can draw on any of the methodologies as outlined in Chapters 3–6 of this book, that is, surveys/questionnaires; qualitative ethnographic or discourse analytic; or quantitative/experimental approaches.

This section will give a brief overview of various typical educational research methods, drawing on the work of Cohen et al. (2011). Initially, we will discuss these methods broadly in terms of conducting educational research and will give some examples of interpreter education research studies that utilize the method under discussion. Later in the chapter, we will focus more specifically on a range of interpreter education topics and provide further samples of published research for consideration.

7.4.1 Surveys

Using some kind of survey or questionnaire instrument, you can gather information about educational experiences or outcomes at a particular point in time, and thus make observations about any patterns that are evident. Survey methods include:

- Opinion polls
- Test scores
- Student preferences
- Teaching evaluations

As discussed in Chapter 3, internet-based questionnaires are becoming increasingly popular for the purposes of expediency and cost-effectiveness, but they can also be problematic in terms of reach (see Cohen et al. 2011 for a discussion of the advantages and disadvantages of using online questionnaires for educational research). A survey can also include follow-up interviews that are organized after receipt of questionnaire responses. The interviews can also 'survey' the views of respondents, and can be conducted face-to-face, by telephone, or via videoconference technology (such as FaceTime, Skype or Oovoo). An example of an interpreter education research study that included both online surveys and follow-up interviews is Sameh's study of student perceptions of the balance between theory and practice in their interpreter training programme (2009).

7.4.2 *Naturalistic/qualitative methods*

Cohen et al. (2011) advocate for the use of naturalistic/qualitative methods in educational research in order to generate rather than test hypotheses, that is, providing a 'thick' description of an educational phenomenon (as discussed in detail in Chapter 4). The kinds of naturalistic educational inquiry that they suggest include:

- Case study – investigation into a specific instance of teaching in a real-life classroom or training programme context (e.g. Sadlier 2009);
- Comparative study – several case studies compared;
- Retrospective study – focus on biographies of participants (teachers/students) or which ask participants to look back on teaching/learning events/issues;
- Snapshots – analyses of particular educational situations, events or phenomena at a single point in time (values/policy/provision rather than classroom teaching);
- Longitudinal studies – investigation of issues or people over time (Petronio and Hale 2009);
- Phenomenology/ethnography – seeing things as they really are and establishing the meanings of things through illumination and explanation rather than through taxonomic approaches or abstractions, explanation of social groups and situations in their real-life educational contexts;
- Grounded theory – developing theories to explain educational phenomena, with theories emerging from the data rather than being pre-determined; and
- Biography – individual or collective experiences.

In addition to the above qualitative methods, discourse analysis (see Chapter 5) can be used in relation to case studies or comparative studies in order to analyse the language that is used in the classroom, as seen in Example 7.1.

> ### Example 7.1: Discourse analytical case study
>
> Napier (2010) used discourse analysis to analyse classroom discussions among interpreting students. She conducted a systemic functional linguistic case study of university classroom talk in order to evaluate the storytelling that occurred and how it functioned as a pedagogical tool. The data consisted of two hours of naturalistic classroom talk with interpreting students who were discussing the topic of interpreting ethics. The 'chunks' of the text comprising storytelling were identified, and the stories were classified into genres. The study revealed exemplum stories to be the most common story genre and that story genres were used, by both the teacher and the students, to make meaning within the learning process. The findings of this study demonstrated that storytelling is a feature of pragmatic teacher-student interaction, and is a pedagogical tool used to engage with interpreting students in order to relate practical experience to theoretical constructs.

The main methods that could be used for data collection in line with any of the above approaches to inquiry include:

- Participant or non-participant observation of classes/meetings
- Audio/video recording of classroom interaction
- Interviews, focus groups and consultations
- Documents and field notes
- Written accounts (e.g. reflective essays from students)

Cohen et al. (2011) suggest that there are 12 key stages that are necessary for any effective qualitative educational study:

1 Locating a field of study
2 Formulating a research question
3 Addressing ethical issues
4 Deciding on the sampling technique
5 Finding a role and managing entry into the context (cooperation, access, permission)
6 Finding informants/participants
7 Developing and maintaining relations in the field

8 Data collection in situ – use of a variety of techniques

9 Data collection outside the field – context outside of the educational institution that might influence behaviour of students?

10 Data analysis

11 Leaving the field – how to conclude research, terminate roles, disengage

12 Write the report – target audience, output, dissemination

They advise a note of caution when using educational case studies, as results cannot be generalized, and researchers should pay heed to reliability and validity. For this reason, be careful who and what you select as the focus of your case study. Any good case study needs to present in-depth data (i.e. a thick description). See Section 7.6.2 for a couple of examples of interpreter education case studies.

7.4.3 *Experimental methods*

Often in educational research it is not possible to undertake true experiments, as the experimental design cannot always control for all conditions (Cohen et al. 2011). Nevertheless, there are examples of experimental interpreter education studies, such as Ko's (2008) empirical study of interpreter training, which compared students taught by distance mode with a control group of those taught face-to-face. However, it is more likely that educational studies are quasi-experimental. The following list presents possible examples of experimental studies in education (refer back to Chapter 6 for more detailed explanation of each experimental approach):

1 A pre-experiment design with a one group pre-test post-test: The experiment would involve testing a group of students on a particular skill, introducing a new curriculum innovation, and then testing them again to see how the change affected the skills in question (see Hale and Ozolins, forthcoming in 2014 for an example of this methodology.)

2 One group time series: The one group is the experimental group and is given more than one pre-test and more than one post-test.

3 Single-case research: The design involves continuous assessment of some aspect of human behaviour over a period of time (e.g. a semester), with administration of procedures on multiple occasions, and 'intervention effects' are replicated with the same subject(s) over time.

7.4.4 *Historical/documentary*

This method of inquiry for educational research involves drawing on existing documents to examine records of an event or process. These documents can be sourced from written, printed, electronic (internet), audio or video sources. Ideally, primary documents should be used (Cohen et al. 2011), including books (based on research), textbooks, magazines or newsletters (e.g. from professional interpreting associations), published reports (e.g. the Australian government Orima report, which documented the supply and demand of Auslan interpreting), diaries or journals of different stakeholders (e.g. interpreting students, practitioners, educators, consumers) and letters or emails between individuals or organizations/educational institutions.

Archives from national libraries and other stakeholder organizations can also be used to locate relevant documents. These days with the availability of documents electronically on the internet, this research method is much more feasible and also not as time-consuming as it used to be. Documentary analysis can involve historical, content and thematic analyses of a range of different documents within one project and needs to take into account broad educational, social, political and economic contexts that were prevalent at the time of publication of the document(s).

A good example of a documentary study of interpreter education is Carolyn Ball's (2007) PhD thesis, which focussed on the history of American Sign Language (ASL) interpreting education. Her study provides a chronological history of the development of ASL interpreter education, drawing on data from records of several organizations that date back as far as the eighteenth century and from interviews with key ASL interpreter practitioners. Her study also provides an overview of the social, political and legal perspectives that influenced the development of the interpreter education field in the United States.

7.4.5 *Role-plays*

An innovative educational method is to use role-plays to get participants to consider different perspectives and experience how people behave in different situations (DeNeve and Heppner 1997). Role-plays are commonly used in interpreter training to provide simulated, but authentic-like, experiences for interpreting students in different contexts, for example, in doctor-patient consultation, solicitor-client interaction or teacher-parent interview (Metzger 2000). Using role-plays as a training activity encourages a problem-based approach to learning and enables participants to learn 'on the job' (Auer 1998).

However, Cohen et al. (2011) contend that role-plays can also be used effectively as a research method. They state that by using role-plays as a form of research design and data collection, you can:

- observe human behaviour;
- explore different points of view;
- alter variables as the research unfolds;
- provide planned or spontaneous prompts/stimuli to participants;
- investigate patterns of behaviour;
- and involve participants as co-researchers.

One of the keys to the success of role-plays as research is that all participants must be actively involved in the research process. The role-plays can be structured to become incrementally more or less challenging and can be controlled by stopping, pausing or extending the activity. An educational research design on interpreting, for example, could compare student participation in role-plays as opposed to classroom or online discussions for identifying problems in interpreting. Cohen et al. (2011) suggest, however, that researchers need to be careful when using role-plays in educational research, as they are context-bound and localized.

7.4.6 Action research

Although action research (AR) can be used as a framework for the analysis of individual interpreting practice (see Chapter 4, § 4.5.3.2), this methodological approach is most popular in educational research. AR has particularly been used extensively in curriculum innovation in the fields of education, second language acquisition and language teaching and more recently in interpreter education (Slatyer 2006). According to Sagor (2010), AR can be used for 'macro' level projects that investigate issues on an institutional level, or 'micro' level projects that focus on single student learning attributes, rather than broad programme goals. In such AR research, the dependent variable would be what you hope to see changed as a result of actions (e.g. the development of graduates with high level interpreting skills), and the independent variables would be the student traits which cannot be changed (e.g. bilingual status, interpreting experience, personality, etc.).

AR involves repetitive, reflective cycles of planning, information gathering/ data collection and implementation referred to as the action research 'spiral' (Burns 2010), and the reflective process involves four key stages: sensing the problem, reading the problem (e.g. literature review, data collection and analysis), matching the problem (making recommendations for change) and acting on the problem (implementation) (Scott 1999).

One of the most important elements of applying AR in educational research is the collaborative nature of the approach, which should involve a partnership between stakeholders, such as interpreter educators and researchers, who together investigate classroom practice (Burns 1999), curriculum innovation (Slatyer 2006) or educational change (Fullan 1991; Scott 1999).

AR can be an effective catalyst for educational change and promotes 'reflection in and on action', which should be encouraged of educational institutions (Schön 1995). In a study of long-term outcomes of educational action research projects, Kember (2002) identified the benefits of action research as follows: (1) lasting improvements in teaching in terms of deeper understanding of teaching and willingness to employ more innovative teaching strategies, (2) a shift towards more student-centred teaching approaches and a better understanding of students' needs, (3) teachers' development of action research abilities and recognition of action research as a natural framework for the educational change process, (4) improved capacity and competence to reflect upon, and monitor quality of own teaching, (5) development of teamwork skills and (6) changing attitudes and development of valuable skills.

Scott (1999, p. 119) identifies a series of attributes that distinguish action research as an effective approach to supporting educational change or innovation, which can be adapted for research on interpreter education as follows:

a On-going identification and investigation of interpreting practices requiring improvement or enhancement;

b Development of interpreter practitioners' skills in problem identification and problem solving;

c Ensuring that results of enquiry actually get translated into interpreting practice;

d Greater collaboration among interpreting practitioners, educators and students;

e Developing strategies for change or innovation that take into account or seek to influence positively the local interpreter educational context.

Any educational AR project ideally needs an action plan, clear objectives and a timeline. The plan outlines the problem 'sensed' (e.g. interpreting students are not being given enough opportunities for autonomous learning and skill development); how the problem will be 'read' (e.g. literature review combined with mix of data-gathering techniques); how the problem will be 'matched' (e.g. revision of the curriculum); and the plan on how to 'act' (i.e. implementation). At each stage of the AR spiral, the researchers reflect on the process and after implementation may sense further problems and changes needed, and thus enter a new phase of the research cycle (e.g. after implementation of new curriculum, there is identification of resources needed to support students' autonomous learning).

Drawing on Scott's work, the following set of questions can be used to determine the nature of an action plan (1999, p. 29):

- Which learning objectives should guide what happens in the programme?
- What content must the learning programme cover?
- What teaching and learning strategies are most appropriate?
- What learning resources will best enhance these learning strategies?
- What is the most appropriate way to sequence learning segments?
- What assessment approaches and tasks should be used?
- Where should learning take place?

Example 7.2 is an example of an action plan taken from an action research project that was set up to instigate a change in the delivery of a postgraduate sign language interpreting programme (Napier 2005b). The goal of the project was to research and develop a new curriculum and delivery mode for the programme so that it could be offered in external (distance) mode, and therefore be made accessible to potential students from all over Australia.

Educational change typically occurs due to 'a unique mix of external, system and local factors' (Scott 1999, p. 7). External factors in interpreter education may include changes in professional accreditation/certification requirements, recognition of a language (e.g. the New Zealand Sign Language Act led to recognition of the need for postgraduate level training of sign language interpreters in that country), supply and demand issues or changes in government regulations (e.g. migrant student visa requirements in Australia). Organizational factors can include, for example, introduction of new institutional (university/college) policies for entry/exit requirements, assessment conditions, higher education sector policies that filter down to universities and university calls for scholarship of teaching. A good example of how external factors have impacted on organizational factors is in Europe and the establishment of the Bologna Declaration of 1999, requiring all European universities to align their programmes at undergraduate and postgraduate levels to promote mobility of students across borders. This has had an impact

Example 7.2: Example of an interpreter education action research plan

One-year project – seven key stages:

1 Research and literature review of distance education and sign language interpreter training programme curricula and delivery modes worldwide.

2 Establishment of a focus group with stakeholders (representatives from the University, including the Centre for Open Education, Centre for Professional Development (Learning and Teaching), Department of Linguistics, Translation and Interpreting programmes, and other experts in interpreter education).

3 Survey of potential students (those that had already expressed an interest in the programme) as to what delivery modes they would prefer, and would most meet their learning needs.

4 Survey of enrolled students as to which components of the (then weekly) delivery mode they feel they most benefit from.

5 Writing and development of new curriculum outline, including proposals for delivery format.

6 Writing of draft student reading packages and investigation of online delivery formats.

7 Application for funding to develop online resources and products needed to deliver the whole programme in blended mode.

at organizational level as universities have had to review their programs and revise their *curricula* accordingly. This change has filtered down to impact on interpreter education programmes in the form of what entry criteria can be determined for enrolment to study and shifts in pedagogy to more student-centred approaches (Rico 2010). Likewise, the agreement has had an impact on when and how interpreters are tested at admission and completion of an interpreter education programme (Salaets and Vermeerbergen 2011).

Exercise 7.3

Following on from the research questions you devised in Exercise 7.2, consider what methodology or methodologies you may use to answer your questions. How do you justify the methodological choices that you have made? How easy will it be for you to collect your data? What permissions will you need to receive?

7.5 Planning and designing educational research

This next section follows on from Sections 7.2, 7.3 and 7.4 in providing general guidance in planning and designing an educational research project. Here we will begin to relate the broader educational research principles for interpreter education research, but more specific examples will be given in Section 7.6.

7.5.1 Choosing and planning an educational research project

As with Interpreting research generally, educational research is often more effective if it is problem-based, that is, that the question of interest arises in the researcher's everyday work. This question could be as a result of reading about a particular teaching theory or activity, observation of student behaviour in the classroom or results at the end of a course or your own experience as an interpreting student.

The approach you choose should be based on what you want to know, as there are different kinds of research purposes, and thus different kinds of research that may lead you to answer your questions. Table 7.1 (taken

Table 7.1 Purposes and kinds of research

Kinds of research purpose	Kinds of research
Does the research want to test a hypothesis or theory?	Experiment, survey, action research, case study
Does the research want to develop a theory?	Ethnography, qualitative research, grounded theory
Does the research need to measure?	Survey, experiment
Does the research want to understand a situation?	Ethnographic and interpretative/ qualitative approaches
Does the research want to see what happens if . . .?	Experiment, participatory research, action research
Does the research want to find out 'what' and 'why'?	Mixed methods research
Does the research want to find out what happened in the past?	Historical research

from Cohen et al. 2011, p. 116) provides a breakdown of the kinds of questions you can ask to interrogate what you want to know (i.e. identify the purpose) and then the approach you may consider (i.e. the kinds of research).

The sequence and design of the research depend on the methodological paradigm that you select, that is, whether your hypothesis drives or emerges from the research. This will then dictate whether you do the literature review first, then define the research questions and design; or whether you identify a topic, do the literature review and then define the research questions. In conducting a literature review, you will need to contextualize your study of interpreter education by drawing on the broader educational (as well as Interpreting studies) theories, any available literature on the particular educational phenomenon under investigation and any relevant interpreting-specific classroom research. (Refer to Chapter 2 for a detailed overview of how to write a critical literature review).

7.5.2 Operationalization *of educational research questions*

In terms of operationalization of educational research questions, here we present a sample research study on interpreter education that is based on an adaptation of an example presented by Cohen et al. (2011). First, we consider the overall aim of the educational research project, which is to 'ascertain the level of continuity between different modules in a postgraduate interpreter education program'.

This research aim is broad, but is too general to stand alone, so in order to come up with a list of research questions more specifically, we can deconstruct the term 'continuity' into different components:

- experiences
- syllabus content
- teaching and learning styles
- skills
- concepts
- organizational arrangements
- aims and objectives
- ethos
- assessment

The notion of continuity can be narrowed down even further by focussing on the identification of aspects of the continuity of *pedagogy*:

- level of continuity of pedagogy
- nature of continuity of pedagogy
- degree of success of continuity of pedagogy
- responsibility for continuity
- record keeping and documentation of continuity
- resources available to support continuity

So if you are conducting an interpreter education research project that focuses on elements of continuity of pedagogy as outlined above, the research questions can be operationalized as follows:

- What pedagogical styles operate in each curriculum area (e.g. language and culture, interpreting theory, interpreting techniques, note-taking, ethics and professionalism, consecutive interpreting, simultaneous interpreting)?
- What are the most frequent and most preferred pedagogical styles (from the perspective of teachers and/or students)?
- What is the balance of pedagogical styles (teacher-led/student-led, lectures/discussion/practical)?
- How are the pedagogical styles influenced by the resources available (literature, teachers, interpreting laboratories, source texts, role-play participants)?
- To what extent is continuity planned and recorded (vision/mission of the programme, entry selection criteria, curriculum, learning outcomes, competencies, assessment criteria, moderation)?
- On what criteria will the nature of continuity be decided (external interpreting accreditation/regulatory body requirements, educational institutional requirements, graduate capabilities)?

In considering the research questions above, we need to pay heed to the kind of evidence that is required to answer these questions, for example, by utilizing desk research and sourcing available texts (e.g. programme handbook/study guides, exams, assessment criteria and tasks) as well as engaging in additional data collection. Following on from the methodological framework chosen for the study (i.e. quantitative or qualitative), any of the following methodologies or instruments could be selected to collect data for this study:

- Questionnaires to students, teachers, administrators
- Interviews/focus groups with students, teachers, administrators
- Participant/non-participant observation of interpreting classes
- Discourse analysis of classroom interactions
- Collection of interpreting test results
- Comparative analysis of entry and exit outcomes
- Case studies of interpreting students or teachers
- Role-plays/simulations

7.5.3 Educational research data

Much educational research is complex. For a project to be effective and truly evaluate educational experiences or outcomes, the research will often need to involve many layers of data collection over a period of time. Consequently, it is worth documenting what will be collected, when and how in a 'data matrix'. An example of a data matrix for the above sample study on the level of continuity of pedagogy between different modules in a postgraduate interpreter education programme can be seen in Table 7.2.[2]

When collecting such extensive amounts of data, it is important to be mindful of any ethical issues that might arise during the data collection. The principles around ensuring that research is conducted ethically discussed in Chapter 2 of this book are also applicable to interpreter education research. As researchers, we need to be sensitive to our relationships in the educational context, especially when involving research with students. If we are in a teacher-student relationship, we need to ensure that students do not feel coerced to be involved, or that their grades will be influenced in any way by their involvement. Teachers are in a potentially powerful position in this context, and need to be mindful that students might not feel that they can say no. Also, it is worth considering what will happen to your research if they refuse to be involved. If we are seeking to collect data through classroom observations, we also need to be conscious of how our teacher peers (if you are an educator) or student peers (if you are a student) will feel about being observed. These considerations should be thought through and accounted for in the design phase and in the process of seeking ethical approval for the study.

Finally, as also reported in Chapters 3–6 for studies that focus on Interpreting, the form of data analysis that you choose for educational research will be influenced by the theoretical framework and methodological approach(es) that you select.

Table 7.2 Example of data matrix

Task/measure	Type of data	Procedure for data collection	Method of analysis
Analysis of curriculum	Curriculum information/ textual	Internet search; Email contact with programme administrator	Thematic analysis
New student enrolment surveys: Expectations of pedagogy in the programme	Anonymous survey (range of item types: Likert scales; qualitative)	Hard copy on enrolment day or online	Quantification of responses, content/thematic analysis of qualitative, statistics
End-of-year student surveys: Reflections on the pedagogy used in the programme	Anonymous survey (range of item types: Likert scales; qualitative)	Hard copy in last face-to-face class or online	Quantification of responses, content/thematic analysis of qualitative, statistics
End-of-semester Teacher Evaluation Surveys	Anonymous survey (range of item types: Likert scales; qualitative)	Hard copy in last face-to-face class or online using institutional teacher evaluation service/ instruments	Quantification of responses, content/thematic analysis of qualitative, statistics
Former student/ graduate surveys: Reflections on the pedagogy used in the programme	Anonymous survey responses (range of item types: Likert scales; qualitative)	Snowball sampling – via email to alumni, teacher and student networks, Facebook	Quantification of responses, content/thematic analysis of qualitative, statistics
Student entry status cf. exit status	Quantitative	Data gathered from administration records	Statistics
Student final interpreting exam results	Quantitative	Data gathered from teacher/ administration records	Statistics

Table 7.2 (Continued)

Task/measure	Type of data	Procedure for data collection	Method of analysis
Teacher surveys	Anonymous survey responses (range of item types: Likert scales; qualitative)	Online	Quantification of responses, content/thematic analysis of qualitative, statistics
Teacher reflections on pedagogy at team meetings	Observation notes		Content/thematic analysis, discourse analysis
Teaching observations	Observation notes, Audio/video-recorded records, transcripts	Email contact with teachers to arrange observations, using pre-established observation schedule	Content/thematic analysis, discourse analysis
Focus groups: teachers, students, graduates	Audio/video-recorded records, transcripts	Direct approach by phone/email via research team networks; meetings organized at range of different times to suit participants and to ensure representative sample	Thematic analysis

Exercise 7.4

Revisit your responses to Exercises 7.2 and 7.3, and create a data matrix for your educational research project that reflects the types of data you will collect, the method(s) of data collection and the analytical approach. Also consider the relationships between the participants and any sensitivities that may need to be considered. How will you incorporate consideration of these ethical issues into your research design?

7.6 Examples in interpreting education and assessment research

The majority of interpreter education literature to date has been descriptive, either providing an overview of teaching and learning issues in training and educating interpreters (e.g. Wilson 2013), trends in interpreter education (e.g. Hubscher-Davidson and Borodo 2012), suggested curricula based on teaching experience (e.g. Rudvin and Tomassini 2011; Salaets and Vermeerbergen 2011) or a description of specific teaching activities (e.g. Cornwall 2011). Pöchhacker (2010c) presents an explanation for this, stating that there are 'significant methodological challenges involved in answering some of the major curricular or didactic questions on the basis of controlled experimental designs' (p. 9). Thus, he suggests that it would be more effective for interpreter educational researchers to conduct 'fieldwork in the classroom setting, often on the basis of case studies drawing on a range of predominantly qualitative data; and given the considerable time and effort required for such studies, [he advocates] a move toward participatory research in the classroom setting, done by those who teach in collaboration with those who learn, ultimately empowering the latter and inducting them early on into the community of professional practice' (p. 9).

Nonetheless, as stated in the introduction to this chapter, there is an emerging body of research literature on interpreter education, which draws on different theoretical frameworks. Before presenting a list of published research across different interpreter education and assessment topics as food for thought for your own research, first we give an example of how an interpreter education research proposal on the same topic can be presented from two different theoretical perspectives, with reference to the adult education theory as discussed in Section 7.2.

7.6.1 Sample interpreter education research proposal: From two educational theoretical perspectives

In this section we explore two educational research perspectives with the purpose of comparing different questions that may be asked in a potential interpreter education research project. The two theoretical research perspectives that will be considered are critical theory and post-structuralist perspectives to examine the training and accreditation of interpreters in Australia, with a focus on Interpreting quality standards. To contextualize the potential research project, it is worth providing brief information about Interpreting standards in Australia.[3]

An accreditation system for the qualification of interpreters has been available in Australia for over 30 years, under the auspices of the National Accreditation Authority for Translators and Interpreters (NAATI).

Accreditation is offered through three different routes: (a) completion of a NAATI approved course; (b) sitting a one-off accreditation examination in the specific language of the candidate; or (c) assessment of specialized interpreter/translator qualifications obtained from overseas. In awarding accreditation, NAATI is 'indicating that at the time of the award, the person concerned has reached the level of competency in interpreting or translating required for work at the standard of the level of accreditation which has been granted' (Bell 1997); and accreditation is available at several levels. In interpreting: paraprofessional, professional, conference and senior conference; in translation: professional, advanced and senior.

NAATI recognizes the benefits of interpreters completing training or education that leads to accreditation (NAATI 2013). Attendance at a training course is not mandatory, however, meaning that many interpreters receive accreditation without being trained. NAATI-approved training courses are available at further education colleges throughout Australia for people to become accredited at paraprofessional or professional level. There are also a handful of university courses approved by NAATI whereby graduates attain an undergraduate or postgraduate qualification and NAATI professional level accreditation. All these courses have to meet strict requirements in terms of contact hours, content and interpreting practice in order to be approved by NAATI (Bontempo and Levitzke-Gray 2009). Yet NAATI does not make any key distinction between vocational 'training' or more academic 'education' of interpreters, a situation which is considered to be problematic if research and theory is 'divorced' from practical elements of training (Angelelli 2004b).

The proposed project would be designed to investigate whether NAATI course approval adds any value to the educational experience of interpreters and whether graduates are better interpreters than those who attain accreditation through passing a one-off test. The structure of data collection for each project would be the same, but the questions asked would be different, dependent on the research perspective adopted.

Accordingly, a 2-year project could be designed, adopting the following methodology:

- Survey (through online questionnaires) of teachers, students, recently accredited interpreters (through both testing and training), experienced interpreters, service providers and consumers with regard to notions of quality in interpreting, values around training, accreditation and NAATI and values around professional development in order to collect quantitative data;

- Separate and mixed focus groups with the above stakeholders to collect further in-depth qualitative data;

- Observation of teaching practices in further education college and university classrooms;

- Observation of interpreters practising in the workplace;

- Review of NAATI test development across a range of languages;

- Contrastive analysis of NAATI test (for those who sat a test) and final exam scores (for those who completed a training course) of recently accredited interpreters;

- Evaluation of NAATI course approval regulations;

- Development of recommendations in relation to training, education and accreditation;

- Interviews with stakeholders to gain feedback on recommendations;

- Proposal to NAATI regarding process of course approval.

From the perspective of critical theory, the research aim would be to show how NAATI approval potentially oppresses the interpreter education industry as a whole, as well as individual providers/institutions, teacher/educators and administrators, and subsequently detracts from the educational experience of students.

A number of questions that contribute to the overall research aim could be asked and may be answered using the combined quantitative and qualitative methods outlined above. Accordingly, the goal would be to design an action research project, where educator-researchers would be encouraged to analyse and critique their own involvement with course approval and accreditation issues and how this may impact on their teaching practices and ultimately, upon their students. Action research has been used by other interpreter researchers and educators to investigate stakeholders' perceptions of interpreter competencies (Witter-Merithew and Johnson 2005).

This proposed project from a critical theory perspective may consider the following questions:

- What are the indirect or 'hidden' costs of gaining course approval? For example, the cost of person-hours that may have been otherwise directed towards teaching and/or resources.

- Of all the accreditations and course approval matters at issue, which of these are regarded as most important by students that will directly influence their 'purchase' of education as opposed to just sitting for a NAATI test?

- Similarly, which of all the accreditations and course approval matters at issue are most important to teachers (as decided by teachers), and which will directly influence their choice to teach as well as practice as an interpreter?

- Does NAATI approval lead to a better system of quality assurance from the different perspectives of all stakeholders?

- Is Australia's system of accreditation of interpreters an assurance of quality interpreter education?

- Should NAATI's system of accreditation be expanded to include re-validation of interpreter 'licence' for quality assurance purposes (as currently being proposed by NAATI)? If so, how would this impact on the training institutions?

From a post-structuralist perspective, the project would aim to uncover the effects of NAATI approval on the discourses that drive decision-making by stakeholders within the interpreter education community.

The alternative project would be framed around the same questions outlined above; however, the focus would be on the power relationships among the stakeholders and how those who hold power effect changes to the landscape of interpreter training and accreditation in Australia.

Rather than freeing providers and/or students from oppression, the goal of the project would be to reveal how the language, discourse and texts of the interpreter education community are affected by the conditions laid down by NAATI and for those seeking accreditation and who therefore must comply. For example:

- How have the requirements of NAATI course approval and accreditation affected the language of stakeholders within the Australian interpreter education community?

- Which stakeholders have benefited and which have suffered from the type of language used?

- How has the language of approval and accreditation affected students' decisions to 'purchase' their education?

- Similarly, how has the language of approval and accreditation affected teachers' decisions to choose whether to work for a training programme or provide ad-hoc professional development workshops?

- What effect have the current levels of approval and accreditation had on discourses between external third parties and administrators? Between administrators and students? Between teachers and students? Between students themselves?

- What benefits might accrue from the rationalization and simplification of approval and accreditation requirements? Are there any stakeholders that would benefit more than others? Would any stakeholders suffer from these changes?

In a post-structuralist sense, it would be important to establish a localized case study project wherein a single provider would be encouraged to contextualize the answers to the above questions, as well as to make any other knowledge claims they believe are appropriate in relation to approval and accreditation and the effects on their relationships with stakeholders and their ability to provide a quality education for their students.

Within this text, it would be imperative to ask some additional questions of a reflexive nature, considering any changes to the positioning of the researchers that occur during the research process. Thus, further key questions to consider include:

- What are the values and assumptions that have underpinned the research?

- How does this influence what can and may be said in the research?

- Are there other risks that the positioning of the researchers brings to the project? For example, what has the research NOT said?

- What forms of knowledge and specific knowledge claims are being generated by the research?

- To what extent does the research empower or disempower the people involved in it?

- What kind of reality is the research constructing?

As can be seen from the above example, the same interpreter education research project could be tackled in different ways, depending on the theoretical underpinning. The critical theory approach would set out to critique the current policy ideology and would serve the interests particularly of interpreter educators in exposing the ideologies that protect the interests of the current accreditation system. The post-structuralist approach, however, would seek the truth through exploration of the discourse, with the goal of exposing how the established training and accreditation options may be constrained. In addition, the post-structuralist approach would adopt a strong reflexive focus, considering the position of the researcher.

7.6.2 Sample of interpreting education and assessment research studies

The following list presents examples of interpreter education and assessment research studies that have been conducted as PhD theses, or appear as published journal articles. We have included the abstracts written by

Exercise 7.5

Read the following two articles on different types of interpreter education research and provide a critique of each study with consideration of the following questions (refer back to Chapter 2 on critical reading and writing):

1 How much does the abstract reveal about the study in relation to general educational research principles?

2 What is the theoretical foundation for the study? Does it draw on educational theory, interpreting studies theory or both? Is there enough of a theoretical framework to justify the research design?

3 What is the methodological approach selected for the study? Could the study have been conducted using any other methodololologies?

4 What are the strengths and weaknesses of the study?

5 What do the findings reveal and what are the implications of the study?

6 Could this study be replicated in your own interpreter education context?

   a Hartley et al. (2003). Peer- and self-assessment in conference interpreter training. Unpublished research report. Available: http://www.llas.ac.uk/resourcedownloads/1454/hartley.rtf

   Abstract: This article reports the key findings of a project aiming to promote learner autonomy in interpreter training by providing learners with detailed and applicable guidelines when practising peer-assessment and self-monitoring. This was done by observation of the practice of expert interpreters when conducting interpreting classes, interviews with trainers and end-users, using these results to establish peer assessment criteria and evaluating their subsequent use with participating groups of learners at two UK HEIs.

   b Clifford, A. (2005). Putting the exam to the test: Psychometric validation and interpreter certification. *Interpreting*, 7(1), 97–131.

   Abstract: In this article, the author makes a distinction between the quality-oriented assessment prevalent in translation and interpreting and the psychometric evaluation common in other disciplines. He suggests that the latter is a more appropriate approach for interpreter certification, an assessment situation where inferential decisions are made. He demonstrates how such research might be carried out in interpreting by validating both an existing conference interpreter certification test and a new test constructed according to measurement and evaluation principles.

the authors for each study so that you can see the variation in research methodologies used across this domain of research.

a   Assessment in interpreter education programmes and interpreter testing

- Huang, T.-l. (2006). *A Study of applying portfolio assessment in an interpreter training course*. National Taiwan University of Science and Technology.

  The purpose of the study is to investigate the feasibility of integrating portfolio assessment with quality assessment as an alternative evaluation method in an interpreter-training course. Based on the theories of Smith and Tillema's training portfolio and Riccardi's interpretation quality evaluation sheet, an action research project was conducted at a sight translation class in an extension MA programme at a university in Taiwan. The participants consisted of seven students, one teacher, and the researcher herself.

  The data were collected from questionnaires, a pre-test and a post-test, grades of in-class role-play activities, class observations, interviews and the students' training portfolios. The results of the existing study confirm that process-oriented portfolio assessment, integrated with performance-based quality assessment, benefits both teachers and students in evaluating and presenting actual learning process and in identifying oral interpreting quality of each student in interpretation course.

- Valero-Garcés, C. and Socarrás-Estrada, D. (2012). Assessment and evaluation in labs for public services interpreting training. *International Journal of Interpreter Education*, 4(2), 7–23.

  This study reports on the development and application of two bilingual interpreting tests given to master's students during three academic years (2009–12) at the University of Alcalá, Madrid, Spain. Its main objective is to compare trainees' test performance at two different points in time. The study analyses the degree of accuracy and the speed of response, considering the variables of mother tongue, gender, age and undergraduate education. Our customized tests drew upon two aptitude tests developed by Pöchhacker (2009a) and Russo (2009) and combine oral-aural exercises with tasks requiring listening skills, expressional fluency and public-service-setting terminology. The tests are administered in a 24-seat multimedia lab, which allows recording students' performance for further evaluation. The results show the validity of the tests (Baker 2004) to measure the students' aptitudes before and after training, and thus the tests prove to be useful tools to predict professional performance as well.

- Timarová, S. and Ungoed-Thomas, H. (2008). Admission testing for interpreting courses. *The Interpreter & Translator Trainer,* 2(1), 29–46.

  Admission testing is an integral part of interpreter training, yet it is surrounded by much controversy and scepticism. This paper first looks into some general principles of designing an admission test (its purpose, link with curriculum, effectiveness and efficiency of testing), emphasizing the dissociation between skills to be tested and tests used for tapping them. The authors then present data from a small-scale study in which 18 interpreting schools provided information on their admission testing practice and answered questions related to the skills tested and tests employed, and to the overall efficiency of their admission procedure. Based on this analysis, they conclude that there is a reasonable consensus among schools in terms of which tests are best suited to test which skill, but that new approaches to admission testing are needed to improve their efficiency. More specifically, the authors suggest that schools improve their recording systems, that soft skills are included in formal testing, and that new testing methods are explored.

b Perspectives of interpreting students

- Bartłomiejczyk, M. (2007). Interpreting quality as perceived by trainee interpreters: Self-evaluation. *The Interpreter and Translator Trainer,* 1(2), 247–67.

  This paper discusses quality assessment of the performance of both professional and student interpreters working in various contexts, using a wide range of methods. It then focuses on self-evaluation by trainee simultaneous interpreters as examined in two empirical studies. The first project applied retrospective verbal protocols to investigate interpreting strategies used by 36 advanced student interpreters working in both directions between Polish (A) and English (B). The results concerning self-evaluation, which are presented here, were a by-product of this first study, but they gave rise to questions that are further explored in the second project. Eighteen subjects at the same stage of training were asked to interpret a text from English into Polish and to evaluate their performance, linking it to the strategic processing they had applied. The results suggest a significant trend towards negative assessment, combined with most attention being devoted to faithfulness to the original message and to completeness. Issues of presentation (including monotonous intonation, hesitant voice and long pauses), on the other hand, were hardly ever mentioned.

- Lim, L. (2013). Examining students' perceptions of computer-assisted interpreter training. *The Interpreter & Translator Trainer*, 7(1), 71–89.

  Audio-cassette recorders have traditionally been central to interpreter training facilities, including labs and interpreting suites. With the growing ubiquity of information and communication technologies, however, integrating computers in the interpreting classroom and exploring their pedagogical potential has moved higher up the research agenda of interpreter trainers. This study explores the effectiveness of a Computer-Assisted Platform (CAP) in assisting student interpreters with their interpreting practice. Rather than examining the usefulness of this platform from the teacher's viewpoint, this research focuses on the students' perception of what computer-assisted training offers them, comparing it with their learning experience using audio-cassette recorders. Subjects in this study identified five attributes as central to their perceptions of CAP-based interpreting training. The findings also suggest that subjects prefer the computer-assisted approach to the traditional form of interpreting practice involving audio-cassette recorders. The paper articulates the reasons for their preferences, and explores the potential of the CAP as an alternative approach to interpreter training.

c Curriculum innovation and review

- Sawyer, D. (2004). *Fundamental aspects of interpreter education.* Amsterdam: John Benjamins.

  The author offers an overview of the Interpreting Studies literature on curriculum and assessment. A discussion of curriculum definitions, foundations, and guidelines suggests a framework based upon scientific and humanistic approaches – curriculum as process and as interaction. Language testing concepts are introduced and related to interpreting. By exploring means of integrating valid and reliable assessment into the curriculum, the author breaks new ground in this under-researched area. Case studies of degree examinations provide sample data on pass/fail rates, test criteria and text selection. A curriculum model is outlined as a practical example of synthesis, flexibility and streamlining.

- Dean, R. K. and Pollard, R. Q. (2011). Context-based ethical reasoning in interpreting: A Demand Control Schema perspective. *The Interpreter & Translator Trainer*, 5(1), 155–82.

  Ethical interpreting practice must be predicated on an ongoing analysis of relevant contextual factors that arise in the interpreting situation. Although endorsed to some degree in interpreting pedagogy, this assertion runs counter to much of the history and continuing rhetoric of the interpreting field. Interpreting students receive a mixed message when educators assert a non-contextual, rule-based approach to ethics while simultaneously responding to both ethical and translation questions with 'It depends' – an obvious reference to the centrality of context in decision making. This article elucidates a teleological (outcomes-focused) ethical reasoning framework that hinges on a continuing analysis of the dynamic context of the interpreting situation. Grounded in the construct of practice profession responsibility, this approach scrutinizes the co-created dialogue between the interpreter, the consumers who are present, and the context of their collective encounter. It is argued here that critical reasoning in the service of work effectiveness equates to ethical reasoning, even if an ethical dilemma per se has not arisen. The authors' approach to context-based interpreting work analysis and decision making, the demand control schema (DC-S), has been the subject of several research studies, including a recently-concluded dissemination project involving 15 interpreter education programmes across the United States.

- Schafer, T. (2011). Developing expertise through a deliberate practice project. *International Journal of Interpreter Education,* 3, 15–27.

  Ericsson defines expertise as follows, 'Expert performers can reliably reproduce their performance any time when required such as during competition and training' (2001, p. 194). Merely practicing a skill repeatedly will not result in expert performance. However, 'deliberate practice' can improve performance. Deliberate practice is defined as '. . . tasks that are initially outside of their current realm of reliable performance, yet can be mastered within hours of practice by concentrating on critical aspects and by gradually refining performance through repetitions after feedback' (Ericsson 2001, p. 692). Mindset effects deliberate practice. Dweck (2006) describes two types of mindset: fixed and growth. A fixed mindset perceives intelligence and ability as static despite effort. A growth mindset embraces effort as a means to improve ability. Closing the gap between graduation and certification may be facilitated by deliberate practice. This action research project describes the introduction of deliberate practice and mindset in an interpreter education programme.

- Cho, J. and Roger, P. (2010). Improving interpreting performance through theatrical training. *The Interpreter & Translator Trainer,* 4(2), 151–71.

Aspiring interpreting professionals need to possess skills that allow them to think quickly in order to deal with unexpected situations that will inevitably arise in the course of interpreting assignments. The complex and inherently unpredictable nature of interpreting can be a major source of anxiety for student interpreters, particularly when they are called upon to perform in a language in which their proficiency and confidence levels are limited. Specific techniques for managing this anxiety, however, are often lacking in interpreter training programmes. This study examines the effects of a programme based on theatrical techniques commonly used in the training of professional actors but tailored specifically for novice interpreters. Two groups of interpreting students each received seven weeks of training in a sequential manner, allowing an external rating of the participants' performance to be carried out before and after the training took place. Results of the external ratings and the participants' own evaluation of their learning revealed significant benefits, with gains particularly evident in the areas of confidence, delivery and rapid problem solving abilities.

d Case studies

- Rico, C. (2010). Translator training in the European Higher Education area: Curriculum design for the Bologna process. A case study. *The Interpreter & Translator Trainer,* 4(1), 89–114.

  All across Europe, universities are currently engaged in a process of curricular reform to meet the requirements of the Bologna Declaration (1999) and, in doing so, create the European Higher Education Area by 2010. As part of this reform process, European higher education institutions aim to adopt easily comparable curricular structures, establish a common system of credit transfer, promote student mobility and develop shared quality assurance methodologies. This paper examines a number of pedagogical principles inspired by the Bologna agenda, including the growing pervasiveness of student-centred methodologies that encourage active learning and rely on new channels for trainer-trainee interaction. It is argued that this new pedagogical trend runs parallel to recent developments in translator training, such as social constructivism (Kiraly 2000) or task-based learning (Gonzáles-Davies 2004; Hurtado Albir 1999), which also revolve around the student as the centre of the learning process. The paper then focuses on a pilot adaptation experience within the Spanish higher education system: the reform of the translation degree programme at Universidad Europea de Madrid. This account begins by placing the chosen case study within the wider context of legislative reform in Spain;

it then moves on to outline the steps taken to ensure that the reformed curriculum meets the institutional requirements, as well as the rationale for the proposed distribution of curricular contents within the new degree structure. The advantages of using digital portfolios as instructional tools underpinning the implementation of key principles in the Bologna reform process are also examined.

- Boéri, J. and de Manuel Jerez, J. (2011). From training skilled conference interpreters to educating reflective citizens: A case study of the Marius action research project. *The Interpreter & Translator Trainer,* 5(1), 41–64.

  This paper reflects on how to initiate transformative training practices that set out to enhance social awareness of the role of conference interpreting in an asymmetrical society. Adopting a narrative perspective, the authors focus on two successive teaching innovation projects run at the University of Granada – 'Elaboration of Multimedia Didactic Material for Interpreting Classes' and 'Virtualization of Multimedia Didactic Material for Interpreting Classes'. The two projects together are referred to as 'Marius'. Marius's training research methodology, based on emancipatory principles of participation and horizontality, is elaborated for and with students. Drawing on new technologies, the project accommodates a plurality of voices and cosmovisions, not only to ensure that future interpreters develop the ability to work with both dominant and resistant discourses in society, but also to encourage them to reflect on these discourses and on their own role as professionals and citizens. This case study is particularly helpful in exploring how a socio-critical pedagogy, particularly action research, allows for a shift from training practitioners for the market towards educating reflective citizens, at the same time as problematizing the ethics of training research methodologies.

Exercise 7.6

Think back to your ideas for your own interpreter education research project, as developed through the exercises in this chapter. Consider your own plans in relation to the abstracts of previous interpreter education projects, as presented above. Are there any studies outlined in Section 7.6.2 that could be replicated by you in your own interpreter education research; with different languages, in a different educational context, or triangulated with other data?

7.7 Conclusion

This chapter has discussed how to apply various quantitative and qualitative Interpreting studies methodologies to the exploration of interpreter education, by contextualizing research questions within a framework of educational theory. Different types of interpreter education research have been presented, and in particular the chapter has examined how one research question can be investigated in different ways depending on the educational theoretical perspective adopted. In summary, a range of examples of interpreter education research projects have been given, which reveal the varying approaches to conducting research on learning and teaching in interpreter pedagogy.

Further reading

Angelelli, C. and Jacobson, H. (eds) (2009). *Testing and assessment in translation and interpreting studies*. Amsterdam: John Benjamins.
Cohen, L., Manion, L. and Morrison, K. (2011). *Research methods in education* (7th edn). Abingdon, Oxon: Routledge.
Sawyer, D. (2004). *Fundamental aspects of interpreter education*. Amsterdam: John Benjamins.

Notes

1   Thanks to Dr Raquel de Pedro Ricoy and PhD students at Heriot-Watt University for the discussion around this point, which crystallized the introductory component of this chapter.

2   This example is adapted from a data matrix created for an action research project conducted at Macquarie University in Sydney: Napier, J. et al. (2008–11). A new vision for Translation and Interpreting education in the twenty-first century: A research embedded review project. http://www.ling.mq.edu.au/translation/review.htm.

3   Note: at time of writing, a report has just been released that provides results from Phase I of a project to review potential improvements in the NAATI testing system (see Hale et al. 2012). The proposed project in this book is completely hypothetical and not related in anyway to the recent real project, and does not present any opinion from the authors of this book on the need for NAATI to improve its interpreting standards.

CHAPTER EIGHT

Conducting and disseminating interpreting research

This chapter will provide an overview of aspects of Interpreting research that are critical for consideration in conducting and disseminating Interpreting research:

- Deciding on your research design: traditional versus innovative
- Positioning yourself and your research
- Reporting the results
- The thesis: styles, structures and formats
- Disseminating your results
- Applying your research findings
- Becoming an interpreting researcher

8.1 Introduction

In each chapter of this book, you have been guided through the various stages of conducting a research project: from defining concepts of research and research design and developing your research proposal (Chapter 1); to how to conduct a critical literature review and considering ethical aspects of your research design (Chapter 2); to applying different research methodologies in conducting your research – including survey questionnaires (Chapter 3), qualitative ethnographic approaches (Chapter 4), discourse analysis (Chapter 5) and experimental design (Chapter 6); to considering how any of these research methodologies could be utilized in interpreter education research (Chapter 7). Each chapter has featured exercises for you to undertake, which have been designed to engage you in thinking about the research process and to walk you through developing your own research project. The primary target audience of this book is research students undertaking Masters or PhD research projects.

However, we envisage that any person interested in conducting Interpreting research will benefit in some way from this book – whether they are practitioners considering doing a PhD or embarking on an individual action research (interpreter fieldwork) project, or early career researchers, or established university educators who are either looking for a resource to help their students or are themselves exploring what other methodologies can be applied in their own research on Interpreting. So now we come to the final chapter of the book. By the time you read this chapter, you will either have a fully fleshed out research proposal ready to go, or you may well have completed your research project. So what now? The goal of this chapter is to tie together the content of the previous seven chapters, and to focus particularly on critical things that we feel are important for any Interpreter researcher to consider in conducting and disseminating Interpreting research. Completed research ideally needs to be shared with all stakeholders. This can be done through publications (Napier 2011b), but there are other ways to ensure the findings of your research can be disseminated, so we will give you some tips on the best ways to go about that. Before we discuss key issues to consider in conducting and disseminating Interpreting research, we would like to revisit the notion of research design, and give you some further food for thought for your current or future studies.

8.2 Which research design? Traditional or innovative?

Depending on what stage you are at in your research design, you may have a clear idea of the research methodology or methodologies that you intend to use. Chapters 3–6 of this book have presented and critiqued more traditional research methods, outlining standard quantitative and qualitative approaches to collecting and analysing data. We know that there is a wide range of models and methods utilized in Interpreting research (Mason 2000), and because it is still an emerging research discipline, we can afford to explore different research methods (Riccardi 2002).

8.2.1 Mixed methods research

Throughout the book (particularly Chapters 1, 4, 6 and 7) we have mentioned how research designs can incorporate triangulation of research data using different methodologies in order to test or explore the same phenomena from different perspectives (or through different 'lenses'). This approach is typically referred to as 'mixed methods' (Johnson et al. 2007) or 'multi-method' research (Brewer and Hunter 2006), and is particularly popular in social science research. Some researchers would consider this as one of the major research paradigms equal to, and alongside, quantitative and qualitative paradigms (Johnson et al. 2007) and is of 'widespread use in practice . . . a style in its own right; a style that provides increased power of persuasion and strengthened claims to validity' (Brewer and Hunter 2006, p. xi). Furthermore, Brewer and Hunter claim that multi-method research has far wider uses and implications than just for triangulation purposes: 'Theorizing and theory testing, problem formulation and data collection, sampling and generalization, hypothesis testing and causal analysis, social problem and policy analysis, and even the writing and publication of results may benefit from bringing a multi-method perspective to bear on social research' (2006, pp. xi–xii).

Pöchhacker (2011a) considers that the use of mixed-methods research designs in Interpreting studies are appropriate in order to account for the level of complexity in exploring interpreting processes and practices. Therefore, we encourage interpreter researchers to explore the possibilities of using a mixed methods research design. Employing such an approach will allow you to draw on traditional research methodologies, but will also allow scope for innovation in research design.

8.2.2 *Innovation in research design*

As recommended by Luker (2008), as social science researchers we need to 'play out of our shoes' and 'think at a higher level of generality' (p. 218), which means considering which research method(s) will enable us to answer the questions we have about interpreting.

'Playing out of our shoes' can mean embarking on interdisciplinary study, as suggested by Shlesinger (1998) for Interpreting scholars, or adopting more innovative, less traditional approaches to conducting research on Interpreting. Some examples of innovative Interpreting research methods include the use of:

- newspaper archives (Phelan 2011)
- retrospection protocols (Ivanova 2000; Vik-Tuovinen 2000)
- think-aloud protocols (Stone 2007)
- eye tracking (Shreve et al. 2010), and
- cognitive-experimental studies (Moser-Mercer 2010).

If you are at the stage of developing a research proposal, and considering which university to enrol in for your PhD candidature, then consider what methodologies you may want to employ, and how traditional or innovative you would like to be in your research design. This can help you to determine the best PhD supervisor to meet your needs. PhD supervisors will have their own areas of expertise and methodological preferences, so choose your university and your supervisor accordingly and wisely.

8.3 Positioning yourself and your research

In order to contextualize your research, it is worth considering how to position yourself and your role as an Interpreting researcher, and also how to position your research in the field generally, that is, where does your research fit into the wider picture of Interpreting studies?

8.3.1 Positioning yourself: *Your role as an interpreting researcher*

Where you position yourself as an Interpreting researcher is influenced by institutional, political and attitudinal factors. In 1995, Franz Pöchhacker gave an overview of the profile of Interpreting researchers at that time, by examining their publication record, their affiliations with universities and 'schools' of Interpreting studies, and their role as academics and professional interpreter practitioners. He found that most interpreter researchers were affiliated with five key centres of Interpreting studies: Georgetown, Paris (ISIT and ESIT), Trieste and Vienna. He also found that the majority of researchers were still practicing professional (conference) interpreters.

Since the 1995 publication, the Interpreting studies field has grown exponentially. Greater numbers of people from countries outside Europe including Australia, China and Canada are conducting research; and we are also seeing more spoken and signed language community interpreting researchers making a contribution – as evidenced through the range of references provided throughout this book. Professional interpreter practitioners still have an important position in Interpreting studies, as evidenced through Shlesinger's (2009) review of ten years of articles published in the journal 'Interpreting – International Journal of Research and Practice in Interpreting'. She noted that much of the research published during that time was led by professional interpreters seeking to explore questions resulting from their own practice. Non-practitioner 'career academics', however, still have a place in pioneering aspects of Interpreting and Translation studies research (Pollitt 2011), and together we all form a 'community of practice' of researchers (Meyerhoff 2008).

As Pollitt (2011) and others suggest, depending on the theoretical framework that you draw upon as the foundation of your work, it can be important to position, or 'situate', yourself as an interpreter researcher. In order to better place the research project, it is worth outlining your role in the research context, by inserting a small section in the introduction of your thesis or research report. You may like to cover the following kinds of information:

- Educational qualifications

- Language status (bilingual, trilingual?)

- Interpreter qualifications and experience

- Interpreter education experience

- Other roles in the interpreting community

- Any particular theoretical frameworks that you ascribe to and why

- How you came to Interpreting research

- What has led you to this particular research question or questions

Exercise 8.1

Select one of the research ideas that you have been working on while reading this book, or refer to your final research proposal, and write a paragraph to position yourself in the research. Use the list of questions above as a guide. What do you think consumers of the research will need to know about you in order to understand your relationship to the research and your research agenda?

8.3.2 *Positioning your research: Where and how does it fit?*

In addition to positioning yourself as an individual, in considering where and how your research fits within the wider Interpreting studies field, you can position your research and give yourself a clear picture of how your research will make a contribution to the field.

Holmes' (2000) 'name and nature of the field of translation studies' is considered by many to be 'the founding statement for the field' of translation studies (Gentzler 2001, p. 94). Holmes suggested a map of translation studies, in an attempt to provide an overview of the nature of translation studies and the position of research within the field (see Figure 8.1).

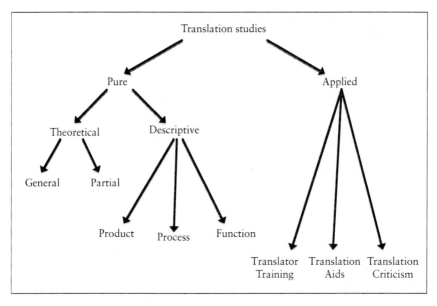

FIGURE 8.1 *Holmes' map of translation studies (Cited in and adapted from Toury 1995)*

Holmes makes a distinction between pure and applied research, and what the outcomes of translation studies research might be. Holmes' map has been critiqued by Vandepitte (2008), Pym (2010) and others, but still provides a valuable conceptual model for us to consider how to position our research. Is it pure or applied? Is it theoretical or descriptive? How will the research be applied? (See Chapter 1).

In relation to Interpreting studies research, Pöchhacker (2004, 2006, 2009b) has mapped Interpreting studies in terms of the central themes and ideas that have emerged through the growing body of work and the changing paradigms in Interpreting studies. Following on from Holmes' translation studies map, there is a similar need to produce Interpreting studies research that is pure and applied, theoretical and descriptive. In their discussion of signed language interpreting, Leeson et al. (2011) state that there is a need for three types of applied Interpreting studies research that: (1) feeds directly into teaching by describing skills and strategies that interpreters need to develop; (2) produces technical tools that interpreters and interpreting students can use: and (3) expands our understanding of interpreting practices, the role of the interpreter and the interpreting context. The same could be said for studies of spoken language interpreting. So where and how does your own interpreting research fit in this context?

Exercise 8.2

Read Pöchhacker, F. (2009). The turns of interpreting studies. In G. Hansen, A. Chesterman and H. Gerzymisch-Arbogast (eds), *Efforts and models in interpreting and translation research*. Amsterdam: John Benjamins, pp. 25–46.

Create an interpreting studies map (cf. Holmes' translation studies map)

Reflect on the various references you have been given throughout this book – what types of research do we see in interpreting studies? Where do they fit on your interpreting studies map? Do we have enough theoretical (pure) research? Is the field dominated by any particular kind of research?

Identify where your research fits in your interpreting studies map, that is, how would you position your own research?

8.4 Reporting the results

In Chapter 4, and our discussion of qualitative research methodology, we cautioned against making sweeping generalizations about your research findings. This is important to remember when interpreting (sic) and reporting the results of your research. Generalizations can only be made to broader interpreting populations, depending on the research methodology and design that you have used. This is one of the benefits of replicating the research of other Interpreting researchers, in order to identify similarities and differences across countries, languages and cultures (Shlesinger 2009).

It is your role as a researcher to interpret what you think the findings of your research mean, why they are significant and for whom they are significant. As Pöchhacker (2010d) outlines, Interpreting research matters potentially to various stakeholders, including educators, the interpreting research community as well as the practice, the profession and the institutional (user) context. The relevance of your research to each of these stakeholder groups will depend on how your research is positioned, that is, what kind of research it is. Therefore any claims that you make about your research need to be contextualized and conclusions need to be appropriately drawn. Conclusions can only summarize what you have found in your study, and how they apply specifically to, or are significant for, the target population. For example, a case study of interpreting can reveal insights into how interpreters work, but cannot conclusively demonstrate that all interpreters work the same way.

When reporting the results of your research, consider that you are telling the story (Clough and Nutbrown 2007) of how the research was developed and conducted, and the end point. In making the research public, keep in mind that 'social research is persuasive, purposive, positional and political' and that 'research is not complete until it finds a public' (p. 183). Finally, 'the research report should not only tell the story but also *justify* the enquiry' (p. 183, italics in original).

8.4.1 *The thesis: Styles, structures and formats*

Regardless of whether your research is being reported through submission of a PhD thesis, a research report, or publication of a book, journal article or book chapter; it is always worth writing several drafts and getting feedback from others before you submit the final polished version. As you write, you get very close to your own project and it can be hard to objectively see what readers who know nothing about the project will glean from reading. There may be gaps in the description of the methodology, or assumptions made about the context of the study.

The writing style you use will be influenced by the discipline with whom your research aligns (i.e. psychological, sociological, anthropological, etc.) and the methodological approach you have taken. Some disciplines and related journals insist on a more passive voice in academic writing, always writing in the third person. Others allow use of first person and encourage the active voice of the author to be visible throughout the text. See Example 8.1 for an extract taken from the Cambridge Guide to English Usage for guidance on the use of 'I' in writing. For general tips on *writing up* and completing a thesis or writing for publication from different disciplinary perspectives, see the following sources: management (Burton and Steane 2004), social science (Wolff and Pant 1999), Translation studies (Williams and Chesterman 2002) and Interpreting studies (Gile et al. 2001).

Example 8.1: Use of the 'I' in writing

'I'

When can I be used in writing? It depends on what's being written. Personal letters, diaries and autobiography are the natural medium for **I**, talking about opinions, attitudes and feelings ('I think', 'I know', 'I feel' etc.). **I** occurrs naturally in scripted dialogue and many types of fiction. But in professional writing we conventionally avoid **I** even when expressing individual opinions. Thus a reviewer is less likely to say:

I was delighted by the freshness of the performance . . .

than

The performance was delightfully fresh.

Personal opinion is less obvious in the second sentence, where it's blended into the description with an attitudinal adverb ('delightfully'). It implies that anyone viewing the performance would see it that way, as if there's a weight of opinion behind the comment. By avoiding the use of I, the writer masks the subjectiveness of the reaction.

The need to sound authoritative and professional no doubt underlies the convention of avoiding I in academic and bureaucratic writing. It also applies in science, though it was not always so. Newton and other pioneering scientists used I quite freely. The pronoun was not regularly suppressed in science writing until late C19 (Halliday 1988), since when an impersonal style replete with passive verbs has been conventional for scientific writers. Yet one school of scientists – the US Council of Biology Editors – has since the 1960s actively encouraged the use of I, and others are allowing it back in. In the United Kingdom, a study of science and engineering writing by Kirkman (1980) found a sprinkling of the pronoun I in many of the papers published in academic journals. The study also showed that scientists hardly noticed low levels of I, though they reacted negatively to its frequent use, finding it either amateurish or arrogant. Kirkman concluded that 'judicious' use of I was no problem.

More systematic use of I can be found in other contexts. In some government departments, ministerial letters bearing the chief's signature make strategic use of the first person. The motivation may be as much to project the image of a strong executive head as to avoid an impersonal bureaucratic style. Proactive editors of academic manuscripts sometimes make a point of turning every 'it was found that' into 'I found that', in the interests of readability. This practice can however impair the line of argument, which the author has built in.

So, the reasons for using I in writing, or suppressing it, are complex and vary with the context. Writers who avoid it may be adhering to older conventions, or trying to divert attention from the lack of evidence for their opinion. Saying 'This is not acceptable' sounds much more powerful than 'I can't accept this', whether or not there's anything to support it.

Let the reader beware!

(Extract taken from Pam Peters 2004, p. 262)

Exercise 8.3

Write a brief 200 word abstract for your proposed research study, and write it in two different ways: (1) in a passive style, using only third person; and (2) in an active style, using first person and use of 'I'. Which style do you prefer? What message does each abstract convey?

The style and structure of the thesis you write will also be influenced by the following factors:

a   Theoretical framework of the research

b   Methodology and research design

c   Supervisor experience and preference

d   University guidelines and requirements

Typically there are expectations of how a research report or thesis should be structured, according to whether it is a quantitative or qualitative study. Example 8.2 outlines typical quantitative and qualitative formats, as outlined by Cresswell (1994). However, given what we discussed in Section 8.2 of this chapter about using mixed-methods or taking innovative approaches to conducting Interpreting research, then the expected writing formats may be more flexible.

Example 8.2: Overview of research writing structures (Cresswell 1994)

Qualitative writing format

Introduction

    Statement of the problem
    Purpose of the study
    The grand tour question and sub-questions
    Definitions
    Delimitations and limitations
    Significance of the study

Review of literature
Procedure

    Assumptions and rationale for a qualitative design
    The type of design used
    The role of the researcher
    Data collection procedures
    Data analysis procedures

Methods for verification
Outcome of the study and its relation to theory and literature
Appendices

Quantitative writing format

Introduction

> Context (Statement of the problem)
> Purpose of the study
> Research questions or objectives or hypotheses
> Theoretical perspective
> Definition of terms
> Delimitations and limitations
> Significance of the study

Review of literature
Methods

> Research design
> Sample, population or subjects
> Instrumentation and materials
> Variables in the study

Data analysis
Appendices: Instruments

8.4.1.1 Thesis by publication

Some universities are beginning to promote theses produced in journal-article-format rather than traditional 'book' format. This is also sometimes referred to as 'thesis by publication' (TBP). The idea behind TBP is to encourage PhD students to produce a series of thematically linked stand-alone journal articles that have either been published, are in press, have been submitted or are in preparation for submission by the time the thesis is submitted. Essentially, one article equals one chapter in the thesis.[1] The research design can involve a series of thematically linked projects or one major project that is broken down into components and discussed in each article. The introductory and conclusion chapters are written to 'book end' the various chapters, giving an overview of how each article is linked, and summing up the implications of the research and making suggestions for further research. The TBP format requires each chapter of the thesis to read as a self-contained journal article (or book chapter), with its own introduction, literature review, methods, results and discussion and conclusion sections. The rationale behind the TBP approach is that PhD graduates may already have several publications to their name (or at least in press) by the time they complete their PhD, which means that they have already begun their publication track record, and this places them in a better position when applying for academic positions or research grants (see § 8.7 of this chapter).

Choosing a TBP format can be beneficial to interpreter practitioners and others not undertaking full-time PhD study, as the process provides a series of milestones to work towards (Karen Bontempo, in press); but this approach is not evident yet everywhere, and is still frowned upon by some universities who only endorse traditional format theses. Therefore if you are interested in choosing this format for your thesis, make sure you make some enquiries first and ensure that your preferred supervisor and university are willing to allow you to make that choice. Examples 8.3 and 8.4 illustrate the summarized Table of Contents from two recently completed PhD theses. Each thesis differs in two respects: (1) one is a qualitative discourse analytical study, and the other is a quantitative experimental study; and (2) one follows a traditional format and the other a TBP format.

Example 8.3: Qualitative discourse analytical study – Traditional format

Healthcare interpreting as relational practice (Major 2013)

Table of Contents

Chapter 1: Background to the study

Includes positioning of the researcher, brief overview of the literature in relation to interpreting and discourse analysis as a rationale for the study, outline of the thesis, and summary.

Chapter 2: Discourse analysis of signed languages and interpreting

Literature review chapter focusing on discourse analysis of signed language interaction (introducing discourse markers, turn exchanges and politeness) and discourse analysis of interpreted interaction (introducing interpreters as active participants, interpreters and relational work); and summary.

Chapter 3: Healthcare interaction and healthcare interpreting

Literature review chapter focusing on healthcare discourse, patients from minority groups and the healthcare setting, interpreted healthcare interpreting; and summary.

Chapter 4: Research method

Includes overview of data collection process, ethics approval, and full description of naturally-occurring and role play data; and summary.

Chapter 5: Clarification requests in simulated interpreted healthcare interaction

Data analysis chapter focusing on discussion of clarification requests used by interpreters in the role play data, and their perceptions of their clarification requests gleaned through post-simulation interviews; and summary.

Chapter 6: Clarification in naturally-occurring interpreted healthcare

Data analysis chapter focusing on discussion of clarification requests used by interpreters in the natural-occurring data, and the nature of clarification as a joint activity by all participants; and summary.

Chapter 7: Managing relational difficulties

Data analysis chapter focusing on discussion of interpreters' strategies for managing relational difficulties in the natural-occurring data; and summary.

Chapter 8: Building and maintaining positive relationships

Data analysis chapter focusing on discussion of interpreters' strategies for enabling positive doctor-patient relationships in the natural-occurring data; and summary.

Chapter 9: Healthcare interpreting as relational practice

Conclusion chapter, giving a summary of the thesis, the implications, applications and limitations of the research, recommendations for further research and concluding remarks.

Complete Reference List

Example 8.4: Quantitative experimental study – TBP format

Working memory and signed language interpreting Wang (2013b)

Table of Contents

Chapter 1: Introduction

Includes background to the research, positioning of the researcher, brief literature review, overview of the goal of the study and the overall research design, and the structure of the thesis; reference list.

Chapter 2: Measuring bilingual working memory capacity of professional signed language interpreters: A comparison of two scoring methods

Includes an overview of methodological differences in verbal working memory span tasks, description of the method of data collection and two

(Continued)

Exercise 8.4 (Continued)

scoring methods, breakdown of results according to scoring method, discussion, acknowledgment of limitations, suggested implications and conclusions; reference list.

Chapter 3: Bilingual working memory capacity of professional signed language interpreters

Includes overview of working memory capacity literature, description of the method of data collection, reporting of quantitative results from working memory span tasks and qualitative results from interviews with interpreters, discussion and conclusion with recommendations for further research; reference list.

Chapter 4: Signed language working memory capacity of signed language interpreters and deaf signers

Includes overview of literature in relation to working memory theories in speech and sign, description of the method of data collection, results and comparison of deaf and interpreter participants' working memory capacity, discussion, conclusion and suggestions for further research; reference list.

Chapter 5: Using rubrics to assess a corpus of signed language interpreting performance

Includes background information in language testing, assessment of interpreter performance and development of rubrics, overview of the experimental corpus (method of data collection) and assessment method, presentation of results and inter-rater reliability, discussion, conclusion and suggested implications; reference list.

Chapter 6: Directionality in signed language interpreting

Includes overview of literature on directionality and working languages in interpreting, description of the method of data collection, reporting of quantitative results of directionality effects on interpreting performance and qualitative results of self-assessment of performance from interviews with interpreters, discussion and conclusion with recommendations for further research; reference list.

Chapter 7: The relationship between professional signed language interpreters' working memory capacity and their simultaneous interpreting performance

Includes overview of literature on working memory models, description of the method of data collection, reporting of quantitative results comparing working memory results with interpreting performance and qualitative results of reporting on working memory overload from interviews with interpreters, discussion and conclusion with recommendations for further research; reference list.

Chapter 8: Conclusion

Includes review of Chapters 2–7, discussion of strengths and limitations of the research, the implications of the study and suggestions for further research; reference list.

Complete Reference List

You can see from each Table of Contents that Major's thesis follows a typical traditional thesis structure, including several literature review chapters before detailing the method, and then combining data analysis and discussion in subsequent chapters that focus on different elements of the data, and then wrapping up with a conclusion chapter. Wang's thesis, however, is a series of self-contained journal articles, with each chapter incorporating a review of the relevant literature, giving a description of the method, and then providing results followed by discussion, then conclusion, and including its own reference list. These two theses are just samples of how different research paradigms can influence the structure of a thesis (i.e. qualitative or quantitative), and also illustrate the differences in following a traditional or TBF format. We are not suggesting that you follow these structures exactly in your own write-up, but that you consider the alternatives to presenting your research work.

8.5 How to disseminate?

On completion of your thesis, it is important to disseminate the findings to all relevant audiences – don't just let your thesis sit on the shelf! Of course you can write for publication, and if you have completed a TBP format then you will have articles already published or ready to publish. The merits of publishing Interpreting research and of also making it accessible to practitioners have been discussed in detail elsewhere (Hale 2007; Napier 2011b), but we do recommend that you think carefully about how to disseminate your research. When you consider publishing, think about whom you want to reach out to. Who needs to know about your research? And how will you get the information to them?

8.5.1 Publishing

Refer back to your map of Interpreting studies that you created in Exercise 8.2, and where you consider that your research fits in the field

Table 8.1 Interpreting-specific journals and publishers

Interpreting: International Journal of Research and Practice in Interpreting	John Benjamins
International Journal of Translation and Interpreting Research	University of Western Sydney, Australia
International Journal of Interpreter Education	Conference of Interpreter Trainers
Interpreter and Translator Trainer	St Jerome
Journal of Interpretation	Registry of Interpreters for the Deaf
Meta	Les Presses de l'Université de Montréal
Translation and Interpreting Studies: The Journal of the American Translation and Interpreting Studies Association	John Benjamins

of Interpreting studies. If it is a theoretical study, then you will need to publish in scholarly journals to share your work with other Interpreting scholars, and possibly researchers in related disciplines (e.g. if you have adopted a psychological approach to examining the interpreting process, then your findings may be of interest to psychologists or psycholinguists). You can target appropriate journals according to the nature of your study. A list of Interpreting-specific journals and publishers can be seen in Table 8.1.[2] If you would like to reach scholars in other related disciplines, then you will need to submit to the journals that they read. For example, if you have completed a study of healthcare interpreting, then you could consider journals such as the Journal of Healthcare Communication, Communication and Medicine, or the International Journal of E-health and Medical Communications; if you have completed a study on legal interpreting, you may consider submitting articles to law journals or forensic linguistic journals, such as The journal of Speech, Language and the Law. Referring to journals that you have featured in your own reference list is a good starting point, as they are obviously publishing research that is relevant to your own study.

When you submit to a scholarly journal, you can expect that your manuscript will enter a double-blind peer review process (see Chapter 2). This means that your paper will be anonymously reviewed by (typically) two experts in the field, as determined by the editor of the journal. You will then receive anonymous feedback from the reviewers, with a recommendation for any necessary revisions before the manuscript can be published. The editor of the journal takes guidance from the reviewers' comments, but has the final say as to whether a paper will be accepted or rejected. You are then usually given time to make any revisions, with a deadline for response. Some journals can take up to two years to publish a submission, depending on the number of manuscripts they receive. The better quality the journal, the harder it is to get published in it!

If yours is an applied study, then you will still need to publish in scholarly peer-reviewed journals, as described above. But you may also like to consider how to reach other audiences that need to know about your research results. If, for instance, your study focuses on interpreter education, then you may like to write a short piece for a newsletter or in a blog aimed at interpreter educators. For example, in relation to a longitudinal project concerning whether deaf people can serve as jurors by accessing courtroom information sufficiently through signed language interpreters, several publications were produced over the life of the project that targeted different audiences, as follows:

- Monograph published by the New South Wales Law Reform Commission (who commissioned the study), targeted at policymakers (Napier et al. 2007);

- Book chapter in an edited volume entitled 'Interpreting in legal settings', targeted primarily at signed language interpreter researchers (Napier and Spencer 2008);

- Chapter in a peer-reviewed conference proceedings 'Critical Link 5', targeted at spoken and signed language interpreter practitioners, researchers and educators (Napier et al. 2009);

- Short article in the journal Reform, targeted at lawyers and other interested parties working in the area of law reform (Napier and Spencer 2007);

- Brief reports on outcomes of the study, targeted at the Australian Deaf community and featured in the magazine of the peak community organization Deaf Australia (previously known as the Australian Association of the Deaf) (Napier 2007; Napier and Shearim 2012)

- Brief article overview of the implications of the research for interpreters in the magazine produced by the Australian Sign Language Interpreters Association (Napier 2009).

You can see from the above list that information about the research study was disseminated to different relevant audiences: lawyers, deaf people, signed language interpreters, and Interpreting researchers, by the nature of the publications produced.

Exercise 8.4

Consider who needs to know about your research.

Write a list of journals that you would like to target for the possible publication of your research findings. Include both interpreting-specific journals and those from other relevant disciplines (do a search through Google Scholar to identify appropriate journals if necessary).

Identify other suitable sources of publications to inform other stakeholders about your research.

8.5.2 Conference presentations

Another way to disseminate information about research is through presenting conference papers. As with the strategy for targeting appropriate journals, you can also target conferences depending on the nature of your study, and the audience you want to reach. You can consider attending academic conferences to present to other researchers, as well as to conferences of professional interpreting associations. You may also consider presenting at conferences in related disciplines: for example, conferences for lawyers or judicial officers if your research is in legal interpreting, for medical practitioners, if it is in medical interpreting, and so forth. To refer back to the same example study presented in section 8.5.1, and the ensuing publications, the list below illustrates the range of conference presentations that resulted from the deaf juror study:

- 'Auslan interpreters and the law: Shaping the future picture for deaf people to serve as jurors'. Presentation to the Annual National Conference of the Australian Sign Language Interpreters Association, Adelaide, 24–6 August 2012.

- 'Please just translate word-for-word and let me interpret the meaning': Understanding linguistic and role issues for courtroom interpreters. Keynote paper presented at the National Legal Interpreting Conference hosted by the Institute for Legal Interpreting, Denver, Colorado, USA, 12–14 April 2012.

- 'Legal interpreting research: An example – can deaf people serve as jurors?' Panel presentations to the National Legal Interpreting Conference hosted by the Institute for Legal Interpreting, Denver, Colorado, USA, 12–14 April 2012.

- 'Interpreters and the law: Research on signed language interpreting in NSW courts'. Paper presented at the Language and The Law Symposium at the Applied Linguistics Association of Australia conference, 30 November-2 December 2011.

- 'Research on signed language interpreting in NSW courts'. Paper presented at the Legal and Police Interpreting conference. RMIT University, Melbourne, 18 November 2011.

- 'Interpreting access in Australian courts: An overview of recent research'. Keynote presentation at the 3rd Community Interpreting Research Conference, Trinity College Dublin, 10–11 February 2011.

- '"We find the defendant not guilty": An investigation of Deaf jurors' access to court proceedings via sign language interpreting'. Paper presented at Critical Link: the 5th International conference on community interpreting, Sydney, Australia, 11–15 April 2007.

Conference presentations can occur throughout the process of a research project, as it can be valuable to present earlier research design plans, preliminary findings, or definitive conclusions at different stages of the study, in order to get feedback from peers and other interested parties. This feedback can help to shape the nature of your study and ensure that it is relevant to all stakeholders. Attending conferences is also an important opportunity to network with scholars in your field, and get an overview of what other researchers are working on so that you can identify research trends to which you can also contribute (see Chapter 2).

Exercise 8.5

Consider where you can present your research.

Do a search for interpreting conferences (or other relevant conferences), which are being advertised for the next two years. Write a list of conferences that you would like to present at.

8.5.2.1 Submitting conference abstracts

When you have identified which conferences you would like to attend, the next step is to submit an abstract for consideration. Many universities provide limited funding for PhD students to attend international conferences, but there is typically a requirement that you have to be giving a presentation; and this also applies for staff in academic positions. The earlier you start submitting abstracts the better, and it does get easier. Our key tips are as follows:

- Read the Call for Papers carefully:

  o   What is the conference theme?

  o   Are there any particular strands that your research fits into?

- o   What kinds of submissions are they looking for (papers, workshops, panels)?

- o   What is the word limit?

- o   What is the required format of the abstract?

- o   What is the deadline for submission?

- o   Write your abstract according to the theme – so ensure that you make the link between your research and the theme.

- o   Give a very brief background to the project (do not refer to too much literature as this uses up your word count), describe the goal of the project, where you are at in the project (i.e. collecting data, data analysis, reporting preliminary results, etc.), what the potential implications of the project are for the conference audience, and how the research fits with the conference theme.

- o   Do not go over the word limit!

Example 8.5 provides a sample of a Call for Papers from an interpreting-specific conference held in the United Kingdom in 2010.

Example 8.5: Sample of call for papers

6th International Critical Link Conference

26–30 July 2010, Aston University, Birmingham, United Kingdom

Interpreting in a Changing Landscape

Call for Papers

The Organising Committee of Critical Link 6 would like to invite you to submit an abstract for a presentation at the Critical Link 2010 Conference. This Call includes submissions for papers, poster sessions, discussion panels, workshops, round table discussions, and pre- and post-conference workshops.

The Conference will bring together representatives from every sphere of the public service interpreting community: academics, interpreting practitioners, employers, trainers, policy makers, service providers and service recipients to shed new light on the vital role that public service/ community interpreters play in our world. The conference theme is Interpreting in a Changing Landscape. The aim is to explore political, legal, human rights, trans-national, economic, socio-cultural, and sociolinguistic aspects of public service/community interpreting. Abstracts of papers relating to the following key strands in interpreting research and practice will be prioritized for inclusion in the programme:

1 Commissioning of interpreting services
   a National and political responsibility for service provision
   b Public awareness of costs and benefits
   c The role of national and multinational interpreting agencies
   d The practice of outsourcing interpreting services
   e The role of the state in the certification of public service interpreters
   f Analysing demand for interpreting services

2 Professional governance within public service/community interpreting
   a Codes of Ethics and Conduct, disciplinary procedures
   b The role of professional associations
   c. Professional registers, local lists and trade unions
   d Performance management of interpreters – monitoring, feedback and supervision
   e Regulation of interpreters and of interpreter services
   f Quality assurance mechanisms and external validation systems
   g Advocate, mediator, culture broker, interpreter: one job or many?
   h The rights of immigrants and asylum seekers to communication services

3 Using innovative practice and new technologies to improve public service interpreting
   a Telephone, Video, Remote interpreting
   b Telecommunication and Webstream interpreting
   c Terminology storage and retrieval
   d The virtual courtroom
   e Interpreting in conflict zones

4 Interpreter training and education
   a Who sets the standards and what are they?
   b Who should provide training and who should fund it?
   c Technology in interpreter education

(*Continued*)

Exercise 8.5 (Continued)

  d   Access to training

  e   Assessment, accreditation and qualifications

  f   Training the trainers

  g   Less widely taught languages

  h   Role of private accrediting bodies

5 Continuing Professional Development (CPD)

  a   Models of CPD for interpreters

  b   Language enhancement programmes

  c   Progression routes and rewards for excellence

  d   In-service training for public sector staff

6 Research

  a   Social impact of research

  b   Innovative research methods

  c   Interdisciplinary research in legal, medical, social services and local government settings

  d   Interpreting in humanitarian or military intervention

  e   Practitioners as researchers

Abstracts should be approximately 300 words and written in English. When submitting your abstract, please specify the format and which of the strands your contribution will address: paper (20 minutes + 10 minutes discussion), poster, workshop, panel, round table discussion (90 minutes). Proposals for pre-and post-conference workshops are also invited and should be labelled accordingly.

From the above Call for Papers, it can clearly be seen what kind of presentations the conference organizers were looking for. The focus of the conference was interpreting in community settings, and there are clear strands that they were targeting in order to explore different aspects of community interpreting practice, pedagogy and policy. Example 8.6 includes a selection of three abstracts taken from the conference programme booklet, from papers that were presented at the conference (i.e. abstracts that were accepted). Look closely at the titles of the papers, and how the authors have made the connection between their research, the proposed presentation and the conference theme.

Example 8.6: Sample conference abstracts

1   Teruko Asano, Nagoya University of Foreign Studies, and Masako Mouri, Nanzan University, Japan

Rapid Changes in the Interpreters' Landscape as premised by the Introduction of new Investigation and Trial Procedures in Japan

Currently the Japanese legal system is being updated, in line with Japan's efforts to achieve greater globalization within its society. In this respect, Japan recently introduced a citizens'/lay judge system and by doing so, has opened up the trial process to greater public participation. This innovative change, however, has created some new challenges for legal interpreters.

Firstly, the prosecutor's office has moved to introduce DVD recorded interrogations so as to provide greater transparency and enhanced visualization of the investigation process, and to discourage the obtaining of false confessions. However, one issue that arises in this context is interpreter-mediated investigations of suspects who are foreign nationals and lack Japanese language skills. The processes involved in such investigations are currently under consideration, in view of the fact that to prepare investigative reports, interpreters are asked to interpret sentence by sentence, and all interpretations are required to be double checked and confirmed. This paper examines the issues posed by interpretation induplicate as related to linguistic equivalency during the investigation. It also proposes a process of single interpretation investigation sessions accompanied by investigative statements drawn up by the prosecutors so as to achieve fairer and more accurate investigations.

Secondly, the Japan Federation of Bar Associations has introduced a new system of legal defence for suspects before and after indictment. Under this system, the legal defence team for the suspect can now remain unchanged both during the investigative and the trial stages of the case. However, the interpreters for the legal defence team prior to the trial and those used during the trial are most likely to be different, which could lead to miscommunication and discrepancies in interpretation due to the lack of continuity in the interpreting team. In view of the above changes, and in an effort to maintain fairness and justice within these new systems, attention needs to be given to eliminating discrepancies in the background information and the legal vocabularies used by interpreters in cases involving foreign national defendants. This paper proposes the following solutions to these issues.

- Bilingual text and standardized vocabularies to be made available to all interpreters
- A certified interpreter system in Japan to ensure a uniform standard of ability for a legal interpreters.

(Continued)

Exercise 8.6 (Continued)

- A register of suitable legal interpreters that is shared and accessed across the legal profession, from the courts to the prosecutors and to the bar associations.

2 María Brander de la Iglesia, University of Salamanca, Spain

From 'should' to 'could' in the Ethos of the Interpreting Community: Landscaping the Critical Garden

With the pedagogical purpose of applying a critical approach to existing paradigms on Ethics in Interpreting Studies (see, for instance, Martín Ruano 2008) we could ask ourselves whether laws may be to justice what a deontological code is to ethics.

Prescriptive 'codes of practice', also known as 'codes of conduct', have traditionally attempted to tell professional interpreters of each specialty what 'should' be done in specific cases where problematic issues had arisen, time and again, in the practice of interpreting. When perusing the literature on the subject of Ethics in Interpreting, whether descriptive or empirical in nature, we see most studies have sought to either describe or prove what it is that interpreters ought to do when confronted with ethical disjunctives. However, Marzocchi (2005) shows us that normative discourse is not static; established norms in practice 'could' or perhaps 'should' change with the times and the ethos –spirit, tone or sentiment– of a given community, or communities. Furthermore, the identity of any community and its sense of cohesiveness may depend largely on whether its members are allowed to participate in the creation of its rules.

This paper seeks to reflect upon issues relative to the Interpreting Community's Ethos and ideas of right and wrong within our 'collective intelligence' (Lévy 1997), especially among educators. Access to training has evolved, as has the social impact teaching methodologies influenced by certain ethical or ideological positions (Freire 1970). The connection of ethics to pedagogical approaches such as Critical Pedagogy or Social Constructivism will be discussed, with the aim of exploring the changing landscape and understanding critical ways of approaching Ethics in the interpreting class.

3 John Walker, University of Sussex

Interpreting Between Two Signed Languages: Changing the Landscape of Interpreting

With over 50 sovereign states in Europe, of which 27 are members of the European Union (EU), these nations have one or more sign languages in each country. The European Council has recommended that each

European nation recognize their sign language(s), since 1988. There are 7339 interpreters in Europe across 23 countries (de Witt 2008), working between their national sign language and national spoken language, and fewer are able to work into English or international sign (as a lingua franca). The European Commission (2009) acknowledges that resorting to a lingua franca cannot replace the effectiveness of interpreting between two parties and their native languages.

Deaf entrepreneurs are venturing into Europe to bring bespoke services to Deaf people in other areas; in a multilingual Europe, this is proving a challenge. The cost of employing three interpreters working in a relay chain from British Sign Language (BSL) to Lingua deSignos Espanola (LSE) via spoken English and Spanish (for example) was simply prohibitive. Deaf people (and some hearing people) who are fluent between two or more sign languages have often provided a service within the community and often without remuneration (Adam/Stone 2007). There is a demand for interpreters to be trained, qualified and registered (Collins/Walker 2005) that will make this specialized resource available in which to increase Deaf people's movement across Europe.

The EuroSign Interpreter project will provide a learning resource for educational institutions to include sign language to sign language interpreting in their programmes, especially in the UK, France, Germany and the Czech Republic. There are several barriers to be overcome: the benchmarking of sign languages against the European Language Framework (CEFRL); the assessment of interpreting between two sign languages where the L2 is not taught or assessed in the host country; and how the teaching of interpreting applies to interpreters working between two sign languages. The project was funded by the EC for a total of €336k over two years and includes a consortium of Universities (Sussex and Hamburg), a UK employment agency in France (Dering Service de l'Emploi) and a professional body of interpreters (CKTZJ). This paper will report on the research progress with support from the consortium and their expert panels.

Exercise 8.6

Refer back to the list of conferences that you wrote down for Exercise 8.5.
   Download the Call for Papers for one of the conferences.
   Write an abstract in response to the Call for Papers, referring to the tips above and the sample abstracts in Example 8.6.

8.5.3 Professional development presentations

The results of research can also be presented by giving professional development workshops or seminar presentations to relevant groups of interpreters or other professionals. For example, Hale's body of research on the discourse of courtroom interpreting (2001, 2002, 2004, 2007, 2011) has led to the regular delivery of sessions about interpreting to judicial officers, tribunal members and lawyers as part of their training (e.g. annual magistrates' conferences, training sessions organized by the different state judicial commissions, by the national judicial college of Australia and the Judicial Institute of Judicial Administration (AIJA) and annual conferences and training sessions organized by the different state and federal tribunals such as the Refugee/Migration Review Tribunal and the Law Society and Bar Association). In this sense, when contemplating the presentation of results to these kinds of audiences, you are beginning to consider how your research can be applied.

8.6 Application of findings

Interpreting research findings can be applied to policy, practice and pedagogy. More recently the trend seems to be to refer to these types of application as 'knowledge transfer and exchange'. Research Councils UK (RCUK) defines 'knowledge transfer' as follows:

> Knowledge transfer describes how knowledge and ideas move between the knowledge source to the potential users of that knowledge. The Research Councils [UK] encourage knowledge transfer by supporting schemes and activities to transfer good ideas, research results and skills between, for example, universities and other research organisations, business, the third sector, public sector and/or the wider community (Research Councils UK 2013b).

Hand in hand with knowledge transfer comes 'knowledge exchange and impact'. RCUK (2013a) states that 'Impact is the demonstrable contribution that excellent research makes to society and the economy. Impact embraces all the extremely diverse ways in which research-related knowledge and skills benefit individuals, organisations and nations by: fostering global economic performance . . . increasing the effectiveness of public services and policy; [and] enhancing quality of life, health and creative output'.

Thus to successfully apply your Interpreting research findings, and have greater impact, you need to consider how to transfer the knowledge from your study to the stakeholders that matter. This means working collaboratively in partnership with those stakeholders to translate research findings into a realistic form of application, making research 'on, for and with' stakeholders (Turner and Harrington 2000). Examples of knowledge transfer from Interpreting research projects include:

- A project on video remote signed language interpreting in court, commissioned by the NSW Department of Justice and Attorney General in Australia, led to recommendations for policy and a trial of signed language interpreting provision via video conference facilities (Napier 2011a);

- Information from Hale's body of research (e.g. 2004; 2011) into court interpreting has been incorporated into benchbooks[3] used by judges in NSW and into different state language policies. Some of Hale's research has been funded by external legal bodies (such as the AIJA, the Victorian Department of Justice or the NSW Department of Attorney General and Justice) and protocols on working with interpreters in the legal system are being discussed based on the results of Hale's research;

- Training has been developed for medical students, medical professionals and interpreters based on healthcare communication research and healthcare interpreting research (Friedman-Rhodes and Hale 2010; Major 2012; Tebble 2003).

8.7 Your future as an interpreting researcher

So, now you have finished your PhD. What is next after graduation? Depending on your background before you entered Interpreting research, you may be considering a career as an interpreter researcher, an interpreter educator or a practitioner; or perhaps all three. If you are keen to continue to engage in Interpreting research, you can either elect to be a 'practisearcher' (Gile 1994) or seek out an academic position. When looking for a job, remember that positions may be available in a variety of different departments, not just interpreting schools. For example, the list of departments listed in Pöchhacker's (1995) profile of 'those who do' Interpreting research, include: Translation and Interpreting, Languages, Economics, Linguistics, Slavic Languages and English.

If you decide to pursue a career as an academic, there is merit in continuing to practice as an interpreter, as interpreter intuitions are often instrumental in guiding research agendas. Practice can inform research, which informs teaching, which then continues to inform practice in a cyclical process (see Hale 2007; Napier 2005a, 2011b). However, balancing the demands of being an academic and maintaining experience as a practitioner can be difficult to juggle (Monikowski, in press).

8.7.1 *Applying for funding*

If an academic teaching-research position is not available, then you could consider applying for a postdoctoral fellowship. Different countries will offer various funding schemes through their research councils or other funding bodies. It is worth affiliating yourself with a university to develop a proposal, and either continue to work with your PhD supervisor or collaborate with other researchers in a different institution (some postdoctoral funding schemes actually encourage moving to a different institution after completing your PhD).

Even if you successfully obtain an academic position, if you are based in a research university, you will be encouraged (if not expected) to apply for research grants, and produce research outputs (i.e. publications), and participate in public engagement and knowledge transfer. One of the keys to success in obtaining research funding is to develop a solid research track record, which includes evidence of publications and research income. So get publishing as soon as you can! Many universities offer internal research grant schemes to support early career researchers to begin to develop a track record, with an expectation that you will go on to secure external research income either through grants (from funding bodies such as research councils), or through commissioned research from government, industry or community organizations. Depending on the type of research you want to conduct, you can explore various sources of grants housed within arts and humanities or social sciences.

The classification of the grant application is important, as your proposal will be reviewed by a panel of experts, so you need to ensure that they understand your approach, methodology and rationale for the project. You cannot guarantee that a grant reviewer will know anything about your field of research, so you need to write in such a way that they can clearly appreciate your work, and be convinced that yours is the project worth funding. Example 8.7 features a letter written to grant writers, with tips from a grant reviewer's perspective. The letter was read out to a session on innovation in research hosted at Macquarie University in Sydney in 2012 by Karina Luzia (with support from Dr Stefan Popenici, the organizer of the event), and was subsequently published as an opinion piece in the Australian Universities' Review journal. With permission, we have reproduced the whole letter here as it provides an excellent, down to earth overview of the best way to approach grant writing, which we felt is said much better by Karina than either of us.

Exercise 8.7

Think about your future career as an Interpreting researcher. Would you like to pursue an academic career? What are your career goals?

Example 8.7: Tips for grant writers (Luzia 2013)

Dear Grant Applicant,

You don't know me but I am a fan. Not just of your current work but of your future work – the work you are going to fund with this grant.

Now I haven't applied for many grants, but I have read a lot of applications – successful and otherwise – and I have sat on quite a few grant committees. And even in this relatively lowly role, I have been at least partly responsible for the passage of a number of applications through the final crucial stages of the grant process. Sometimes I have been partly responsible for applications not getting through. Sometimes I have passionately – and more importantly, successfully – argued for a project I believe in. And sometimes – and there is always a mental fist pump of victory when this happens – I have changed the minds of others regarding what is worth funding.

It's not often I get the chance to address you directly – at least outside my head. Usually any feedback I give on individual applications will be channelled – and somewhat diluted – through the formal committee feedback process and so I am glad to have this opportunity to talk to you, not just as a member of the committee but as someone who has read your application and is now fully prepared to defend you and your ideas – if necessary – to others. So, thank you for this opportunity to tell you directly why I am going into bat for your application.

You've told me a story – the story of your project. And it's a fascinating story too: the tale of an issue or a problem and your quest to find or implement a solution. You have presented me with the whole kit and caboodle, all the juicy detail, from the big, BIG picture stuff down to the work that only lacks funding to make it reality. You have shown me how you, your project team, and your project can be the heroes in this story.

You've made the proper introductions. Because your application is an introduction – not only an introduction to an issue and to a project, but also to your academic/ research/technical/professional field, expertise, profession, maybe even your passion. You've introduced me to some of the most pressing issues in this field. And of course, your application is an introduction to a particular problem of current and great concern, and it is this well-defined and detailed concern represented in and by this grant application that has made me sit up, even though it is midnight and I have just made my way through so many other applications and that wine is looking good.

You've hooked me. In the very first line cast through this application to fund your quest, you've provided me with the broad context and the wider meaning of your project. You've done this by making reference to a broad issue or concern – a reference that captures my interest straight away, no matter who I am or what field I work in; a reference that makes me think

(Continued)

Exercise 8.7 (Continued)

straight away 'Yes. This is important'. Then you have narrowed down that broad frame of reference to focus on one particular aspect to this broader issue, which happens to be the very problem that this project will address. All this within the first few paragraphs.

You've made me mind the gaps. For example, in the opening sections, you've made reference to the relevant literature and to the past and current research, and to the important gaps in this knowledge – enough to show that what you are addressing or trying to do in your project has not yet been researched, achieved, implemented, or even attempted. And it needs to be; now! You have also reassured me. After you have stated the importance and/or urgency and/or necessity of this project or this problem in a scholarly yet accessible way, you have told me – again in a scholarly, accessible way – that you are going to (try to) fix this problem or fill in the gaps with your project and you have told me precisely how you are going to do this.

You've approached this application as a scholarly work. You've shown how this particular issue or problem is evidence-based; that other experts in your field also think this is An Issue. You've presented background research in this area; you are clearly familiar with the literatures related to both field and specific topic; and importantly, you've made reference to the related . . . literature. In doing so, it is apparent that this hasn't been a last-minute pawing through any old text that happens to be lying around or an unthinking use of Big Names and Buzz Words. No, instead, you have demonstrated that this is something that you have been thinking about for some time, and from different angles, and with input from other key thinkers in this area.

You care about my properly understanding what you are trying to accomplish. You've remembered that while I'm a colleague and a peer, I might also be someone who is not necessarily well-versed in your field, and I might need to be informed about some things – concepts, definitions, philosophies, debates – that you have long ago come to terms with during your own extended immersion in this area. Thank you for using up precious application space to succinctly inform me on these important details.

You also care about good communication. You're a good [academic] . . . because your grant application includes succinct and straight-forward explanations of foundational or difficult or complex concepts while minimising jargon; you've explained any necessary technical terms; all the while keeping your sentences short, clear, and to the point. In other words, you haven't forgotten what makes for good written communication in any field from the sciences to the humanities, from IT to HR: clear argument; clear structure; clear sentences; clear explanation of relevant and/or difficult and/or discipline-specific concepts; and last, but perhaps most importantly, clear and engaging writing. And at 11pm, the night before the early-morning grant committee meeting, I am grateful for this clarity that cuts through the fog in my brain that has risen from reading 30 other grant applications that haven't been so focused.

You made it really easy for me to say 'yes' from the outset because you've made sure to provide all the required information outlined in the grant application guidelines. For example, your project rationale includes broad and specific descriptions of the challenge, issue or problem. It details exactly what you, your project collaborators, and the project itself are going to do, and how. You've described exactly how you will be the instigators of change; the providers of evidence-based solutions; the innovators. Your project methodology makes sense, even to someone who is not familiar with the particular methods or techniques used in your field. You've answered the basic methodological questions –what you are going to do; where you are going to do it; how you are going to do it; who you are going to do it with; and why. You've shown that you and your colleagues are primed and ready to go. You've done this by having a realistic project schedule/timeline that includes all resources – financial, human, and material – as well as clearly delineated roles and responsibilities; dissemination strategies; and project milestones. And by 'realistic', I mean you never made me think 'Hmm – I wonder just how they are going to do THAT in that tiny amount of time' or worse – 'They are NEVER going to be able to do that in that timeframe!'. You've been explicit about both the specific project deliverables and the tangible and non-tangible outcomes of the project.

You've provided a realistic and legitimate budget with realistic and legitimate expenses. You haven't asked for non-allowable items such as laptops and iPads. These tempting items are usually only funded if they are only ever going to be used in and for this one project – something that is rather hard to demonstrate. Crucially too, your budget hasn't made the calculator appear, whether the night before the meeting, or when somebody calls (yells) for one in the grant committee meeting. You don't want to be the application with the weird figures that makes the calculator appear because you know that if the calculator appears, and if your budget doesn't add up, your ability to pay attention to the details that are critical to any project's success will be in doubt.

Admiring your attention to detail regarding your budget reminds me of another thing that reassures me as to your ability to manage this project successfully – your adherence to the relatively few and simple formatting rules. You've used the right font (Times New Roman) and font size (12pt), line spacing (single) and paragraph spacing (6pt) and length (6 pages). You've shown you care enough about this application to not distract your reader with ostensibly minor formatting errors that nonetheless put your ability to follow the simplest of instructions in doubt. I could rant about the experience of reading an application written in 10pt Arial with no paragraph spacing and after reading eleventy-hundred other applications that didn't test my

(*Continued*)

Exercise 8.7 (Continued)

eyesight or bring on migraines. Or how much I resent reading one word over the 6 page limit. But I won't. I'll just say that the formatting and length of your document is not the place to get innovative or creative.

You've also got a plan to show success (or otherwise). In other words, your project has evaluation strategies that will monitor the effectiveness (or otherwise) of:

the project methodology
the strategies you have used for implementing the project
the dissemination strategies
project outcomes and
project's potential to support change, innovation and/ or reform.

You've made it known that others – important others – think this project is not only a great idea but a needed intervention. You've included the necessary endorsements from respective staff (Head of Departments, Associate Deans, Executive Dean etc.) however, it is also clear that you have had advice and feedback from trusted colleagues and mentors on your application, because this application is obviously not a first or even a second draft.

Where possible too, you've referred to whatever local support is available, whether through additional funds, reduced workload, administrative assistance, thereby showing that your department is willing to put its money where its mouth is – in this time of widespread budget deficits, a powerful indicator of project value. Think of this as the support from your local village to go on your heroic quest.

And by doing all of the above, you have been clever and you have made your application work for you in a number of ways. You have made your application a multi-functional document that is not only a funding instrument, but also a valuable dissemination device that shows your willingness to use every opportunity to let people know about this important work that needs to be done. You have also made this application work for you as a key reference document for your project. As such, this application is not only going to get you money, it is going to be your first port of call whenever you need to check that the project is on track and for reporting back to the funding body.

Perhaps most importantly . . . you've shared your vision. I am not in your area or in your field. But your application has made me see the gaps – or chasms – that exist in your field, and your application has left me in no doubt as to how your project can start to fill some of these gaps. Even – and this is important – even if this project fails, it will be a splendid failure born of a red-hot go.

In reading your application I've learnt something beyond your immediate need for funds. I've learnt about your field and discipline, about its methods and its concerns, but also a little about what makes working in your field so exciting. In fact you've made me want to learn more – I want to sit in on one of your lectures, or work with you on a project, or at very least, chat some more about this particular project with you. You've made me blurt out things like 'Nifty!', 'Oh, now that is cool!' or 'Excellent!' You've made me fantasise, however briefly, about working on this project with you, not just because you've engaged me through a well written and presented application but you've shown that this project matters.

Most of all you've invited me to become invested. . . . You've shown that you care, not only about a particular issue, but also about the themes and intent of the grant programme itself; enough to spend your valuable time putting together a tight, well-written, strictly-formatted application for a scholarly, methodologically rigorous, evidence-based project that will contribute to positive change.

So thank you – not just for doing this all so well that you have made it easy for me to go into that meeting and argue (if necessary) for your application, but also for giving me the opportunity to play a tiny part in your quest.

Yours in innovation and scholarship,

Your grant application reader and committee member,
Karina Luzia,
Macquarie University

Featured in Australian Universities' Review, 55(1), (2013), pp. 66–8. Reproduced with permission.

8.8 Conclusion

In wrapping up this book, this chapter has discussed essential elements of conducting and disseminating Interpreting research, including suggestions for conducting mixed-methods or innovative research, your role as an interpreting researcher and positioning your research; how to report and disseminate research through theses, publications and conference presentations. Finally, we have considered life after the PhD, and provided ideas for your future as an interpreter researcher. For some light-hearted reading about doing social science research and balancing life with doing research, we recommend that you read Luker (2008), who provides a witty and common-sensical approach to developing a research proposal, doing a literature review, conducting research, and writing-up.

We hope we have been able to assist you in your research journey and look forward to reading the results of your studies!

Further reading

Gile, D., Dam, H. V., Dubslaff, F., Martinsen, B. and Scholdager, A. (eds) (2001). *Getting started in interpreting research: Methodological reflections, personal accounts and advice for beginners*. Amsterdam: John Benajmins.

Luker, K. (2008). *Salsa dancing into the social sciences: Research in an age of info glut*. Cambridge, MA: Harvard University Press.

Nicodemus, B. and Swabey, L. (eds) (2011). *Advances in interpreting research: Inquiry in action*. Philadelphia: John Benjamins.

Winston, E. and Monikowski, C. (eds) (in press). *Evolving paradigms in interpreter education: Impact of interpreting research on teaching interpreting*. Washington, DC: Gallaudet University.

Notes

1   For an example of university guidelines that promote TBP, see Macquarie University in Sydney – http://mq.edu.au/policy/docs/hdr_thesis/guideline_by_publication.html.

2   For a more comprehensive list of translation and interpreting studies journals, see Napier, J. (2011). If a tree falls in the forest, does it make a noise? The merits of publishing interpreting research. In B. Nicodemus and L. Swabey (eds), Advances in Interpreting Research: Inquiry in Action. Philadelphia: John Benjamins, pp. 121–52.

3   See for example http://www.judcom.nsw.gov.au/publications/benchbks/local/interpreters.html.

REFERENCES

Adamowicz, A. (1989). The role of anticipation in discourse: Text processing in simultaneous interpreting. *Polish Psychological Bulletin*, 20(2), 153–60.

Ainsworth-Vaughn, N. (2001). The discourse of medical encounters. In D. Schiffrin, D. Tannen and H. Hamilton (eds), *The handbook of discourse analysis*. Massachusetts and Oxford: Blackwell, pp. 453–69.

Alvstad, C., Hild, A. and Tiselius, E. (2011). Methods and strategies of process research: Integrative approaches in translation studies. In C. Alvstad, A. Hild and E. Tiselius (eds), *Methods and Strategies of Process Research*. Amsterdam: John Benjamins, pp. 1–12.

Amato, A. (2007). The interpreter in multi-party medical encounters. In C. Wadensjö, B. E. Dimitrova and A. Nilsson (eds), *The Critical Link 4: Professionalisation of interpreting in the community*. Philadelphia: John Benjamins, pp. 27–38.

Andres, L. (2012). *Designing & doing survey research*. London: SAGE.

Angelelli, C. (2004a). *Medical interpreting and cross-cultural communication*. London: Cambridge University Press.

— (2004b). *Revisiting the interpreter's role: A study of conference, court and medical interpreting in Canada, Mexico, and the United States*. Amsterdam: John Benjamins.

Angelelli, C. and Jacobson, H. (2009). Introduction: Testing and assessment in translation and interpreting studies: A call for dialogue between research and practice. In C. V. Angelelli and H. E. Jacobson (eds), *Testing and Assessment in Translation and Interpreting Studies*. Amsterdam: John Benjamins, pp. 1–12.

Auer, P. (1998). Learning how to play the game: An investigation of role-played job interviews in East Germany. *Text: An Interdisciplinary Journal of Language, Discourse & Communication Studies*, 18(1), 7–38.

Austin, J. (1962). *How to do things with words*. Oxford: Oxford University Press.

Bain, K. (2004). *What the best college teachers do*. Harvard: Harvard University Press.

Baker, D. (2004). *Language testing: A critical survey and practical guide*. London: Edward Arnold.

Ball, C. (2007). *The history of American Sign Language interpreting education*. Unpublished doctoral dissertation, Capella University, Minneapolis, MN, USA.

Banna, K. (2004). Auslan interpreting: What can we learn from translation theory? *Deaf Worlds*, 20, 100–19.

Bargiela-Chiappini, F., Nickerson, C. and Planken, B. (2007). *Business discourse*. Basingstoke: Palgrave Macmillan.

Barik, H. A. (1975). Simultaneous interpretation: Qualitative and linguistic data. *Language and Speech*, 18, 272–97.

— (1994). A description of various types of omissions, additions and errors of translation encountered in simultaneous interpretation. In S. Lambert and B. Moser-Mercer (eds), *Bridging the gap: Empirical research in simultaneous interpretation*. Amsterdam: John Benjamins, pp. 121–38.

Barnett, R. (1994). *The limits of competence: Knowledge, higher education and society*. Buckingham: Open University Press, pp. 140–53.

Bartlomiejczyk, M. (2006). Strategies of simultaneous interpreting and directionality. *Interpreting*, 8, 149–74.

— (2007). Interpreting quality as perceived by trainee interpreters: Self-evaluation. *The Interpreter and Translator Trainer*, 1(2), 247–67.

Bax, S. (2011). *Discourse and genre*. Basingstoke: Palgrave Macmillan.

Bell, S. J. (1997). The challenges of setting and monitoring the standards of community interpreting: An Australian perspective. In R. Roberts, A. Dufour and D. Steyn (eds), *The Critical Link: Interpreters in the community*. Amsterdam: John Benjamins, pp. 93–108.

Bendazzoli, C. (2012). From international conference to machine-readable corpora and back: An ethnographic approach to simultaneous interpreter-mediated communicative events. In F. S. Sergio and C. Falbo (eds), *Breaking ground in corpus-based interpreting studies*. Bern: Peter Lan, pp. 91–118.

Berk-Seligson, S. (1990). *The bilingual courtroom: Court interpreters in the judicial process*. Chicago: The University of Chicago Press.

— (2002). *The bilingual courtroom: Court interpreters in the judicial process*. Chicago: The University of Chicago Press.

Biagini, M. (2012). Data collection in the courtroom: Challenges and perspectives for the researcher. In F. S. Sergio and C. Falbo (eds), *Breaking ground in corpus-based interpreting studies*. Bern: Peter Lan, pp. 231–52.

Biber, D. (2012). Register and discourse analysis. In J. P. Gee and M. Handford (eds), *The Routledge handbook of discourse analysis*. New York: Routledge, pp. 191–208.

Bloch, A. (2004). Doing social surveys. In C. Seale (ed.), *Researching society and culture*. London: SAGE, pp. 163–78.

Blommaert, J. (2005). Bourdieu the ethnographer. *The Translator*, 11(2), 219–36.

Boéri, J. and de Manuel Jerez, J. (2011). From training skilled conference interpreters to educating reflective citizens: A case study of the Marius action research project. *The Interpreter & Translator Trainer*, 5(1), 41–64.

The Bologna Declaration (1999). Report from the European Commission. Available: http://www.bologna-bergen2005.no/Docs/00-Main_doc/990719BOLOGNA_DECLARATION.PDF

Bontempo, K. (in press). The chicken and the egg dilemma: Academizing a semiprofession. In E. Winston and C. Monikowski (eds), *Evolving paradigms in interpreter education: Impact of interpreting research on teaching interpreting*. Washington, DC: Gallaudet University.

Bontempo, K. and Levitzke-Gray, P. (2009). Interpreting down under: Sign language interpreter education and training in Australia. In J. Napier (ed.), *International perspectives on sign language interpreter education*. Washington, DC: Gallaudet University Press.

Boud, D. and Feletti, G. I. (eds) (1997). *The challenge of problem-based learning* (2nd edn). London: Kogan Page.

Brennan, M. and Brown, R. (1997). *Equality before the law: Deaf people's access to justice*. Durham: Deaf Studies Research Unit, University of Durham.

Brewer, J. and Hunter, A. (2006). *Foundations of multimethod research: Synthesizing styles*. Thousandoaks, CA: SAGE.

Brown, G. and Yule, G. (1983). *Discourse analysis*. Cambridge: Cambridge University Press.

Brown, P. and Levinson, S. (1987). *Politeness: Some universals in language usage*. Cambridge: Cambridge University Press.

Brunette, L., Bastin, G., Hemlin, I. and Clarke, H. (eds) (2003). *The Critical Link 3: Interpreters in the community*. Amsterdam: John Benjamins.

Bryman, A. (2004). *Social research methods*. New York: Oxford University Press.

Buogucki, L. (ed.), (2010). *Teaching translation and interpreting: Challenges and practices*. Newcastle-Upon-Tyne: Cambridge Scholars Publishing.

Burns, A. (1999). *Collaborative action research for English language teachers*. Cambridge: Cambridge University Press.

— (2010). Action research. In B. Paltridge and A. Phakiti (eds), *Continuum companion to research methods in applied linguistics*. London: Continuum, pp. 80–97.

Burns, R. B. (1994). *Introduction to research methods* (2nd edn). Melbourne: Longman Cheshire.

— (1997). *Introduction to research methods* (3rd edn). Melbourne: Addison Wesley Longman.

Burton, S. and Steane, P. (eds) (2004). *Surviving your thesis*. London: Routledge.

Cambridge, J. (1999). Information loss in bilingual medical interviews through an untrained interpreters. *The Translator*, 5(2), 201–19.

Carr, S., Roberts, R., Dufour, A. and Steyn, D. (eds) (1997). *The Critical Link: Interpreters in the community*. Amsterdam and Philadelphia: John Benjamins.

Carspecken, P. F. (1996). *Critical ethnography in educational research; A theoretical and practical guide*. NY: London: Routledge.

Chernov, G. V. (2004). *Inference and anticipation in simultaneous interpreting*. Amsterdam: John Benjamins.

Chesterman, A. and Wagner, E. (2004). *Can theory help translators: A dialogue between the ivory tower and the wordface*. Manchester: St. Jerome.

Chincotta, D. and Underwood, G. (1998). Simultaneous interpreters and the effect of concurrent articulation on immediate memory: A bilingual digit span study. *Interpreting*, 3(1), 1–20.

Cho, J. and Roger, P. (2010). Improving interpreting performance through theatrical training. *The Interpreter & Translator Trainer*, 4(2), 151–71.

Christoffels, I. K., De Groot, A. M. B. and Kroll, J. F. (2006). Memory and language skills in simultaneous interpreters: The role of expertise and language proficiency. *Journal of Memory and Language*, 54(3), 324–45.

Christoffels, I. K., De Groot, A. M. B. and Waldorp, L. J. (2003). Basic skills in a complex task: A graphical model relating memory and lexical retrieval to simultaneous interpreting. *Bilingualism: Language and Cognition*, 6(3), 201–11.

Cicourel, A. (1999). The interaction of cognitive and cultural models in health care delivery. In S. Sarangi and C. Roberts (eds), *Talk, work and institutional order*. Berlin and New York: Mouton de Gruyter, pp. 183–224.

Cirillo, L. (2012). Managing affective communication in triadic exchanges: Interpreters' zero-renditions and non-renditions in doctor-patient talk. In C. J. Kellett (ed.), *Interpreting across genres: Multiple research perspectives*. Trieste: EUT Edizioni Universtà di Trieste, pp. 102–24.

Clayman, S. E. and Gill, V. T. (2012). Conversation analysis. In J. P. Gee and M. Handford (eds), *The Routledge handbook of discourse analysis*. New York: Routledge, pp. 120–34.

Clifford, A. (2005). Putting the exam to the test: Psychometric validation and interpreter certification. *Interpreting*, 7(1), 97–131.

Clough, P. and Nutbrown, C. (2007). *A student's guide to methodology* (2nd edn). London: Sage.

Cohen, L., Manion, L. and Morrison, K. (2011). *Research methods in education* (7th edn). Abingdon, Oxon: Routledge.

Cokely, D. (1992). Effects of lag time on interpreter errors. In D. Cokely (ed.), *Sign language interpreters and interpreting*. Burtonsville, MD: Linstok Press, pp. 39–69.

Converse, J. M. and Presser, S. (1986). *Survey questions: Handicrafting the standardized questionnaire*. Newbury Park: Sage.

Cordella, M. (2004). *The dynamic consultation. A discourse analytical study of doctor-patient communication*. Amsterdam and Philadelphia: John Benjamins.

Cornwall, F. (2011). Creating your own materials for use in the interpreting classroom. *International Journal of Interpreter Education*, 3, 49–55.

Coulthard, M. (1985). *An introduction to discourse analysis*. London: Longman.

— (2004). Whose voice is it? Invented and concealed dialogue in written records of verbal evidence produced by police. In J. Cotterill (ed.), *Language in the legal process*. New York: Palgrave Macmillan, pp. 19–34.

Coulthard, M. and Johnson, A. (2007). *An introduction to forensic linguistics: Language in evidence*. London and New York: Routledge.

Cragg, S. (2002). Peeling back the skins of an onion. *Deaf Worlds*, 18, 56–61.

Cresswell, J. (1994). *Research design: Qualitative and quantitative approaches*. London: Sage.

Crowley, K. (2007). The literature review: Not sinking, writing. In C. Denholm and T. Evans (eds), *Supervising doctorates downunder*. Camberwell: Acer Press.

Dal Fovo, E. (2012). Topical coherence in television interpreting: Question/answer rendition. In F. S. Sergio and C. Falbo (eds), *Breaking ground in corpus-based interpreting studies*. Bern: Peter Lang, pp. 187–209.

Davidson, B. (2000). The interpreter as institutional gatekeeper: The social-linguistic role of interpreters in Spanish-English medical discourse. *Journal of Sociolinguistics*, 4(3), 379–405.

Dean, R. K. and Pollard, R. Q. (2011). Context-based ethical reasoning in interpreting: A demand control schema perspective. *The Interpreter & Translator Trainer*, 5(1), 155–82.

Delbridge, A., Bernard, J., Blair, D., Butler, S., Peters, P. and Yallop, C. (eds) (2003). *The Macquarie Dictionary*. Sydney: Macquarie Library.

DeNeve, K. M. and Heppner, M. J. (1997). Role play simulations: The assessment of an active learning technique and comparisons with traditional lectures. *Innovative Higher Education*, 21(3), 231–46.

Denny, T. (1978). *Story Telling and Educational Understanding. Paper #12 in Occasional Paper Series*. Paper presented at the Annual Meeting of the International Reading Association.

Dickinson, J. (2002). Telephone interpreting-Hello, is anyone there? *Deaf Worlds*, 18, 34–8.

— (2010). *Interpreting in a community of practice: A sociolinguistic study of the signed language interpreter's role in workplace discourse*. Heriot-Watt University, Edinburgh, Scotland.

Dickinson, J. and Turner, G. H. (2008). Sign language interpreters and role conflict in the workplace. In C. Valero-Garces and A. Martin (eds), *Crossing borders in community interpreting: Definition and dilemmas*. Amsteram: John Benjamins, pp. 231–44.

Dollerup, C. and Appel, V. (eds) (1996). *Teaching translation and interpreting 3: New horizons*. Amsterdam: John Benjamins.

Dollerup, C. and Loddegaard, A. (eds) (1991). *Teaching translation & interpreting: training, talent & experience*. Amsterdam: John Benjamins.

— (1994). *Teaching translation & interpreting 2*. Amsterdam: John Benjamins.

Dörnyei, Z. (2007). *Research in applied linguistics*. Oxford: Oxford University Press.

Drew, P. (1992). Contested evidence in courtroom cross-examination: The case of a trial for rape. In P. Drew and J. Heritage (eds), *Talk at work: Interaction in institutional settings*. Cambridge: Cambridge University Press, pp. 470–520.

Durranti, A. (ed.). (2009). *Linguistic anthropology: A reader*. Chichester, West Sussex, UK: Wiley-Blackwell.

Dweck, C. S. (2006). *Mindset: The new psychology of success*. NY: Ballantine.

Edwards, R. (1998). A critical examination of the use of interpreters in qualitative research. *Journal of Ethnic and Migration Studies*, 24(1), 197–208.

Engel, C. E. (1992). Problem-based learning. *British Journal of Hospital Medicine*, 48(6), 325–9.

Englund Dimitrova, B. and Hyltenstam, K. (eds) (2000). *Language processing and simultaneous interpreting: interdisciplinary perspectives*. Amsterdam: John Benjamins.

Ericsson, K. A. (2001). Expertise in interpreting: An expert-performance perspective. *Interpreting: International Journal of Research and Practice in Interpreting*, 5(2), 187–221.

Evans, D. and Gruba, P. (2002). *How to write a better thesis*. Melbourne: Melbourne University Press.

Fairclough, N. (1992). *Discourse and social change*. Oxford: Polity Press.

Fern, E. F. (1983). Focus groups: A review of some contradictory evidence, implications, and suggestions for future research. *Advances in Consumer Research*, 10, 121–6.

Finton, L. (2005). Compression strategies: ASL to English interpreting. *Journal of Interpretation*, 49–64.

Flowerdew, L. (2012). Corpus-based discourse analysis. In J. P. Gee and M. Handford (eds), *The Routledge handbook of discourse analysis*. New York: Routledge, pp. 174–87.

Foxcroft, L. (3/1/2012). This much we know: There's fat chance of staying slim. *The Sydney morning Herald*, p. 9. Retrieved from http://www.smh.com.au/action/printArticle?id=2869626

Friedman-Rhodes, E. and Hale, S. (2010). Teaching medical students to work with interpreters. *The Journal of Specialised Translation*, 14, 121–44.

Fullan, M. G. (1991). *The new meaning of educational change*. London: Cassell.

Gavioli, L. and Baraldi, C. (2011). Interpreter-mediated interaction in healthcare and legal settings. Talk organization, context and achievement of intercultural communication. *Interpreting*, 13(2), 205–33.

Gee, J. P. (2011). *An introduction to discourse analysis: Theory and method* (3rd edn). New York: Routledge.

Gee, J. P. and Handford, M. (2012). Introduction. In J. P. Gee and M. Handford (eds), *The Routledge handbook of discourse analysis*. New York: Routledge, pp. 1–6.

Geertz, C. (1973). *The interpretation of cultures*. New York: Basic Books.

Gentzler, E. (2001). *Contemporary translation theories* (2nd edn). Clevedon, UK: Multilingual Matters.

Gibbons, J. (1990). Applied linguistics in court. *Applied Linguistics*, 11, 229–37.

— (2003). *Forensic Linguistics*. Malden; Oxford: Blackwell.

Giddens, A., Duneier, M. and Appelbaum, R. P. (2009). *An introduction to sociology* (7th edn). London: W. W. Norton & Company.

Gile, D. (1990). Scientific research vs.personal theories in the investigation of interpretation. In L. Gran and T. Christopher (eds), *Aspects of applied and experimental research on conference interpretation*. Udine: Campanotto Editore, pp. 28–41.

— (1994). Opening up in interpretation studies. In M. Snell-Hornby, F. Pöchhacker and K. Kaindl (eds), *Translation studies: An interdiscipline*, Vol. 2. Amsterdam: John Benjamin, pp. 149–58.

— (1995). *Basic concepts and models for interpreter and translator training*. Amsterdam; Philadelphia: J. Benjamins Pub. Co.

— (1998). Observational studies and experimental studies in the investigation of conference interpreting. *Target,* 10(1), 69–93.

— (2009). *Basic concepts and models for interpreter and translator training* (revised edn). Amsterdam; Philadelphia: John Benjamins Pub. Co.

— (ed.) (2001). *Getting started in interpreting research: Methodological reflections, personal accounts and advice for beginners*. Amsterdam; Philadelphia: J. Benjamins Pub. Co.

Gile, D., Dam, H. V., Dubslaff, F., Martinsen, B. and Scholdager, A. (eds) (2001). *Getting started in interpreting research: Methodological reflections, personal accounts and advice for beginners*. Amsterdam: John Benajmins.

Glaser, B. G. and Strauss, A. (1967). *Discovery of grounded theory: Strategies for qualitative research*. New York: Aldine.

Goffman, E. (1981). *Forms of talk*. Oxford: Basil Blackwell.

Gonzáles-Davies, M. (2004). *Multiple voices in the translation classroom: Activities, tasks, and projects*. Amsterdam; Philadelphia: John Benjamins.

Grice, P. (1975). Logic and conversation. In P. Cole and J. Morgan (eds), *Syntax and semantics*, Vol. 3. New York: Academic Press, pp. 41–58.

Gumperz, J. J. (1981). The linguistic bases of comunicative competence. In D. Tannen (ed.), *Analyzing discourse: Text and talk*. Washington D.C.: Georgetown University Press, pp. 323–34.

— (ed.) (1982). *Discourse strategies*. Cambridge: Cambridge University Press.

Hale, S. (2001). How are courtroom questions interpreted? An analysis of spanish interpreters' practices. In I. Mason (ed.), *Triadic exchanges studies in dialogue interpreting*. Manchester: St. Jerome, pp. 21–50.

— (2002). How faithfully do Court interpreters render the style of non-English speaking witnesses's testimonies? A data based study of Spanish-English bilingual proceedings. *Discourse Studies*, 4(1), 25–47.

— (2004). *The discourse of court interpreting. Discourse practices of the law, the witness and the interpreter*. Amsterdam and Philadelphia: John Benjamins.

— (2007). *Community interpreting*. Hampshire: Palgrave Macmillan.

— (2011). *Interpreter policies, practices and protocols in Australian Courts and Tribunals. A national survey*. Melbourne: Australian Institute of Judicial Administration.

Hale, S., Bond, N. and Sutton, J. (2011). Interpreting accent in the courtroom. *Target*, 23(1), 48–61.

Hale, S., Garcia, I., Hlavac, J., Kim, M., Lai, M., Turner, B., and Slatyer, H. (2012). *Improvements to NAATI Testing: Development of a conceptual overview for a new model for NAATI standards, testing and assessment*. Sydney: University of New South Wales.

Hale, S. and Ozolins, U. (forthcoming in 2014). Monolingual short courses for language-specific accreditation: Can they work? A Sydney experience. *The Interpreter and Translation Trainer*, 8(2), TBA.

Hale, S., Ozolins, U. and Stern, L. (eds) (2009). *Critical Link 5. Quality in interpreting: A shared responsibility*. Amsterdam/Philadephia: John Benjamins P/C.

Hall, J. K. (2002). *Teaching and researching language and culture*. London: Longman Pearson.

Hall, R. (2008). *Applied social research: Planning, designing and conducting real-world research*. South Yarra, Vic.: Palgrave MacMillan.

Hammersley, M. (1990). *Reading ethnographic research: A critical guide*. London: Longman.

Harmer, J. (2007). Relay interpretation: A preliminary study. In F. Pöchhacker, A. Jakobsen and I. M. Mees (eds), *Interpreting studies and beyond*. Copenhagen: Samfundslitteratur Press, pp. 73–88.

Hartley, A., Mason, I., Peng, G. and Perez, I. (2003). *Peer- and self-assessment in conference interpreting training*. York, UK: Subject Centre for Languages, Linguistics & Area Studies, Higher Education Academy.

Hema, Z. (2002). Dialogism. *Deaf Worlds*, 18, 62–5.

Hess, J. M. (1968). Group Interviewing. In R. L. King (ed.), *ACR fall conference proceedings*. Chicago, Illinois: American Marketing Association, pp. 193–6.

Heyl, B. S. (2001). Ethnographic interviewing. In P. Atkinson, A. Coffey, S. Delamount, J. Lofland and L. Lofland (eds), *Handbook of ethnography*. London: Sage, pp. 368–83.

Holmes, J., Marra, M. and Vine, B. (2011). *Leadership, discourse and ethnicity*. Oxford: Oxford University Press.

Holmes, J. S. (2000). The name and nature of translation studies. In L. Venuti (ed.), *The translation studies reader*. London; NY: Routledge, pp. 172–85.

Huang, T.-l. (2006). *A study of applying portfolio assessment in an interpreter training course*. Unpublished thesis, Department of Foreign Language Studies, National Taiwan University of Science and Technology, Taipei.

Hubscher-Davidson, S. and Borodo, M. (eds) (2012). *Global trends in translator and interpreter training*. London: Continuum.

Hull, S. (2002). To interpret . . . or not to interpret. *Deaf Worlds*, 18, 50–5.

Hurtado Albir, A. (1999). *Enseñar a traducir*. Madrid: Edelsa.

Hutchings, P. and Shulman, L. S. (1999). The scholarship of teaching: New elaborations, new developments. *Change*, 31(5), 10–15.

Hyland, K. (2004). *Disciplinary discourses: Social interactions in academic writing* (Michigan classics edn). Ann Arbor: University of Michigan Press.

Hymes, D. (1974). *Foundations in sociolinguistics: An ethnographic approach.* Philadelphia, PA: University of Pennsylvania Press.

Hyönäa, J., Tommolaa, J. and Alaja, A. M. (1995). Pupil dilation as a measure of processing load in simultaneous interpretation and other language tasks. *The Quarterly Journal of Experimental Psychology Section A: Human Experimental Psychology,* 48(3), 598–612.

Isham, W. and Lane, H. (1994). A common conceptual code in bilinguals: Evidence from simultaneous interpretation. *Sign Language Studies,* 23, 291–317.

Ivanova, A. (2000). The use of retrospection in research on simultaneous interpreting. In S. Tirkkonen-Condit and R. Jääskeläinen (eds), *Tapping and mapping the processes of translation and interpreting.* Amsterdam: John Benjamins, pp. 27–52.

Jacobsen, B. (2008). Interactional pragmatics and court interpreting An analysis of face. *Interpreting,* 10(1), 128–58.

Jarvis, P. (2004). *Adult education and lifelong learning: Theory and practice* (3rd edn). London: RoutledgeFarmer.

Jefferson, G. (1974). Error correction as an interactional resource. *Language in society,* 2, 181–99.

Johnson, D. M. (1992). *Approaches to research in second-language research.* New York: Longman.

Johnson, D. W. and Johnson, R. T. (1994). *Learning together and alone: Cooperative, competitive, and individualistic learning* (4th edn). Boston: Allyn and Bacon.

Johnson, R. B., Onwuegbuzie, A. J. and Turner, L. A. (2007). Toward a definition of mixed methods research. *Journal of Mixed Methods Reseach,* 1(2), 112–33.

Johnston, T. and Schembri, A. (2007). *Australian sign language (Auslan): An introduction to sign linguistics.* Cambridge: Cambridge University Press.

Johnstone, B. (2009). *Discourse analysis.* Oxford: Blackwell.

Kalina, S. (2005). Quality in the interpreting process: What can be measured and how? *Communication & Cognition,* 38(1–2), 27–46.

Kember, D. (2002). Long-term outcomes of educational action research projects. *Educational Action Research,* 10, 83–103.

Kern, B. (2001). Using role play simulation and hands-on models to enhance students' learning fundamental accounting concepts. *Journal of the Scholarship of Teaching and Learning,* 1(1), 8–24.

Kiraly, D. (2000). *A social constructivist approach to translator education: Empowerment from theory to practice.* Manchester: St. Jerome.

Knowles, M., Holton, E. F. and Swanson, R. A. (2005). *The adult learner: The definitive classic in adult education and human resource development* (6th edn). Boston: Elsevier.

Ko, L. (2008). Teaching interpreting by distance mode: An empirical study. *Meta,* 53(4), 814–40.

Kopczynski, A. (1980). *Conference interpreting: Some linguistic and communicative problems.* Poznan: Adam Mickiewicz Press.

Krathwohl, D. R. (1998). *Methods of educational and social science research. An integrated approach.* (2nd edn). NY: Longman.

Krippendorff, K. (2004). *Content analysis: An introduction to its methodology* (2nd edn). Thousand Oaks, CA: Sage Publications.

Krystallidou, D. K. (2012). On mediating agents' moves and how they might affect patient-centredness in mediated medical consultations. *Linguistica antverpiensia,* 11, 75–94.

Kumar, R. (2011). *Research methodology: A step-by-step guide for beginners* (3rd edn). London: SAGE.

Larochelle, M. and Bednarz, N. (1998). Constructivism and education: Beyond epistemological correctness. In M. Larochelle, N. Bednarz and J. Garrison (eds), *Constructivism and education.* Cambridge: Cambridge University Press, pp. 3–22.

Lee, A. (1992). Poststructuralism and educational research: Some categories and issues. *Australian educational researcher,* 2(1), 1–12.

Leeson, L. and Foley-Cave, S. (2007). Deep and meaningful conversation: Challenging interpreter impartiality in the semantics and pragmatics classroom. In M. Metzger and E. Fleetwood (eds), *Translation, sociolinguistic, and consumer issues in interpreting.* Washington, DC: Gallaudet University Press, pp. 45–70.

Leeson, L., Wurm, S. and Vermeerbergen, M. (2011). "Hey Presto!": Prepraration, practice and performance in the world of signed language interpreting and translation. In L. Leeson, S. Wurm and M. Vermeerbergen (eds), *Signed language interpreting: preparation, practice and performance.* Manchester: St. Jerome, pp. 1–11.

Leigh Smith, B. and MacGregor, J. T. (1992). What is collaborative learning? In A. Goodsell, M. Mather and V. Tinto (eds), *Collaborative learning: A sourcebook for higher education.* University Park, PA: National Centre on Post Secondary Teaching, Learning and Assessment (NCLTA), pp. 9–22.

Lester, S. (1999). An introduction to phenomenological research. Retrieved 10 September 2010, from http://www.sld.demon.co.uk/resmethy.pdf

Liamputtong, P. (2010). *Performing qualitative cross-cultural research.* Cambridge: Cambridge University Press.

Lim, L. (2013). Examining students' perceptions of computer-assisted interpreter training. *The Interpreter & Translator Trainer,* 7(1), 71–89.

Liu, M. (2011). Methodology in interpreting studies. A methodological review of evidence-based research. In B. Nicodemus and L. Swabey (eds), *Advances in interpreting research. Inquiry in action.* Amsterdam & Philadelphia: John Benjamins Publishing Company, pp. 85–119.

Loftus, E. (1979). *Eyewitness testimony.* Cambridge, MA: Harvard University Press.

Luker, K. (2008). *Salsa dancing into the social sciences: Research in an age of info glut.* Cambridge, MA: Harvard University Press.

Luzia, K. (2013). Dear grant applicant. *Australian Universities' Review,* 55(1), 66–8.

Macnamara, B. N., Moore, A. B., Kegl, J. A. and Conway, A. R. A. (2011). Domain-general cognitive abilities and simultaneous interpreting skill. *Interpreting,* 13(1), 121–42.

Major, G. (2012). "What happens truly, not text book!": Using authentic interactions in discourse training for healthcare interpreters. In K. Malcolm and L. Swabey (eds), *In our hands: Educating healthcare interpreters.* Washington, DC: Gallaudet University Press, pp. 27–53.

— (2013). *Healthcare interpreting as relational practice.* Unpublished doctoral thesis, Macquarie University, Sydney.

Major, G. and Napier, J. (2012). Interpreting and knowledge mediation in the healthcare setting: What do we really mean by "accuracy"?. In M. Shuttleworth and V. Montalt (eds), *Linguistica Antiverpiesa*. Antwerp: University Press Antwerp, pp. 207–226.

Malone, E. and Spieth, A. (2012). Team-based learning in a subsection of a veterinary course as compared to standard lectures. *Journal of the Scholarship of Teaching and Learning*, 12(3), 88–107.

Martinsen, B. and Dubslaff, F. (2010). The cooperative courtroom. A case study of interpreting gone wrong. *Interpreting*, 12(1), 21–59.

Mason, I. (2000). Models and methods in dialogue interpreting research. In M. Olohan (ed.), *Intercultural fault lines. Research models in translation studies I. Textual and cognitive aspects*. Manchester: St. Jerome Publishing, pp. 215–32.

— (2004). Conduits, mediators, spokespersons: Investigating translator/interpreter behaviour. In C. Schäffner (ed.), *Translation research and interpreting research. Traditions, gaps and synergies*. Clevedon/Buffalo/Toronto: Multilingual Matters, pp. 88–97.

Massaro, D. and Shlesinger, M. (1997). Information processing and a computational approach to the study of simultaneous interpretation. *Interpreting*, 2(1–2), 13–53.

Maxwell, J. A. (2013). *Qualitative research design: An interactive approach* (3rd edn). Thousand Oaks, CA, USA: Sage Publications.

McGaw, B., Boud, D., Poole, M., Wary, R. and McKenzie, P. (1992). *The impact of educational research*. Canberra: AGPS.

Merten, K. (1983). *Inhaltsanalyse. Einführung in theorie, methode und praxis*. Opladen: Westdeutscher Verlag.

Metzger, M. (1999). *Sign language interpreting. Deconstructing the myth of neutrality*. Washington D.C.: Gallaudet University Press.

— (2000). Interactive role plays as a teaching strategy. In C. Roy (ed.), *Innovative practices for teaching sign language interpreters*. Washington, D.C.: Gallaudet University Press, pp. 83–108.

Meyerhoff, M. (2008). Communities of practice. In J. K. Chambers, P. Trudgill and Schilling-Estes (eds), *The handbook of language variation and change*. Oxford: Blackwell.

Miles, M. B. and Huberman, A. M. (1994). *Qualitative data analysis: An expanded sourcebook* (2nd edn). London: Sage.

Monikowski, C. (in press). The academic's dilemma: A balanced and integrated career. In E. Winston and C. Monikowski (eds), *Evolving pardigms in interpreter education: Impact of interpreting research on teaching interpreting*. Washington, DC: Gallaudet University.

Moser-Mercer, B. (1994). Paradigms gained or the art of productive disagreement. In S. Lambert and B. Moser-Mercer (eds), *Bridging the gap: Empirical research in simultaneous interpretation*. John Benjamins, Philadelphia: Amsterdam, pp. 17–23.

— (2010). The search for neurophysiological correlates of expertise in interpreting. In G. M. Shreve and E. Angelone (eds), *Translation and cognition*. Philadelphia: John Benjamins, pp. 263–87.

— (2011). Identifying and interpreting scientific phenomena: Simultaneous challenges to interpreting research. In B. Nicodemus and L. Swabey (eds),

Advances in interpreting research: Inquiry in action. Philadelphia: John Benjamins, pp. 47–58.

Moser-Mercer, B., Kunzli, A. and Korac, M. (1998). Prolonged turns in interpreting: Effects on quality, physiological and psychological stress (Pilot study). *Interpreting*, 3(1), 47–64.

NAATI (2013). Accreditation by approved Australian course: Information booklet. Retrieved 6 March 2013, from http://www.naati.com.au/PDF/Booklets/Accreditation_by_Approved_Australian_Course_booklet.pdf

Napier, J. (2002). *Sign language interpreting. Linguistic coping strategies*. England, UK: Douglas McLean.

— (2004). Interpreting omissions: A new perspective. *Interpreting: International Journal of Research and Practice in Interpreting*, 6(2), 117–42.

— (2005a). Linguistic features and strategies of interpreting: From research to education to practice. In M. Marschark, R. Peterson and E. Winston (eds), *Sign language interpreting and interpreter education: Directions for research and practice*. New York: Oxford University Press, pp. 84–111.

— (2005b). Making learning accessible for sign language interpreters: A process of change. *Educational Action Research*, 13(4), 505–23.

— (2007). Research shows deaf people should be jurors. *AAD Outlook: Magazine of the Australian Association of the Deaf*, 16(3), 3.

— (2009). Access to justice: NSW deaf people and jury service. *Across the Board: Magazine of the Australian Sign Language Interpreters Association*, 2, 2–3. Melbourne: ASLIA.

— (2010). A case study of the use of storytelling as a pedagogical tool for teaching interpreting students. *The Interpreter & Translator Trainer*, 10(1), 1–32.

— (2011a). Here or there? An assessment of video remote signed language interpreter-mediated interaction in court. In S. Braun and J. L. Taylor (eds), *Videoconference and remote interpreting in criminal proceedings*. Guildford: University of Surrey, pp. 145–85.

— (2011b). If a tree falls in the forest, does it make a noise? The merits of publishing interpreting research. In B. Nicodemus and L. Swabey (eds), *Advances in interpreting research: Inquiry in action*. Philadelphia: John Benjamins, pp. 121–52.

— (2011c). "It's not what they say but the way they say it." A content analysis of interpreter and consumer perceptions of signed language interpreting in Australia. *International Journal of the Sociology of Language: Special issue Translators and Interpreters: Geographic displacement and Linguistic Consequences*, 207, 59–87.

— (2013). "You get that vibe": A pragmatic analysis of clarification and communicative accommodation in legal video remote interpreting. In L. Meurant, A. Sinte, M. Van Herreweghe and M. Vermeerbergen (eds), *Sign language research uses and practices: Crossing views on theoretical and applied sign language linguistics*. Nijmegen, The Netherlands: De Gruyter Mouton and Ishara Press, pp. 85–110.

Napier, J., Carmichael, A. and Wiltshire, A. (2008). Look-pause-nod: A linguistic case study of a deaf professional and interpreters working together. In P. Hauser, K. Finch and A. Hauser (eds), *Deaf professionals and designated interpreters: A new paradigm*. Washington, D.C. Gallaudet University Press, pp. 22–42.

Napier, J. and Kidd, M. (in press). Limited English literacy as a barrier to accessing healthcare information for deaf people who use Auslan as their primary language. *Australian Family Physician*.

Napier, J. and Rohan, M. (2007). An invitation to dance: Deaf consumers' perceptions of signed language interpreters and interpreting. In M. Metzger and E. Fleetwood (eds), *Translation, sociolinguistic, and consumer issues in interpreting*. Washington, D.C. Gallaudet University Press, pp. 159–203.

Napier, J. and Sabolcec, J. (2012). *Access to preventative and ongoing healthcare information for deaf Auslan users: A qualitative study*. Sydney: Macquarie University.

Napier, J. and Shearim, G. (2012). Can deaf people serve as jurors in Australia? An update on research. *Outlook: Magazine of Deaf Australia*, 21(8), 10–12.

Napier, J., Slatyer, H., Song, S., Kim, M., Inoue, I. and Dong, H. (2008–2011). A new vision for translation and interpreting education in the 21st century: A research embedded review project. Sydney: Macquarie University.

Napier, J. and Spencer, D. (2007). A sign of the times: Deaf jurors and the potential for pioneering law reform. *Reform: A Journal of National and International Law Reform*, 90, 35–7.

— (2008). Guilty or not guilty? An investigation of deaf jurors' access to court proceedings via sign language interpreting. In D. Russell and S. Hale (eds), *Interpreting in legal settings*. Washington D.C. Gallaudet University Press.

Napier, J., Spencer, D. and Sabolcec, J. (2007). *Guilty or not guilty? An investigation of deaf jurors' access to court proceedings via sign language interpreting. Research Report No. 14.*: NSW Law Reform Commission.

— (2009). *A shared responsibility in the administration of justice: a pilot study of sign language interpretation access for deaf jurors*. Paper presented at the Quality in Interpreting: A shared resposibility – proceedings of the 5th International Critical Link Conference.

Nardi, D. and Kremer, M. (2003). Learning outcomes and self Affessment of baccalaureate students in an introduction to nursing course. *Journal of the Scholarship of Teaching and Learning*, 3(3), 43–55.

Neuman, W. L. (2000). *Social research methods. Qualitative and quantitative approaches*. (4th edn). Boston; London: Allyn & Bacon.

Nicodemus, B. (2009). *Prosodic markers and utterance boundaries in American sign language interpretation*. Washington, D.C. Gallaudet University Press.

Noaks, L. and Wincup, E. L. (2004). *Criminological research: Understanding qualitative methods. Introducing qualitative methods*. London: Sage.

Nunan, D. (1992). *Research methods in language learning*. Cambridge: Cambridge University Press.

Ochs, E. (1979). Transcription as theory. In E. Ochs and S. B. (eds), *Developmental Pragmatics*. New York: Academic Press, pp. 43–72.

Patton, M. Q. (1987). *How to use qualitative methods in evaluation*. Beverly Hills: Sage.

Peters, P. (2004). *The Cambridge guide to English usage*. Cambridge: Cambridge University Press.

Petronio, K. and Hale, K. (2009). One interpreter education program, two sites: A comparison of factors and outcomes. *International Journal of Interpreter Education*, 1, 45–61.

Phelan, M. (2011). Legal interpreters in the news in Ireland. *The International Journal for Translation & Interpreting Research*, 3(1), 76–105.

Phillips, N. and Hardy, C. (2002). *Discourse analysis. Investigating processes of social construction.* London and New Delhi: Sage.

Pittarello, S. (2012). Medical terminology circulation and interactional organisation. *Linguistica antverpiensia*, 11, 113–32.

Pöchhacker, F. (2001). Quality assessment in conference and community interpreting. *Meta*, 46(2), 410–25.

— (1995). "Those who do . . .": A profile of research(ers) in interpreting. *Target*, 7(1), 47–64.

— (2004). *Introducing interpreting studies.* London & New York: Routledge.

— (2005). From operation to action: Process-orientation in interpreting studies. *Meta: Translators' Journal*, 50(2), 682–95.

— (2006). "Going Social?" On the pathways and paradigms in interpreting studies. In A. Pym, M. Shlesinger and Z. Jettmarová (eds), *Sociocultural aspects of translating and interpreting.* Amsterdam: John Benjamins, pp. 215–32.

— (2009a). *Testing aptitude for interpreting: The SynCloze test.* Paper presented at the the Symposium on Aptitude for Interpreting: Towards Reliable Admission Testing at Lessius University College, Antwerp, Belgium.

— (2009b). The turns of Interpreting Studies. In G. Hansen, A. Chesterman and H. Gerzymisch-Arbogast (eds), *Efforts and models in interpreting and translation research.* Amsterdam: John Benjamins, pp. 25–46.

— (2010a). Interpreting studies. In Y. Gambier and L. Van Doorslaer (eds), *Handbook of translation studies.* Amsterdam: John Benjamins.

— (2010b). The role of research in interpreter education. *The International Journal for Translation & Interpreting Research*, 2(1), 1–10.

— (2010c). The role of research in interpreter education. *Translation & Interpreting*, 2(1), 1–10.

— (2010d). Why interpreting studies matters. In D. Gile, G. Hansen and N. K. Pokorn (eds), *Why translation studies matters.* Amsterdam, The Netherlands; Philadelphia, PA: John Benjamins Pub. Co, pp. 3–13.

— (2011a). Researching interpreting. Approaches to inquiry. In B. Nicodemus and L. Swabey (eds), *Advances in interpreting research. Inquiry in action.* Amsterdam and Philadelphia: John Benjamins Publishing Company, pp. 5–25.

— (2011b). Simultaneous interpreting. In K. Malmkjær and K. Windle (eds), *The Oxford handbook of translation studies.* Oxford; New York: Oxford University Press, pp. 275–93.

Pollitt, K. (2011). Towards a collective biography of spoken/written ~ sign language translating? Retrieved 27 March 2013, from http://www.kyrapollitt.com/wp-content/uploads/2012/05/Edited-version-Towards-a-collective-biography-of-spoken.pdf

Pym, A. (2010). *Exploring translation theories.* London: Routledge.

Rampton, B. (2010). Linguistic ethnography, interactional sociolinguistics and the study of identities. In C. Coffin, T. Lillis and K. O'Halloran (eds), *Applied linguistics methods: A Reader.* London: Routledge, pp. 234–50.

Rasinger, S. M. (2008). *Quantitative research in linguistics.* London & New York: Continuum.

Research Councils UK (2013a). Knowledge exchange and Impact Retrieved 20 March 2013, from http://www.rcuk.ac.uk/kei/Pages/home.aspx

— (2013b). Knowledge transfer portal. Retrieved 20 March 2013, from http://www.rcuk.ac.uk/kei/ktportal/Pages/home.aspx

Riccardi, A. (2002). Interpreting research: Descriptive aspects and methodological proposals. In G. Garzone and M. Viezzi (eds), *Interpreting in the 21st century: Challenges and opportunities.* Amsterdam: John Benjamins Publishing.

Rico, C. (2010). Translator training in the European Higher Education area: Curriculum design for the Bologna process. A case study. *The Interpreter & Translator Trainer,* 4(1), 89–114.

Ridley, D. (2008). *The literature review. A step-by-step guide for students.* LA/London/New Delhi: SAGE.

Roberts, R., Carr, S., Abraham, D. and Dufour, A. (eds) (2000). *Critical Link 2: Interpreters in the community. Papers from the second international conference on interpreting in the legal, health and social service settings.* Amsterdam and Philadelphia: John Benjamins.

Robson, C. (2011). *Real world research: A resource for users of social research methods in applied settings.* Chichester, West Sussex: Wiley Blackwell.

Roy, C. (1989). Features of discourse in an American Sign Language Lecture. In C. Lucas (ed.), *The sociolinguistics of the deaf community.* New York: Academic Press, pp. 231–52.

— (1992). A sociolinguistic analysis of the interpreter's role in simultaneous talk in a face-to-face interpreted dialogue. *Sign Language Studies,* 74, 21–61.

— (1993). A sociolinguistic analysis of the interpreter's role in simultaneous talk in interpreted interaction. *Multilingua: Journal of Cross-Cultural and Interlanguage Communication,* 12(4), 341–64.

— (1996). An interactional sociolinguistic analysis of turntaking in an interpreted event. *Interpreting,* 1(1), 39–68.

— (2000). *Interpreting as a discourse process.* New York and Oxford: Oxford University Press.

Rudestam, K. E. and Newton, R. R. (2001). *Surviving your dissertation: A comprehensive guide to content and process* (2nd edn). Thousand Oaks, Calif.: Sage.

Rudvin, M. and Tomassini, E. (2011). *Interpreting in the community and workplace: A practical teaching guide.* London: Palgrave.

Russell, D. (2002). *Interpreting in legal contexts: Consecutive and simultaneous interpretation.* Burtonsville, MD: Sign Media.

Russo, M. (2009). *Aptitude testing over the years.* Paper presented at the Symposium on Aptitude for Interpreting: Towards Reliable Admission Testing. Lessius University College, Antwerp, Belgium.

Russo, M., Bendazzoli, C., Sandrelli, A. and Spinolo, N. (2012). The European Parliament Interpreting Corpus (EPIC): Implementation and developments. In F. S. Sergio and C. Falbo (eds), *Breaking ground in corpus-based interpreting studies.* Bern: Peter Lang, pp. 53–90.

Sacks, H. S., E. and Jefferson, G. (1974). A simplest systematics for the organisation of turn-taking for conversation. *Language and communication,* 50, 696–736.

Sadlier, L. (2009). Pandora's box: Lifting the lid on issues of testing: A case study of sign language interpreters in training in Ireland. *The Sign Language Translator & Interpreter,* 3(2), 177–201.

Sagor, R. (2010). *Collaborative action research for professional learning communities*. Bloomington, IN: Solution Tree Press.

Salaets, H. and Vermeerbergen, M. (2011). Assessing students upon completion of community interpreting training: How to reshape theoretical concepts for practice? In C. Kainz, E. Prunc and R. Schögler (eds), *Modelling the field of community interpreting: Questions of methodology in research and training*. Vienna: University of Graz, pp. 152–75.

Sameh, H. F. (2009). Exploring MA Students' attitudes to translation theory and practice: An action-research approach. *The Sign Language Translator and Interpreter*, 3(2), 141–55.

Sarangi, S. (2005). The conditions and consequences of professional discourse studies. *Journal of Applied Linguistics*, 2, 371–94.

Savery, J. R. and Duffy, T. M. (1996). Problem-based learning: An instructional model and its constructivist framework. In B. G. Wilson (ed.), *Constructivist learning environments: Case studies in instructional design*. Englewood Cliffs, NJ: Educational Technology Publications, pp. 135–46.

Saville-Troike, M. (1982). *The ethnography of communication: An introduction*. New York: Basil Blackwell.

Sawyer, D. (2004). *Fundamental aspects of interpreter education*. Amsterdam: John Benjamins.

Schegloff, E. and Sacks, H. (1973). Opening up closings. *Semiotica*, 8, 289–327.

Schiffrin, D. (1985). Conversational coherence: The role of well. *Language*, 61(3), 640–67.

— (1987). *Discourse markers*. Cambridge: Cambridge University Press.

Schön, D. A. (1995). The new scholarship requires a new epistemology. *Change*, 27(6), 26–34.

Scott, G. (1999). *Change matters: Making a difference in education and training*. St Leonards, NSW: Allen & Unwin.

Scott, J. W. (1995). The rhetoric of crisis in higher education. In M. Bérubé and C. Nelson (eds), *Higher education under fire: Politics, economics and the crisis of the humanities*. New York: Routledge, pp. 293–304.

Seal, B. (2004). Psychological testing of sign language interpreters. *Journal of Deaf Studies and Deaf Education*, 9(1), 39–52.

Seidman, I. (2006). *Interviewing as qualitative research: A guide for researchers in education and the social sciences*. New York: Teachers College Press.

Seleskovitch, D. (1978). *Interpreting for international conferences*. Washington, D.C: Pen and Booth.

Sergio, F. S. and Falbo, C. (eds) (2012). *Breaking ground in corpus-based interpreting studies*. Bern: Peter Lang.

Setton, R. (2002). A methodology for the analysis of interpretation corpora. In G. Garzone and M. Viezzi (eds), *Interpreting in the 21st century. Challenges and opportunities*. Amsterdam/Philadelphia: John Benjamins, pp. 29–45.

— (2006). Context in simultaneous interpretation. *Journal of Pragmatics*, 38, 374–89.

Sewell, P. and Higgins, I. (eds) (1996). *Teaching translation in universities: Present & future perspectives*. London: Association for French Language Studies.

Shaw, S., Grbic, N. and Franklin, K. (2004). Applying language skills to interpretation: Student perspectives from signed and spoken language programs. *Interpreting*, 6(1), 69–100.

Shlesinger, M. (1998). Corpus-based interpreting studies as an offshoot of corpus-based translation studies. *Meta: Translators' Journal*, 43(4), 486–93.

— (2009). Crossing the divide: What researchers and practitioners can learn from one another. *The International Journal for Translation & Interpreting Research*, 1(1), 1–16.

Shlesinger, M., Déjean, K., Kurz, I., Mack, G., Cattaruzza, L., Nilsson, A., Niske, H., Pöchhacker, F., and Viezzi, M. (1997). Quality in simultaneous interpreting. In Y. Gambier, D. Gile and C. Taylor (eds), *Conference interpreting: Current trends in research*. Amsterdam: John Benjamina, pp. 123–32.

Shreve, G. M., Lacruz, I. and Angelone, E. (2010). Cognitive effort, syntactic disruption and visual interference in a sight translation task. In G. M. Shreve and E. Angelone (eds), *Translation and cognition*. Philadelphia: John Benjamins, pp. 63–84.

Silverman, D. (2006). *Interpreting qualitative data* (3rd edn). London: Sage.

Siple, L. (1996). The use of additions in sign language transliteration. In D. M. Jones (ed.), *Assessing our work: Assessing our worth, Proceedings of the 11th National Convention of the Conference of Interpreter Trainers*. Arkansas: Conference of Interpreter Trainers, pp. 29–45.

Slatyer, H. (2006). Researching curriculum innovation in interpreter education. The case of initial training for novice interpreters in languages of limited diffusion. In C. Roy (ed.), *Advances in teaching interpreters*. Washington, D.C. Gallaudet University.

Smart, G. (2008). Ethnographic-based discourse analysis. In V. J. Bhatia, J. FLowerdew and R. H. Jones (eds), *Advances in discourse studies*. London: Routledge, pp. 56–66.

Spradley, J. P. (1979). *The ethnographic interview*. New York: Holt, Rinehart and Winston.

Stake, R. (1995). *The art of case study research*. Thousand Oaks, CA: Sage.

Starfield, S. (2010). Ethnographies. In B. Paltridge and A. Phakiti (eds), *Continuum companion to research methods in applied linguistics*. London: Continuum, pp. 50–65.

Stenhouse, L. (1975). *An introduction to curriculum research and development*. London: Heinemann.

Stone, C. (2007). Deaf translators/interpreters rendering processes: The translation of oral languages. *The Sign Language Translator & Interpreter*, 1(1), 53–72.

Street, B. (2010). Adopting an ethnographic perspective in research and pedagogy. In C. Coffin, T. Lillis and K. O'Halloran (eds), *Applied linguistics methods: A reader*. London: Routledge, pp. 201–15.

Stubbs, M. (1983). *Discourse Analysis*. Oxford: Blackwell.

Swabey, L. and Mickelson, P. G. (2008). Role definition. A perspective on forty years of professionalism in Sign Language interpreting. In C. Valero-Garcés and A. Martin (eds), *Crossing borders in Community Interpreting*. Amsterdam: John Benjamins P/C, pp. 51–80.

Szabó, C. (2006). Language choice for in note-taking for consecutive interpreting: A topic revisited. *Interpreting*, 8(2), 129–47.

Talmy, S. (2011). The interview as collaborative achievement: Interaction, identity, and ideology in a speech event. *Applied Linguistics*, 32(1), 25–42.

Tannen, D. (2004). Interactional sociolinguistics. In U. Ammon, N. Dittmar, K. J. Matthier and P. Trudgill (eds), *Sociolinguistics: An international handbook of the science of language and society* (New edn). Berlin: de Gruyter.

Tebble, H. (1999). The tenor of consultant physicians. Implications for medical interpreting. *The Translator* 5(2), 179–99.

— (2003). Training doctors to work effectively with interpreters. In L. Brunette, G. Bastin, I. Hemlin and H. Clarke (eds), *The Critical Link 3. Interpreters in the community. Selected papers in legal, health and social service settings. Montreal, Quebec, Canada 22–26 May 2001.* Amsterdam and Philadelphia: John Benjamins, pp. 81–98.

Temple, B. (1997). Watch your tongue: Issues in translation and cross-cultural research. *Sociology,* 31, 607–18.

— (2002). Crossed wires: Interpreters, translators, and bilingual workers in crosslanguage research. *Qualitative Health Research,* 12, 844–54.

Temple, B. and Edwards, R. (2002). Interpreters/translators and cross-language research: Reflexivity and border crossings. *International Journal of Qualitative Methods,* 1(2), 1–12.

Timarová, S. and Salaets, H. (2011). Learning styles, motivation and cognitive flexibility in interpreter training: Self-selection and aptitude. *Interpreting,* 13(1), 31–52.

Timarova, S. and Ungoed-Thomas, H. (2008). Admission testing for interpreting courses. *The Interpreter and Translator Trainer,* 2(1), 29–46.

Titscher, S., Meyer, M., Wodak, R. and Vetter, E. (2000). *Methods of text and discourse analysis* (B. Jenner, Trans.). London: SAGE.

Toury, G. (1995). Part One—Pivotal Position of descriptive studies and DTS. In G. Toury (ed.), *Descriptive translation studies and beyond.* Amsterdam; Philadelphia: John Benjamins, pp. 8–19.

Turner, G. H. and Harrington, F. (2000). Issues of power and method in interpreting research. In M. Olohan (ed.), *Intercultural faultlines: Research models in translation studies I: textual and cognitive aspects,* Vol. 1. Manchester, UK: St. Jerome, pp. 253–66.

Turner, G. H. and Pollitt, K. (2002). Community interpreting meets literary translation: English-BSL interpreting in the theatre. *The Translator,* 8, 25–48.

Usher, R. (1996). A critique of the neglected epistemological assumptions of education research. In D. Scott and R. Usher (eds), *Understanding educational research.* London: Routledge, pp. 9–32.

Valero-Garcés, C. and Socarrás-Estrada, D. (2012). Assessment and evaluation in labs for public services interpreting training. *International Journal of Interpreter Education,* 4(2), 7–23.

van Besien, F. (1999). Anticipation in simultaneous interpretation. *Meta: Translators' Journal,* 44(2), 250–9.

van Dijk, R., Christoffels, I. K., Postma, A. and Hermans, D. (2012). The relation between the working memory skills of sign language interpreters and the quality of their interpretations. *Bilingualism: Language and Cognition,* 15(2), 340–50.

Vandepitte, S. (2008). Remapping translation studies: Towards a translation studies ontology. *Meta,* 53(3), 569–88.

Vargas-Urpi, M. (2011). The interdisciplinary approach in community interpreting research. *New Voices in Translation Studies,* 7, 47–65.

Varney, J. (2009). From hermeneutics to the translation classroom: A social constructivist approach to effective learning. *The International Journal for Translation & Interpreting Research*, 1(1), 27–43.

Vik-Tuovinen, G. V. (2000). Retrospection as a method of studying the process of simultaneous interpreting. In S. Tirkkonen-Condit and R. Jääskeläinen (eds), *Tapping and mapping the processes of translation and interpreting*. Philadelphia: John Benjamins, pp. 63–71.

Wadensjö, C. (1992). *Interpreting as interaction. On dialogue interpreting in immigration hearings and medical encounters*. Linkoping: Linkoping University.

— (1998). *Interpreting as interaction*. London & New York: Longman.

— (2001a). Approaching interpreting through discourse analysis. In D. Gile, H. Dam, F. Dubslaff, B. Martinsen and A. Schjoldager (eds), *Getting started in interpreting research. Methodological reflections, personal accounts and advice for beginners*. Amsterdam and Philadelphia: John Benjamins, pp. 185–98.

— (2001b). Interpreting in crisis: The interpreter's position in therapeutic encounters. In I. Mason (ed.), *Triadic exchanges: Studies in dialogue interpreting*. Manchester: St Jerome, pp. 71–86.

— (2002). The double role of a dialogue interpreter. In F. Pöchhacker and M. Shlesinger (eds), *The interpreting studies reader*. New York: Routledge, pp. 354–71.

— (2004). Dialogue interpreting: A monologising practice in a dialogically organised world. *Target: International Journal on Translation Studies*, 16(1), 105–24.

Wadensjö, C., Englund Dimitrova, B. and Nilsson, A.-L. (eds) (2007). *The Critical Link 4*. Amsterdam and Philadelphia: John Benjamins Publishing Company.

Walker, R. (1985). *Doing research: A handbook for teachers*. London: Meuthen.

Walliman, N. S. R. (2005). *Your research project: A step-by-step guide for the first-time researcher* (2nd edn). London: SAGE.

Wang, J. (2013a). Bilingual working memory capacity in professional Auslan/English interpreters. *Interpreting*, 15(2), 139–67.

— (2013b). *Working memory and signed lanugage interpreting*. Unpublished doctoral dissertation, Macquarie University, Sydney.

Wang, J. and Napier, J. (2013). Signed language working memory capacity of signed language interpreters and deaf signers. *The Journal of Deaf Studies and Deaf Education*, 18(2), 271–86.

Wardhaugh, R. (2010). *An introduction to sociolinguistics* (6th edn). Chichester, West Sussex, UK: Wiley-Blackwell.

Williams, J. and Chesterman, A. (2002). *The Map: A beginner's guide to doing research in translation studies*. Manchester: St Jerome.

Willis, P. and Trondman, M. (2000). Manifesto for ethnography. *Ethnography*, 1(1), 5–16.

Wilson, C. (2013). Teaching and learning of interpreting. In C. A. Chapelle (ed.), *The encyclopedia of applied linguistics*. Oxford: Blackwell Publishing.

Wilson, S. (1982). The use of ethnographic techniques in educational research. *Review of Educational Research*, 47(1), 245–65.

Wittenburg, P., Brugman, H., Russel, A., Klassmann, A. and Sloetjes, H. (2006). *ELAN: A professional framework for multimodality research*. Language Archiving Technology Website, Max Planck Institute of Psycholinguistics, Netherlands.

Witter-Merithew, A. and Johnson, L. (2005). *Toward competent practice: Conversations with stakeholders*. Alexandria, VA: Registry of Interpreters for the Deaf.

Wolff, H. K. and Pant, P. R. (1999). *A handbook for social science research and thesis writing* (2 edn). Kathmandu, Nepal: P. R. Pant.

Wooffitt, R. (2005). *Conversation analysis and discourse analysis. A comparative and critical introduction*. London: Sage Publications.

Wray, A. and Bloomer, A. (2006). *Projects in linguistics. A practical guide to researching language*. New York: Hodder Arnold.

INDEX